Afterglow

AFTERGLOW

A JOURNAL FOR SCOTTIE

A Man in Full Stride

The Memorable Half-life

Of

SCOTT EDWIN GARRETT

August 30, 1964-December 14, 2011

J.B. Garrett

Boulevard Press

This is a true Story. The names, characters, businesses, places, events and incidents are accurate to the best of my recollection. I have tried to recreate events, locales and conversations from my memories of them. In order to maintain their anonymity in some instances I have changed or withheld the names of individuals and places, and some identifying characteristics and details such as physical properties, occupations, and places of residence.

Editor J.B. Garrett
Cover Photo Courtesy of: Kathy Barczak

ISBN   978-0-9832411-26 Hardback
Library of Congress Catalog Number N/A

Publisher: Boulevard Press
80499 Spanish Bay
La Quinta, CA 92253
http://www.BoulevardPress.com

Ordering Information:
Quantity sales. Special discounts are available on quantity purchases by corporations, associations, clubs, and others.
For details, contact: Sales@BoulevardPress.com.

To contact the author:
J.B. Garrett email: Joe.Garrett0@Gmail.com

Contents

FOREWORD

This story, written by his dad and his close friends, chronicles the high points and major achievements of Scott Garrett's shortened life, alternating with vignettes of his epic battle with leukemia and bone marrow transplant.

It is written for his dearest loves: Terry, Jack and Audrey, his mother, father, and brother, his many friends, and for the grandchildren and great grandchildren Scott will not know.

They will recognize his genes in themselves, be influenced by his humor, his energy, his passions, his love of life, his bravery in illness, and his dreams for them.

They will know him and his legacy through these remembrances, helping them to paint his unfinished portrait, picturing him as real to them, seeing him as part of and in their daily lives.

With this book, they can conjure the second half of Scott's life, channeling his counsel, finishing his story, warming in his afterglow.

This story is also for survivors of loved ones lost to blood and other cancers, helping them to grieve, and ultimately to heal, while never forgetting. Cancer impacts virtually every family on earth, defying the best efforts of medicine for the past 5,000 years.

JBG. 7/1/2012

1. Cancer Touches Everyone

"Now that I view the scene in retrospect, I see it as a very gentle and firm deportation, taking me from the country of the well across the stark frontier that marks off the land of malady." [1]

--Christopher Hitchins, Mortality.

Cancer has no soft, subtle edge. One day it is not there…the next day it has invaded and occupied, and turned the host's life upside down. There is no heading it off. There is no barrier which can be put in place to prevent its coming. Its victims are chosen randomly, without provocation. A single mutant gene in one blood cell suddenly decides to divide infinitely and distort the normal mix of blood cells produced by the bone marrow, choking off essential oxygen carrying red cells. The feared

---

1 Mortality, Christopher Hitchins, Hachette Book Group, New York, NY., 2012,1. Written from his hospital bed. He died of esophaogeal cancer on Dec. 15, 201, one day after Scott died.

malady focused on Scott as its primary victim. But we, his family, were its secondary victims. It took us all hostage. We felt his unbearable pain, we went through the tunnel of darkness with him. We suffered as he suffered. With him, we were sleepless and anxious and disoriented and nauseous and humbled. His long days and dreaded nights became ours as well. His hopeful days brought euphoria. His down days brought emotional wreckage. As many before us have realized, we live with trauma as family, not as individuals. We are extensions of each other's physical and mental states.

We survived, but only after a fashion, with disfigured hearts and minds, twisted emotions, crushed spirits.

So this story is primarily about Scott's hopeful and meaningful life cut short in full stride just as his promise was being fulfilled. But to be complete, it also had to be about Terry and Jack and Audrey, and Joan and me and Jon, Terry's parents and siblings, and his many "Jimmy" friends, how we had cancer with him, what we experienced over the seven months of his illness, and how our lives are forever changed by "our" illness.

Cancer takes whole families prisoner! It points the same gun at everyone's head. No survivor is ever the same again.

2. Enter Leukemia

Leukemia entered Scott's blood stream by stealth as stunningly as if a meteorite had fallen on him.   Forty-six years old and in excellent health (according to an executive physical in January), he was now head of litigation and compliance and Associate General Counsel

Scott and Terry in La Quinta, three weeks before his diagnosis.

at A.O. Smith Corporation in Milwaukee.   He had just returned from a twelve-day hurry-up business trip to Shanghai and Nanjing China, and Bangalore, India.

The trip was exhausting both because of the rigorous meeting schedule with Smith attorneys and outside counsel in those locations, but also because of the inverted time schedule. Still, he found time to snap a few pictures of Nanjing and Bangalore with his phone, depicting the best and worst of conditions there.

Bangalore had been his last work destination. He returned from there with a layover in Abu Dhabi, United Arab Emirates, where he changed planes for the long flight to Chicago, during which he slept the entire time, completely out of character for Scott. During the UAE stopover, Scott was entranced by views of Abu Dhabi from the airport. Abu Dhabi is known as the richest city in the world, thanks to abundant oil, and its riches are sculpted into skyscrapers considered architectural masterpieces. He sent pictures of some of these from the airport, one in the shape of a large golden wheel.

Back home, Scott felt unusually depleted by what he was certain was jet lag from the 10 hour time change, the unusual foods he had eaten, and the long days of late night/early morning meetings. Sound sleep had been elusive. Just two weeks before the trip, Scott and Terry and their children, Jack, 11, and Audrey, 10, had spent a joyful week with Joan and me at our home in La Quinta, California. The time together was idyllic for our family. The day they left to return to Milwaukee, I prepared a book of happy photographs commemorating the week and sent it to them.

Scott was strangely ill with flu-like symptoms for two days of their visit, attributing it to stomach upset from something he ate. Given his choice of the spiciest of foods, we all thought a food bacteria might be to blame. He seemed to recover quickly, and no further thought was given to his brief sickness.   During the week, he golfed twice, went horseback riding and to a water park with the kids, swam, played games, and cooked out.

A week after returning home from India, his lethargy continued. He would come home exhausted after spending his days in his Milwaukee office.   Scott continued to think jet lag was the cause of his listlessness and for the edema in his lower legs and ankles.   One morning, Terry commented that his skin seemed to take on a yellow cast.   He agreed, but decided to push on to deal with the heavy backlog on his desk.

The next day, June 7, he attended an early morning staff conference and decided afterwards to excuse himself and go to a nearby walk-in clinic for a precautionary check up.   The thorough physical just five months earlier pronounced him in perfect health except for a slightly low red blood count--- but nothing worrisome.   Scott felt maybe he was iron deficient, and that the doctor might suggest some vitamins.

Blood was drawn and analyzed, and the doctor in charge of the clinic intervened and told Scott he had severe anemia and should go directly to a hospital for closer examination.   Scott called Terry at her work at Wisconsin Junior Achievement, picked her up, and the two drove to Froedtert (pronounced Fraydirt) Hospital, near their home, where he was expected.   The clinic doctor had called ahead, so he was expected.

The clinic doctor then called Scott's cell phone, and told him

"There is a high probability that you have leukemia."

Both Scott and Terry were in stunned disbelief.

Within an hour, he was admitted to Froedtert's leukemia wing and crossed over from the land of wellness into the land of malady. The tentative diagnosis was confirmed through more blood analysis. Leukemia had indeed entered by stealth, without prior notice or fanfare.

From his hospital room, still in shock, Scott made phone calls to family and his office, explaining that he was hospital-confined and would begin chemotherapy and critically needed transfusions that same afternoon. The suddenness of serious illness floored him, but as treatment unfolded over the next few weeks and his knowledge of his disease grew, his confidence also grew that he would soon return to work and resume a different, but full life.

3. The Call

"One day can change your life. All life is three or four big days that change everything."

--*Beverly Donofrio, author.*

On June 7, at 2 PM California time, he made a call to my cell phone, but a poor signal prevented clear communication. I was just about to enter the Apple store in Palm Desert, CA, for an instruction session on my new I-Pad. When the call came, I recognized Scott's voice but the message was garbled. I walked a few steps down the street to get a clearer signal and heard just these words:

"Dad, I have leukemia."

The four words struck me like a lightning bolt, and I became disoriented. I remember thinking this had to be a bad joke, quickly realizing that couldn't be the case. I remember blurting out, "Oh no, no, no. It can't be! Are you serious? Where are you?"

Suddenly, the connection was lost, and I was not even certain I had heard the words correctly. Surely, there was some mistake.

I redialed Scott's cell number, and this time, Terry answered. She was tearful and barely able to speak, but managed to confirm that Scott's words were absolutely true, and that he was now in a hospital bed about to receive red blood transfusions and emergency chemo. She said the kids were in school and knew nothing of this.

I felt weak and short of breath, shaken by the news and incoherent with my questions.

Terry explained that she had called Joan, Scott's mom, while Scott was trying to reach me. She said the doctors told them he would begin intensive chemo and other drugs, be in the hospital at least a month, and, depending on the success of the drugs, might be released, while continuing to receive chemo as an outpatient. Her conversation naturally leaned toward the best case, which was that remission was achievable. Beyond that, the doctors had not told them very much. There had been no time.

His red blood count on admission had been dangerously below normal, and immediate transfusions were begun through a port, or PICC line (acronym for peripherally inserted central catheter) embedded surgically in his right upper arm, feeding across his chest and into a major vein near the heart, allowing medications to be fed directly into his bloodstream. The port had multiple inlet and outlets, allowing vials of blood to be drawn, as well as chemo and other drugs and liquids to be infused.

I called Joan at home. She was in shock, and as tearful as Terry. Neither of us could accept this awful surprise, this terrible news blindsiding us so soon after their recent vacation with us. But our thoughts were with Scott and Terry and what they were thinking and feeling at the moment of realization...the moment when they had confirmation that cancer had randomly moved in and occupied Scott's body, and, in the doing, also captured and held hostage their thoughts, hopes, and dreams.   To the question, "Why Scott? Hitchins' answer for the reason for his own random call from cancer would be, *Why not?"*

It was indeed news which would change Scott's and Terry's lives forever, as well as the lives of Jack and Audrey.   Its implications were huge in terms of how all our lives would have to be reset in a new reality, with different family expectations, modified career goals, a radical change of routine for Terry, and its worrisome impact on their young children.

We knew few details about the disease of leukemia except that it was often deadly. We also knew that as many as half of leukemia sufferers relapse, that the course of treatment is long and painful, and that the disease would be disrupting and life-altering even if cured.

Over the next few weeks, we had a necessary "cliff notes" education in Leukemia 101. We came to understand that the bone marrow is the body's blood factory, and leukemia occurs when mutant cancer genes cause cells to multiply out of control. The mutant cells then invade and hijack the marrow and reprogram it to produce a deadly imbalance of white, red and platelet cells.   In AML Leukemia, the factory produces vastly greater numbers of errant, short-lived, mutant white cells, overwhelming and reducing the hemoglobin concentration in the red nutrient cells, preventing them from carrying adequate oxygen. Literally, the diseased factory begins producing a mix of blood which the body doesn't want and cannot use or store. If not corrected quickly with new oxygen carrying blood, the result is asphyxiation.

Scott's formal diagnosis was ACUTE MYELOID LEUKEMIA, one of the most aggressive types. We learn that the word LEUKEMIA is an adaptation of the Greek words LEUKOS meaning clear, white, and HEIMA, meaning blood. Myeloid also derives from the Greek MYELOS, (marrow), differentiating this disease from leukemic cells originating in the spleen.

Without immediate transfusions and chemo to fight back the mutant cancer cells, the disease can be fatal within a very short time.

In California, we could be of no help to Scott and Terry and the kids. Joan and I made quick plans to drop everything and fly to Milwaukee on June 9. We had one day to prepare and close the La Quinta house, store our cars, cancel any appointments, and pack for what turned out to be a seven-month stay. During the flight, our thoughts were of Scott and Terry and the kids. We didn't talk much, still wrestling with how to absorb what we knew, and what we might find when we arrived.

We called our son Jon, Scott's younger brother, and our extended family and explained what was going on. We knew my younger sister Norma was in hospice and near death from liver cancer in Amarillo and had made the decision that Scott's family needed us more at this moment. Dear sweet Norma died on June 8 after a brave multi-year struggle with melanoma. She was a wonderful and caring human being, a loving mother and grandmother, wife, daughter, and sister. We were sadly unable to attend her service on June 13th. We talked to her husband Ronald and their grown children, Brad and Gina, who understood through their own grief what we were facing.

In Milwaukee, we were picked up by Scott's friend Mike Bressanelli and taken directly to the Froedtert Hospital complex, where we found our way to the leukemia wing and an overwhelmed Scott and Terry. Chemo drugs were being fed through the PICC line, along with the first of eight continuous transfusions of red blood cells and platelets, bags and bags of hydrating fluids and antibiotics.

Scott looked pale and weak and out of place lying in this hospital bed. We were as disoriented as he, grappling with unknowns and our heads filled with questions. We are told that the first treatment phase, known as induction, calls for round-the-clock chemo for a week, followed by intermittent chemo, transfusions as needed, along with a wide variety of other drugs, until remission is hopefully achieved within a month. Steroids would also be a part of the drug mix.

If and when remission is achieved, the consolidation phase starts, calling for additional chemo to kill lingering cancer cells not detectable through normal tests. Consolidation is insurance that the remission can be sustained and a "cure" might possibly be achieved.

Marrow transplant is the third phase, if the patient is healthy enough and chooses the option, and a suitable donor is found. The doctors inject a new replacement marrow factory, bringing with it the potential to produce the correct mix of red and white cells and platelets if not rejected by his immune system.

We got acquainted with the hospital routine, met the leukemia nurses Donna, Amber, and Stacey, and the first of three leukemia doctors who would be primary in his treatment. Dr's. Saad, Atallah, and Palmer would rotate his care, with Atallah and Saad, both Egyptian, playing lead roles in this early stage.   We adjusted ourselves to the notion that Scott would be here for a long time, while we wrestled with the unreality of it all.

Over the next few weeks, we watched incessant testing through dozens of daily patient invasions, the new norm for leukemia patients. Daily drawings of vials of blood, periodic bone marrow biopsies (taken by boring into the pelvic bone), CT scans of kidneys, lungs, and the brain, throat cultures, blood pressure and temperature readings, are the expected routine. Sanitation requires daily PICC line cleanings, room cleanings, bed changing and bathing, all mixed with a constant stream of nurses, doctors, technicians, lab specialists, kidney, lung, and liver specialists coming in and out of his hospital room. ….

Data collectors, people with questionnaires to fill out, meal servers, priests, ministers, social workers, janitors…each had their turn at intruding.   Some would come in the middle of the night or very early morning because that was what their work schedule called for. Ultimately, these constant interruptions became a major nuisance, and, as time went by, Scott became very firm in rejecting the timing of many of their visits.

The first week we stayed at a motel near Scott's home.   On June 15th, we moved into a rental house with rented furniture at 2426 N. 93rd street, about six blocks east of Scott's and Terry's house.   We never dreamed we would stay there until January 13, 2012.

The setting for Scott's treatment is Froedtert Leutheran Hospital, named after its major benefactor. Froedtert is a component and teaching hospital of the University of Wisconsin and Its medical college, attracting students, interns, and residents from all over the world.   It is a major medical center complex with practices in all specialties, much like M.D. Anderson in Houston or Massachusetts General in Boston. The sprawling campus is located in Wauwatosa, Milwaukee County, a few miles west of downtown Milwaukee. The hospital employs 3,000 doctors and 5,000 nurses and support staff.

Most of our days for the remainder of 2011 would be spent in the leukemia and bone marrow transplant wings of this hospital, about three miles from Scott's home.

Gradually, the history and treatment of cancer come into focus for us. One of the oldest of known diseases, it has been found in mummified remains 2500 years BCE. Leukemia has been one of its most vexing forms, confounding medicine men and medieval primitive "cures" as its treatment has evolved through dozens of "breakthroughs", only to realize that long-term cure remains elusive. Leukemia has frustrated the best practitioners and researchers of their eras.

In his Pulitzer-Prize winning book, *THE EMPEROR OF ALL MALADIES*, Dr. Siddhartha Mukherjee, hematologist and oncologist, brilliantly reviews these histories and disappointments, noting the Darwinian nature of cancer cells. As one treatment succeeds in destroying primary or localized cancer cells, stronger "survivor" cells escape and migrate (metastasize) to new locations in the body, forming new types of cancers requiring entirely new therapies. Thus, relapse rates are high for all cancers, but especially for leukemia since these cells cannot be excised surgically.[2]

---

2 Siddhartha Mukherjee, The Emperor of all Maladies, Scribner, New York, 2010

4. In Case You Missed Him

"Country boys learn about soil, plants, farm animals and solitude. City boys learn among crowds, interacting with people and playing games in confined spaces, rarely feeling the soil."

--Unknown

I called him Segwin. To me, the name fit his personality. He used it as his personal Internet handle (Segwin@). He usually called me Joe or Joey, rarely dad. We communicated as equals this way. SEGWIN was a contrivance linking his initials with the second half of his maternal grandfather Henderson's first name, Edwin. He liked it. It was like a private signal between us.

Once in August of 2011, on the course at Blue Mound club, while he was in remission, and again in November, from his hospital bed in the bone marrow transplant wing of Froedtert Hospital, he had said to me:

"Dad, I want to thank you and Mom for all you have done to help keep me alive."

Could he have known? Some say that people do know…

Over the years, he told all of his friends and members of his family, "Don't wait. Do it now! We are all going to die soon".

Prophetic? Perhaps! He didn't postpone his life…he lived it in fast forward, filled with energy, vitality, and drive. He strove for the brass ring, relished the extravagance of owning and driving his Porsche, top down, music blaring. His full half-life held adventure, humor, love and marriage, children, a rising legal career. As an adult, he was firm of purpose and goal inspired. He dreamed of the future, but lived the present. He earned respect as a leader, as a positive force in his community, and as a valued member of his firm. His life was one of "true, meaningful impact," said Jim Stern, his General counsel. He was indeed A MAN IN FULL STRIDE.

In 250 years, he was the first of his Garrett lineage to be born a city boy. But his genes knew the soil.

Eight generations before him had tilled the soil for their survival, moving westward from the original colonies as the country encouraged settlement of new frontiers. Henry Garrett, a tobacco farmer in Virginia who served two stints in George Washington's revolutionary army, moved on to farm in the Carolinas, Kentucky and Tennessee. Some of his sons stayed to farm in Virginia. Other sons and grandsons and their sons continued the westward movement and chose Oklahoma and Texas, where land was still plentiful and productive enough to assure self-sufficiency for their families. Their genes had not evolved in an atmosphere of urban congestion and noise, but in the quiet, isolated, modest homesteads they built with their own hands with wood milled from their own trees. They had no electricity or modern sanitation. With their own hand labor, they cleared their virgin land of mesquite and scrubs and native grasses before planting behind horse-drawn plows. They fought illnesses with home remedies. Their children were born with midwives at home, never in hospitals.

In stark contrast, Scott's early years were stuffed with humanity, noise, color, cultural diversity, and mutual dependency, away from anything agrarian, void of soil and crops and farm animals and farm labor necessary to sustain life. These images and impressions of total urbanity and its displays of extreme wealth and abject poverty in the biggest city in America left an indelible imprint on his psyche... helping to shape his brain and his life views.

Perhaps they helped determine his senses of taste and smell during gestation. How else to explain his lifelong disdain for mustard and undisguised milk? He ingested eggs only as camouflaged ingredients, loved the world's spiciest foods, relished sushi and sashimi and smoked meats. He loved golf and his Porsche, Charles Tyrwhitt custom English shirts, Alan Edmonds shoes, the discipline of the law, five star hotels and Pebble Beach. He prized quality in everything he owned or did, and liked going First Class, saying, "life is too short not to." He saw life as a gift to be experienced in full stride.

He had an uncanny, almost mystical ability to make fast friends of strangers, and to hold on to and nurture them forever. He called most of his true friends "Jimmy," unaware of the irony in his choice of names. In the 1940's, the "Jimmy" fund was one of the very first nationally organized money raising efforts in support of children's leukemia research, founded and promoted by Dr. Sidney Farber at Massachusetts General Hospital, strongly supported by the Albert and Mary Lasker Foundation. This fund-raising effort became the forerunner of the National Cancer Institute and the American Cancer Society, which commanded hundreds of millions of government funds in fighting "The War on Cancer".

He disliked slackers, politicians, dishonesty, and opportunistic plaintiff's lawyers. He loved his wife and children, taking risks, speed, and striving for the top rung. He believed that anything could be accomplished by setting goals and working toward them systematically. He believed, as Buddhists do, that life has the meaning the individual himself assigns to it…and makes it his own mission.

But the important back story of Scott Garrett was the role of his early life in shaping his character and values, forging the qualities which would aid him in his struggle with his greatest challenge, the random unexplained leukemia which was to alter his life vision, shape new values, and define his mortality.

5. Beginning Years

"The whole life of the individual is nothing but the process of giving birth to himself. Indeed, we should be fully born when we die."

--Erick Fromm

On the night of August 29, 1964, the night before Scott was born, he was unaware that he attended a late party on east 32nd street in Manhattan. Joan and I were friends with a cluster of National Airlines flight attendants who shared a lower level garden apartment there. The mood was boisterous and convivial, with drinks and laughter extending to 2 AM Sunday morning.

His home at 15 Park Avenue, apartment 8A, was easy walking distance, and by 2:30 AM, his mother was fast asleep, totally unconcerned with impending events surrounding her child of unknown gender due to arrive perhaps a week later. But by 10:AM on August 30, a quiet and lovely Manhattan Sunday morning, we were focused sharply on the womb bound individual now suddenly determined to escape confinement and make an appearance.

Doctor Shapiro, Joan's OB/GYN was called and made his way quickly to Mt. Sinai hospital, where we were to meet him as soon as possible. After emptying a piggy bank of dimes and quarters barely adequate to cover the 65-block cab fare north to 100th Street and Madison Avenue, the journey was made and Joan was admitted at noon. Mt. Sinai is a teaching hospital complex, officially located in East Harlem, and was the hospital where Dr. Shapiro delivered babies. Until this day, Joan had seen the doctor only in his midtown office.

Fathers in delivery rooms were discouraged in those years. It was suggested that I "take a walk" and have lunch somewhere, at which time the birth would be close.

At 2:00 PM, Scott Edwin Garrett was delivered of Joan Ardith Henderson Garrett, debuting at 7 lbs, 8 ounces, in apparent good health, with all appropriate appendages. My first view was at 2:30 PM, through the window of the infant nursery. All seemed in order! I had nothing to commemorate the event except a small toy metal canon purchased with the residue of piggy bank change at the only shop open in the neighborhood. Forty-eight years later, this toy is still in the family.

His name was a compromise. Mom wanted Steve, after her Swedish grandfather, Steve Johnson, who she adored. Scott somehow won out, with Edwin as a middle name, after his maternal Canadian/American grandfather, Edwin George Henderson.

He was not immediately handsome. However, a slightly pointed head and flat nose from birth compression soon returned to normal. At home on the 8th floor of 15 Park three days later, under the care of his mom and grandmother Alice Henderson, who had flown in from Oakland to help, he was a hit, bringing new life sounds to neighbors accustomed only to city traffic noises and the yelping of small dogs.

One by one, they came to know him. He offered happy smiles, and soon became familiar as the only human baby in the building, competing for attention with an assortment of puppies and cats. He became a male Eloise figure smilingly acknowledged by residents and catered to by local delis and dry cleaners as he and mom made their stroller shopping rounds.

His first year of Manhattan high rise living was progressive and normal except for one personality characteristic which would set him apart for the rest of his life: He was the highest energy, most curious child we or the neighbors had ever seen. Later, the term hyperactive came in vogue. He could not nap until he had opened and closed every box and drawer, touched every button, searched for every electrical outlet, banged every pot and pan, wiggled to every song, toppled everything that could be toppled, leafed through every book he could reach, and, in months to come, vault over the side of his crib.

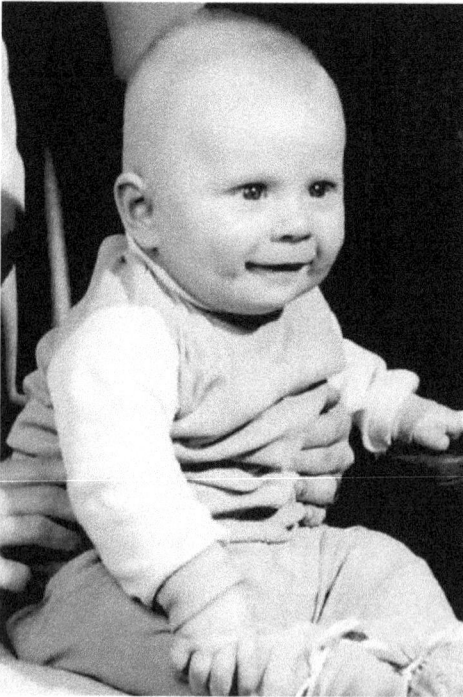

Scott at four months

As soon as he discovered his knees as a means of propulsion, he was unstoppable. He had to be present for all adult gatherings, when he should have been sleeping. On anyone's lap, he was good for 45 seconds before squirming down and moving on. He was overflowing with energy and curiosity always, sometimes jumping up and down in his crib for a good part of the night. His presence could never be denied.

At three months, he monitored the house from his portable crib, hanging on to his bottle. As soon as he cut teeth, he dangled the bottle from his mouth while making rounds. At six months, he and mom were taking the subway uptown to the 59th and Lexington station, exiting a block from central park, and touring his stroller through the park for lunch before the return train ride home. Russell and Tommy, the doormen and elevator operators at 15 Park, became his self- appointed guardians.

15 Park avenue sounds very uptown. Actually, it was in the toney but middle-brow area of midtown Manhattan known as Murray Hill. The area was the ideal jumping off point for busses or subways downtown to Battery Park, Greenwich Village, China Town, and the Staten Island ferry. It was two cross-town blocks from the Empire State building, Altman's department store one block west, Lord and Taylor within four blocks, the J.P. Morgan museum two blocks west. It was also an easy subway or taxi ride uptown to Bloomingdales, Central Park, the Metropolitan museum, the Guggenheim, the museum of Modern Art, the Plaza hotel at 5th and Central Park South, and all of Fifth and Madison Avenue shopping. Murray Hill had its own respectable antique dealers, hardware stores, restaurants, and boutique food markets, like Gristedes on 34th street, a few doors east.

The building had artificially cheap rents under rent control, in effect since WW 2. This subsidy meant turnover was rare. Availability of apartments was by word of mouth, never through advertising. Most residents were long term because they had a great bargain. Joan and I had married just twenty blocks South, in the Fifth Avenue Presbyterian church at 10th street.

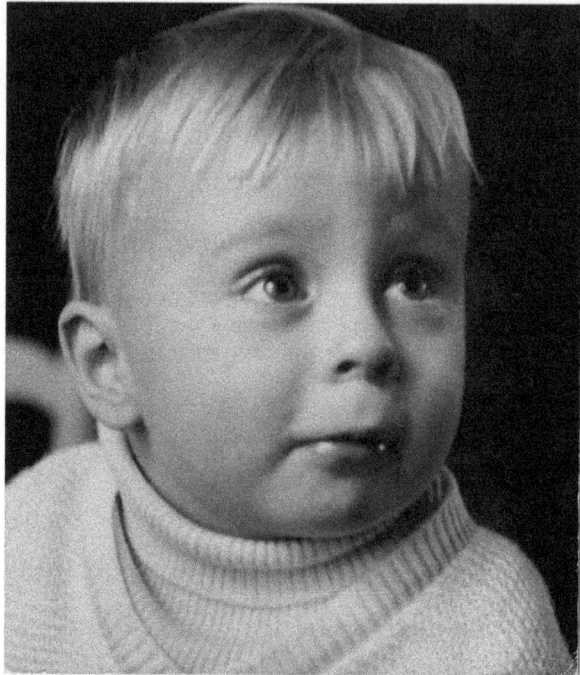

Age 2, A Manhattan native

This setting, a two bedroom, one bath apartment, with prized fireplace and a view directly over Park Avenue, was Scott's home base for his first three years, the last of which he found too confining. More than once, he let himself out the apartment door, descended the stairs to the basement laundry area, and was found there by the doormen and his frantic mother. But convenient shopping and child friendly shopkeepers made the experience memorable. He was often given food or sweets samples, smilingly accepted.

By age two, he graduated to big boy pants and shoes, often walking with mom as she did errands and shopped, with a stroller as back up. His desire and his energy always compelled him to walk or run everywhere, to the point of falling asleep in his tracks. He was rarely cross, always interested and alert. Pictures of him in this period show a happy overall-clad cotton-haired lad exploring his New York digs, or wearing a sailor's white -brimmed hat when on the street.

With little brother Jonathan on the way, and curious Scott needing more roaming space, the family moved to Riverside, Ct., just before his third birthday. The small two story white colonial house there, at 219 Riverside Avenue, had a sizable fenced yard for play, good preschool and kindergarten within a block at the local Episcopal church, and excellent public schools within walking distance. Riverside was a family neighborhood, with plenty of playmates nearby.

Just before making the move, Joan had registered him in a private preschool in Murray Hill, which, she didn't understand at the time, was very selective in its admissions. Scott was interviewed by the headmistress, and two days later his letter of acceptance arrived. Only later did we learn that acceptance at this school usually followed registration at the time of birth, with great weight given to the applicants credentials, financial and otherwise, and the all important private interview one-on-one with the head of the school.

As it turned out, the move to Connecticut precluded Scott's attendance, but we always marveled at our innocence in never doubting that he would be accepted.

So in the summer of 1967, our family decamped Manhattan through Grand Central station and boarded the New Haven railroad for the one- hour ride north, leaving the city behind. Scott was to spend eight of the next thirteen years in Greenwich, Ct., returning to live in Manhattan only as an adult while employed as a paralegal by a large international law firm. But that is another phase of the story.

Scott's early years had been historic in the life of the country, and saw momentous cultural changes. President John Kennedy had been assassinated in November of 1963, nine months before Scott' birth. Lyndon B. Johnson, the vice-president, succeeded him and served the last year of Kennedy's term, then was reelected in November, 1964. Johnson pushed the "war on poverty", and "the great society," setting the stage for the massive social welfare we know today through programs like Medicare, Medicaid, and poverty grants.

Johnson inherited and escalated the Vietnam War by pushing through congressional approvals allowing him great latitude in committing more troops and planes to the effort. The war was highly unpopular with Americans, leading to mass anti-war protests, and ultimately, to Johnson's decision not to seek reelection in 1968. In 1967, the year Scott's younger brother was born, senator John McCain first made news when he was shot down over Vietnam and imprisoned there for a number of years.

Kennedy's goal of space exploration and putting a man on the moon was also championed by Johnson, with the Apollo program bringing notable successes and one disaster in which three astronauts were killed by fire inside their capsule.

Johnson also pushed through and signed the Civil Rights Act of 1964, outlawing segregation in the United States. Race riots followed in Harlem, Atlanta, New Jersey, Minneapolis, Alabama, and Michigan, as segregationists in the South and elsewhere gave way slowly to new rules, and African Americans protested perceived racism and economic inequality.

A cultural revolution was underway in the arts, with Beetlemania sweeping the country and dominating the Billboard charts. Elvis and the Beetles paved the way for Rock and Roll, and later, Rap music. Hell's angels, the motorcycle mounted marauders, were in ascendancy. Zip codes made their debut in the postal system. The first ATM machine was introduced. But there were no personal computers, no signs of the internet to come, no game boxes or I Pads or Kindles. And TV sets were still heavy tube models operated with rabbit ears. Cable had not yet become standard, and there were few program choices. In his early years, Scott saw mostly black and white television on small sets made with technology completely obsolete today.

My Fair Lady, and *Mary Poppins,* sans computerized special effects, were the winning movies of the time. The New York World's Fair opened in 1964, and was underway when Scott was born. The Verranzano Narrows Bridge, the world's longest suspension bridge, spanning the entrance to New York harbor, finally opened to traffic.

And Surgeon General Luther Terry announced on January 1, 1964, conclusive proof that cigarettes can cause lung cancer, leading ultimately to the banning of television advertising of cigarettes in 1971, and the health warnings we see on cigarette packs today.

Scott was a true native of Manhattan, exposed from birth to its ethnicities and international flavors. He rode its subways and busses and saw its parks and museums and famous shops. He visited art galleries, rolled up and down crowded Fifth Avenue, sampled the city's eateries and enjoyed the adoration of shop clerks. His rich imagination was no doubt built on these stored images and sounds.

6. New England

Age 3, a Connecticut Yankee

Life in Connecticut, by contrast, was a coming out party of a different kind for Scott. No longer confined by apartment walls, and free of having his hand held tightly in the city, he soon ventured out in the country-like, tree-lined suburban neighborhood, where older kids and their games drew him in. They began to look out for him as part of their set, and he delighted in companions his own age or slightly older, none of whom he had in the city. He also had plenty of baby sitters with the three Connett sisters next door, and the seven year old Connett twin boys, Quint and Aubrey, to dare him to follow their lead. His energy was every bit equal to theirs, and he was eager for new adventure in these wide-open spaces. At the Connett's historic old colonial era home, ball games, backyard swings, frisbee, hide and seek, and all variations on kids games attracted Scott and many other young kids to their playground, next to an old fashioned red sided barn, where horses had once been stabled.

The setting was idyllic New England, with gentle rolling hills, the Atlantic ocean next door, large old oak and maple trees lining backwater tidal streams, winding narrow streets, tall church steeples, and wide beaches with mild surf perfect for young kids. Summer cookouts with the Connetts at Tod's point, the beach park, were a favorite. The park was nature's playground for all sorts of games, and hot dogs and burgers. It was also a fisherman's paradise, with large stripped bass and blue fish landed regularly.

As a seaside village, water sports dominated, and Greenwich offered perfect deep-water harbors for small and large sail and power-boats. Early on, we joined the Riverside Yacht Club, a bike ride from home. In the junior sailing program there, Scott learned the rudiments of helming single-sail one designs like Sunfish and Optimists. Juniors also competed in racing and diving in the large salt-water pool.

When he was six, we purchased a 23Ft. fiberglass sloop, named it SCOJO after Scott and Jon, and ventured on overnight sailing trips up and down Long Island sound, following rules of the road and navigation learned in Power Squadron courses. The sloop slept four in small bunks, and had only three feet of headroom below, but everyone loved it.

Large 8-10 ft. tidal swings in the Sound had to be factored into every anchorage or mooring to avoid being left aground when the tide rolled out. Favorite anchorages were gunkholes around Oyster Bay on the Long Island side of the sound, and Zeigler's Cove, on the Connecticut side. A small dinghy with oars trailed the sailboat, for rowing ashore.

The Connett's were our old friends and the reason we located next to them when the house became available. Mr. Connett and I had worked together many years. Our social lives were very much tied together. Effie and Gene sort of adopted and introduced us to the neighborhood when we finally got our house cleaned up and painted and moved in. And, of course, they welcomed Scott as the newest toe-head member of their boisterous clan. He was safe with them. Mother Effie would see to that.

Younger Brother Arrives.

The arrival of his brother, Jon, on October 21st, 1967, again brought his grandmother Alice Henderson from the west coast to help with both boys until Joan was up and fully capable of taking over. Scott had been enrolled in nearby St. Paul's Episcopal church pre-k in early September, so he was with playmates there for half of the day, and at home or with neighboring kids for the remaining time. He and Alice spent lots of time on the new rope swing now installed on a sturdy back yard limb.

He also had his first swing set, a difficult to assemble contraption painfully put together soon after Jon was born. But reinforced fencing in the back yard, meant to contain the always curious and highly charged young Scott, proved to be no barrier. On the first day so confined, he scaled the fence and was off to find adventure.

One such day proved to be a painful lesson with school mate Billy Morris, when the two investigated and decided to dissemble a hornet's nest. The enraged hornets fought back, delivering multiple stings while overtaking both boys as they retreated as fast as

Joan and her boys, with Chumley, their dog.

their short legs would carry them. The local pharmacist prescribed lotions and creams which seemed to handle the medical emergency.

Another memorable day, when he had a slight fever, he wandered into the room where his mom sat feeding younger brother Jon. He showed Joan an empty baby aspirin container, and said, "Look, Mom, my *hever* is all gone now." Joan almost fainted, realizing that he had self medicated more than a dozen of the pills. Off they raced, with infant Jon, to the Greenwich hospital emergency room, where Scott was given meds to induce immediate vomiting, clearing his system. Thereafter, all meds were placed out of his reach.

Preparations for Jon's arrival meant new furnishings for Scott's own room at the top of the stairs, now equipped with bright red stacked bunk beds, a dresser to match, and wall to wall blue carpet. He was ready for sleepovers.

He became proficient with tricycles and later, scooters. In the cold Connecticut winters, his playroom was the basement, carpeted with indoor/outdoor material, and warmed by the furnace and washer and dryer there. But the cold and snow outside held more appeal for him. He preferred to 5mix it up with the elements. Later, he and his younger brother would ice skate on frozen Benny Park pond, down the hill from our house, spurring his interest in hockey, which he pursued in his high school years.

A second year of pre-K at St. Paul's brought a wider circle of friends. His fifth birthday party in the back yard of our home drew his circle of regulars, including young Howard Roughan, son of family friends John and Harriet, Mary Irene O'Connor, daughter of New Jersey friends Pat and George, Deirdre McDonald, daughter of Miles and Pat, Katie Grund from across the street, and Teddy Weld from the house behind us. The kids wore cone hats, with noise makers.

Scott and Jon were baptized at St. Paul's Episcopal Church in Riverside, Ct., on Christmas Eve 1967. Scott was three, Jon was two months. Betty Lou and Harry Snyder, old friends, became Godparents, with Effie and Gene Connett, and Joan's brother, Bob Henderson, as sponsors.

PRAYERS

FOR A BIRTHDAY

WATCH over my Godchild, _____
_____, O Lord, as *his* days increase;
bless and guide *him* wherever *he* may be, keeping
him unspotted from the world. Strengthen *him* when
he stands; comfort *him* when discouraged or sorrowful; raise *him* up if *he* fall; and in *his* heart may Thy
peace which passeth understanding abide all the days
of *his* life; through Jesus Christ our Lord. *Amen.*

FOR ANNIVERSARY OF BAPTISM

GRANT, O Lord, that as my Godchild, _____
_____, has been received into
the congregation of Christ's flock and signed with the
sign of the Cross, in token that hereafter *he* should
not be ashamed to confess the faith of Christ cruci-
fied, so *he* may manfully fight under His banner
against sin, the world, and the devil, and may continue Christ's faithful soldier and servant unto *his*
life's end; through the same Jesus Christ our Lord
and Saviour. *Amen.*

FOR ONE ABOUT TO BE CONFIRMED

O GOD, who through the teaching of Thy Son Jesus
Christ didst prepare the disciples for the coming of
the Comforter; Make ready, I beseech Thee, the heart
and mind of Thy servant, my Godchild, _____
_____, who at this time is
seeking to be strengthened by the gift of the Holy
Spirit through the laying on of hands, that drawing
near with penitent and faithful heart, *he* may ever-
more be filled with the power of His divine indwell-
ing; through the same Jesus Christ our Lord. *Amen.*

M-B CO. GODPARENT'S CTF. NO. 1

This is to Certify that

Harry Snyder

is a GODPARENT *to*

Scott Edwin Garrett

who was Born August 30   19 64
and who became
A MEMBER OF CHRIST,
THE CHILD OF GOD, AND
AN INHERITOR OF THE
KINGDOM OF HEAVEN
through

HOLY BAPTISM

in   St. Paul's Church
(CHURCH)
Riverside, Connecticut
(CITY)
on   December 24   19 67

Other Sponsors Eugene Connett
Etheldred Connett
Betty Lou Snyder, Robert Henderson

(Signed) Kenneth R. Franklin

Scott's Baptismal Certificate

Kindergarten at the classic campus-like Riverside Elementary School was
next in order, begun in early September 1969.   Scott and other neighbor
kids often walked the eight or so blocks to school with book bags. The
neighborhood was considered completely safe.

Pee Wee soccer interested Scott as an outlet for his unlimited
energy.   Early school-age boys were formed into teams and leagues,
playing regular games at the community center park in Old Greenwich.

He learned to ride a bike and his range for roaming increased as he rode to school, to the parks, to games, and to friend's houses. At age 7, he had a sleek, bright-red, 26 inch 10 speed that was the envy of his pals. He could barely reach the pedals, but was growing rapidly, and, like a new pair of shoes, the sizes had to take into account the rate of his total body expansion.

In his early years, his paternal grandparents, Frank and Dillie Garrett, came from West Texas to visit him in Connecticut, as did Joan's parents, Edwin and Alice Henderson, who came from Oakland, California. Occasionally, Joan and I and the boys made the trips to see them in Texas and the West Coast, but the distances involved precluded frequent contact. Still, they were very much a part of Scott's and Jon's lives.

Scott's maternal great-great grandparents, Ben and Sophie Johnson, immigrated from Sweden in the late 19th century, settling first in Minnesota before making their way to Danville, California, where they raised a family of three boys and two girls in a closed family compound, and owned a successful construction business.

Scott's mixture of Swedish/English/Irish/and Scottish genes from Northern Europe seemed to program him with intelligence, energy, humor, athletic skill, and drive. Once he formed a goal, he worked endlessly to achieve it, and usually did.

These years in Connecticut were suburban safe, relatively sleepy and all outdoors, with none of the modern electronic distractions to interrupt rough and tumble play. His early lessons about getting along with others were learned through give and take and face-to-face readings of reactions from others. Young boys and girls of the time did not spend time talking on cell phones or texting with I Pods or I phones, or playing passive indoor computer games. Those devices did not even exist, and would not appear for many years to come. Reading real books, not electronic tablets, was in.

His Connecticut environment, Riverside and Old Greenwich, had not yet evolved into red-hot real estate markets they would later become. The now omnipresent McMansions were not then conceived as replacements for modest middle class tear-downs. This transformation occurred slowly as Wall Street financiers and hedge funds moved east to headquarter in Connecticut and drove house and land prices into the stratosphere. This new wealth class changed the character of what had been a mid-level executive community of commuters riding the New Haven railroad to New York City jobs as ad men, sales reps, and corporate climbers.

The national context of Scott's fifth year was major achievement in space exploration amidst cultural and political change. Astronauts Neal Armstrong and Buzz Aldrin landed on the Moon and televised their brief activities there. Scott and Jon were awakened late on the night of July 21st to see the event on TV, which Scott remembered but Jon, of course, did not.

The year was notable also as the first significant withdrawal of troops from Vietnam by newly elected president Richard Nixon, beginning the wind down of that divisive conflict.

Robert Kennedy was assassinated, Edward Kennedy famously drove off the Chappaquiddick bridge on Martha's Vineyard. Sesame

Street debuted on national TV, the Beatles gave their last concert, while the United States Supreme Court ordered "immediate desegregation."

And in June, the little noticed Stonewall riots in New York City, the kickoff to the modern gay rights movement.

Through second grade at Riverside Elementary, Scott's life had been centered in New York city and New England, with little exposure to other geography. Soon enough, that would change.

7. A "Jimmy Friend." The One and Only Scottie G.

By Howard Roughan,
friend and author

Howard and Scott, vacationing with their families
at Rosemary Beach, Fl.

Ask anyone who knew him. Go ahead. They'll tell you this story or that story, the time when he did this thing or said that line you wouldn't believe. They'll tell you the story with relish, with gusto, with a glint in their eye, because this is no ordinary story, no way. This is a Scottie G. story.

How did he do it? How did he make us all laugh so hard, so easily?

It was more than timing, more than a way with words. It was how he saw the world. Not that everything had to be funny. Just that everything didn't need to be so serious. Life was too short for that. Shorter than we all knew.

The phone would ring and I'd see his name on the Caller ID. The number beneath it would change over the years, and change yet again, and in time I'd realize just how many area codes Scott had taught me. Springfield, Peoria, Milwaukee… He was like the back of a concert t-shirt. And everywhere he traveled, the fan base would grow. What a rock star.

Yes, the phone would ring and there he'd be doing his Sean Connery impression or butchering any number of European or Latin American dialects while pretending to be addressing a jury or ordering from the drive-thru at Jack in the Box.

Of course, the real experimental theater was saved for when no one was home. That's when I'd get the official Scottie G. Voicemail. Maybe it would be a riff on Terry's policy of never staying at a motel with "outside doors." Maybe it was revisiting his idea for the great American novel, "Trespass to Chattel," in the hope that he could convince me once and for all that it wasn't a horrible title. Or maybe it was a bit from our ongoing routine about the guys from Moishe's Movers & Storage whose trucks we used to see all the time in Manhattan.

"Oy, my back!" I would say.

"Oy, this box is too heavy!" he would follow.

For sure, no two messages were ever alike but they all still had one thing in common: the automated woman's voice on the answering machine that would announce after Scott had finally finished, "*You have zero minutes of recording time left.*"

Damn, it's so surreal to be writing about him in the past tense. I still don't think of him in that way. I'm not sure I ever will or want to. I'll be in a meeting or out at a restaurant or just running errands when I'll see something funny happening. And like a reflex, my brain will trigger the same thought, the same reminder.

Gotta tell Scott.

The fact that I no longer can then hits me like a sucker punch, but it doesn't stop me from playing the scene out in my head. Because when I do, I can always hear the same thing. It's him laughing...just like he always did. Like no one else. The one and only Scottie G. I miss you like

crazy, buddy.

8. New City, New Friends, New School, New Accent.

Atlanta became his new home in June of 1972. We moved there when Monsanto, the chemical company, transferred us from New York to Atlanta. Scott was two months shy of his eighth birthday. Jon was four. Monsanto had manufacturing plants in Alabama, Florida, and South Carolina, and Atlanta became the management hub for products produced by these factories. My job was to help develop and bring to market new products from these plants.

In the early 70's, Jimmy Carter was Governor of Georgia for one term before becoming President Carter in 1976. The Civil Rights movement was in full swing in the South, and Atlanta tended to be its center for marches, speeches, and protests. The city and the country were absorbing racial change in fits and starts, sometimes with violence.

Scott would soon be entering third grade at Spaulding elementary school in the Sandy Springs area of Fulton county Georgia.

His new home was at 7455 Old Maine Trail in the North Springs subdivision, about ten miles north of downtown Atlanta. The three-story house was quite large compared to Connecticut, with four bedrooms and three baths, and a connected two-story garage with a large playroom on the second level. The design copied the classic Deerfield colonial architectural style, immediately recognizable as exemplifying early Massachusetts clapboard-sided center hall colonials.

The house sat atop a steep hillside covered with towering soft southern pine trees. A protected forest preserve of several hundred acres stretched three miles North from our housing cluster to the south bank of the turbulent Chattahoochee river, the conduit from the Lake Sidney Lanier reservoir thirty miles to the North, from which Atlanta drew its water supply.

After a short acclimation to the new surroundings, this forest became an exploration ground for the two Garrett boys and their new neighborhood friends, Richard and Marty Buckman, who matched ages with Scott and Jon. Jim Schneider, another neighbor was Scott's age, and, with his older brother Bill, joined in the fun, as did their sister Mary, and the Pinkney kids, Donna, Christie, and Donnie, who lived across the street on the corner.

A few miles away, in the long established Buckhead area, lived Monsanto friends Bruce and Barbara English, and their children Robert and Patricia, also good matches as playmates for Scott and Jon.

Scott entered third grade at Spalding Elementary School under Ms. Katrina Gale, his teacher, and quickly became one of her favorites. His academic work was OK, but his energy kept getting in the way of his concentration during class. His doctor prescribed Ritalin briefly, until it was recognized to be working at the wrong times. He was simply into fun and to the development of his life's personality, which would never change. The use of this drug to tone down naturally boisterous boys later

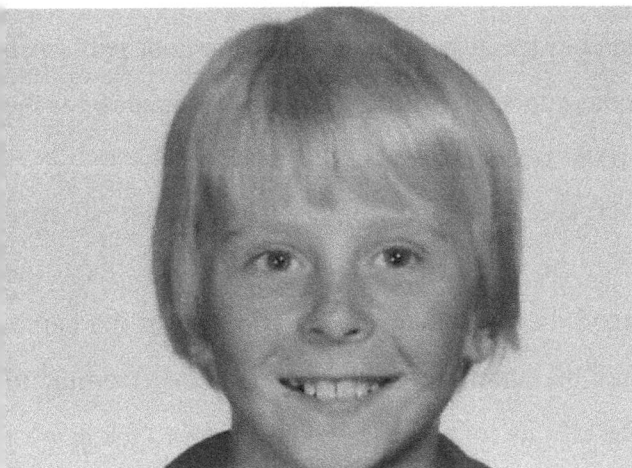

Age 8, ready for Southern adventure

came under great criticism as prescribed too frequently and often wrongfully by doctors at the behest of teachers seeking quieter classrooms.

He saw fun and games in every situation, whether in school, exploring the forest, learning hand standing on skateboards, jumping bicycles over piled up bricks and plywood, swimming and diving in the neighborhood association pool, playing tennis with friends, water skiing at Lake Lanier, playing Pong in the garage playroom, reading a book, telling jokes, or inventing a story.

We impulsively bought a powerboat from our friend Jimmy Dean, the country/western star, and called it BIG ORANGE, its brazen color. It had a powerful six-cylinder inboard engine with plenty of zip for water skiing and tubing, and many summer weekends were spent on the lake. Scott and Jon both became skilled water skiers.

The reservoir was formed by a dam across the Chattahoochee river, the watershed for Atlanta. Sheraton and some investors built a resort hotel and golf course on an island in the lake, with an indoor/outdoor pool open to boaters who tied up at their docks. This area became the hangout for the family on weekends when the skiers got ready for a break.

We joined the Cherokee Town and Country Club, which is where Scott first fell in love with the game of golf at age nine. He liked the junior golf program, learned the fundamentals and etiquette of the game, and it became his preferred life sport, devoting himself in his free time to perfecting his game. Wherever he lived, he located and played the nearest links, later joining private golf clubs when he was able to afford them .
On another whim, we bought a condo in Pinehurst, North Carolina, on a golf course in the middle of this hugely popular golf resort. The location was not far from Charlotte, where Scott's great-grandfather Alexander Morris lived more than a hundred years earlier.

When not on Lake Lanier, the four-hour driving trip to Pinehurst and a round or two of golf and some fishing on Saturday and Sunday became standard. He had a musical love affair with a group named THE MONKEYS, playing their records over and over again, accompanying them with his own drum set, and singing along with them. Joan and I will never be able to erase the sounds of this nascent rock band, banging and singing, "Hey, hey, we're the Monkeys, people say we monkey around, but we're too busy singing to put anybody down."

He became an avid hockey fan, and we often went to pro games in the Atlanta arena. He strapped pillows over his knees and shins and posed for pictures with a hockey stick in his hands, mimicking the goalies.

A driving trip to Disney World in Orlando for vacation, staying at the Disney hotel with a monorail running through it, was a favorite of Scott and Jon. They did not miss a single ride.

A TIME ON THE TEXAS PLAINS:

The Summer of Scott's tenth year, he travelled alone by plane to Lubbock, Texas, transferring planes in Dallas, and was met in Lubbock by his Garrett grandparents, Frank and Dillie, with whom he spent almost the whole summer. Their home was in Plainview, Texas, 45 miles north of Lubbock. His uncles, Cal and Raby, also hosted him and taught him a lot about breeding and raising quarter horses, growing and baling hay, shooting all kinds of guns, chewing tobacco, and riding in small airplanes. The plane adventure came about when Cal loaded Scott into the rear seat of a Piper Cub and flew round trip to Kansas. Scott thought nothing of it.

He also took a turn at dipping snuff and smoking coffee, courtesy of his grandmother, who he loved. But she couldn't convince him to drink milk or eat mustard or eggs. His grandpa Frank took him to play golf at Plainview Country club, a public municipal course.

He spent a lot of time with several cousins who lived in Lubbock and Plainview. Stan Cribbs and Bradley Phinny were his age, and the three got along well, and into mischief. Lynn and Lisa Garrett, Cal's daughters, joined in.

Uncle Cal was the golf professional in Hereford, Texas, some 60 miles northwest of Plainview. Scott was given free rein to roam the Hereford course on a golf cart, and play as much as he wished. He also got free lessons from his uncle, both for golf and shooting a 22 rifle at ground squirrels.

At the end of the summer, his hair was shoulder length, he was ready for braces, and he was taller, stronger and very tanned from the West Texas sun. He had met most all of his Garrett family, many for the first time, as well as many of his grandmother's sisters and brothers and their extended families. He had developed a sense of his Texas roots, and always remembered the summer with pleasure as a time for great freedom to do pretty much as he pleased, with loving family looking out for him. He began a growth spurt that summer.

MAD DOGS:

Back in Atlanta for sixth grade, he joined the soccer team of the local Catholic parish school, where the Schneider kids went. He became a fine player, a forward for the MAD DOGS, and his team became championship quality with good coaching and parental support. They won all games up to and including the state championship for that age group. For the state tournament, the kids were bused to Memphis, Tennessee for playoffs and the big game. It was a memory which would stay with Scott always. He could remember all the players, all the games, and most of the key plays in which he had a part.

At times, his younger brother Jon would sub if the Mad Dogs were shorthanded. Jon was super fast and strong for his age, and a skillful athlete. He had a muscular frame contrasted to Scott's graceful long and lanky makeup.

CAMP KADAHLIA AND OTHER DIVERSIONS:

The next summer, Scott and Rob English chose to go to a month long camp in the highlands of North Carolina, called CAMP KADAHLIA. They slept out, did craft projects, hiked, played games, learned survival skills, and generally exhausted themselves with junk food and lack of sleep. The counselors kept a tight rein, however, and they returned skinnier and well tanned, better for the experience.

Soon afterward, the family took a week's vacation in Acapulco, renting a private home belonging to a friend. The house was near the beach, where both boys swam and parasailed. The caretaker and cook did the food shopping and preparation. Her son was the Pepsi distributor, and the family consumed great quantities of free Pepsi instead of the local suspect water.

His room in Atlanta was big, with a king bed and its own private bath. He relished this space and his privacy. When guests came, he willingly gave up his bed and bunked in with Jon, who now had the twin red-lacquered beds in his room. One of the boys favorite nighttime activities found me lying on the floor between the beds, making up stories about anything, which could go to any length, depending on when the boys fell asleep.

Robert English occasionally slept over and enjoyed hanging out with the boys. So did a variety of other friends of both boys. Rob's younger sister Patricia also liked to mix it up with the boys, and Jon and

Patricia continued their friendship into present day. The Atlanta house had plenty of room. Sleeping bags in the garage playroom was fun for all, followed by pancakes for breakfast in the main house.

Skateboarding became the rage during Scott's Atlanta years, and the neighborhood boys were enthralled with them and the competition and daredevil stunts invented around them. Jumping over obstacles, hand standing on them as they went down steep concrete streets, wiping out with skinned elbows and shoulders and ankles, was to be expected, even with heavy padding and helmets.

Jumping bicycles was inevitably as tempting, and wipeouts were also quite common, but the boys and their friends were fearless, with few lasting ill effects. The endless action and fun was totally consistent with Scott's extroverted personality, encouraged also by the lack of video games or daytime TV or computers or I Pods, which so occupy young people today.

SAILING THE NORTHWEST:

In August, 1976, we flew to Seattle, then by charter aircraft, to Friday Harbor, Washington, to join old friends Halsey and Sharon Burke and their daughter Michelle, for a vacation on their beautiful 65 ft. yawl. Our two families sailed the straits of San Juan De Fuca, Desolation Sound, and on into Canadian waters as part of a two-week live-aboard adventure. The kids and Halsey caught a 40 lb. Link cod fishing from a small rubber dinghy, and, in landing it, punctured the inflated boat. They rushed back to the mother ship before deflating, and the entire crew ate the delicious fish over the next week.

We dug and ate tons of oysters in various harbors, and visited Victoria and Vancouver. Victoria was the birthplace of Scott's grandfather Edwin Henderson. At one anchorage, we rowed ashore and climbed some 300 feet above sea level to swim in an enormous fresh water lake. A cascading waterfall down the mountain formed natural fresh-water bathing pools in the rocks, and we bathed in these stone tubs.

THE HIDEOUT:

Earlier, in Atlanta, Scott confided to me that the boys had built a "hideout" a hike

Our boys with their prized Link Cod

away, and invited me to come and inspect it. The three-mile hike led me and Scott and Jon through the pine forest to the fast flowing Chattahoochee river, then along the river's edge, ascending along a winding trail to a crawl space to the hideout entrance. Inside, the boys had used picks and shovels to dig a cave into the riverbank, some fifty feet above the swirling river below. One slip and one or all of them would have been crashing down to the river to be carried away by the dangerous

current. There were no barriers to prevent just such an occurrence. This isolated setting, with no one nearby to call for help, had the makings of a disaster, and I was alarmed enough to quickly call a halt to the adventure.

I ordered the cave closed, forever, and explained to the boys what might easily happen, and how they would likely never be found in the foaming water filled with logs and rocks and other obstacles. I took an authoritative tone, and, fortunately, Scott and Jon seemed to listen, and never ventured back there, or so they said.

Jon recalls chasing games the boys and their friends played in the woods behind our house. The game involved BB guns, with one team chasing another, and, when in range, shooting them in the back. It was a form of tag. Then the opposing team had a turn shooting. No eyesight was lost, and nobody tattled to the parents. Later, in Connecticut and St. Louis, different versions of the game would be played with sticks and Roman candles, all of them having evolved, they said, from the movie, RUNNING MAN. Scott was the instigator.

FLEXIBILITY, CONVICTIONS, AND MIDDLE SCHOOL:

His sense of adventure and need for full time activity compelled him to try new things, to invent new stunts, to devise new pranks, to extract the most fun from everyday activities. He was tireless, while others ran out of energy and pleaded for breaks. He laughed when others gave in, too easily he thought. And this trait would be uniquely his in whatever he did later in life, in work, in school, in law school, in fighting his illness, in family life, or in leisure at home. He was always working, always planning his next activity, always seeking the humor, building his friendships.

He began forming convictions while in Atlanta. He relished change, loved learning to talk "Southern", liked the experience of Atlanta as broadening to him personally. As an adult, he had trouble imagining why people were reluctant to move to new surroundings, try new things, listen for different accents. He thought it essential to feel at home with diversity, with different cultural and belief systems, and that this sort of change taught adaptability and flexibility. He felt that kids who grew up and spent their lives in one narrow parochial setting were a little deprived, dealing only with the familiar, never outside their comfort zones.

Living these beliefs, he never hesitated to move to a new city, especially if the move meant moving up a rung toward his career goals. And he thought all such moves would make his children stronger in the long run.

As he prepared to enter 8th grade, the Garrett's were transferred back to the New York office, and the family resumed life in another Connecticut home, this one at 21 Cove Road, on Lucas Point in Old Greenwich. The ensuing years in Connecticut were formative and pivotal in Scott's life, but that is another chapter.

9. Phase One Treatment Begins

"If you are going through hell, keep going."
                                   --Winston Churchill

"Man performs and engenders so much more than he can or
should have to bear.
That's how he finds that he can bear anything."
                                   --William Faulkner

The induction phase of leukemia treatment, the literature notes, infuses Cytarabine chemo continuously for seven days through an IV port. This drug suppresses the immune system and slows the growth of cancer cell division. It is followed by Anthracycline, another chemo developed from the streptomyces bacterium, for three consecutive days through an IV push, in a regimen known as "7+3". The expectation is that some 70% of patients will finally achieve remission through this protocol.   The literature names harmful side-effects, but doesn't bother to describe them as a form of going through hell.

Chemotherapy works by poisoning cancer cells, but kills good cells at the same time, greatly reducing the body's normal ability to fight infection. This period of susceptibility to simple or complex infections is known as neutropenia, caused by a shortage of infection fighting neutrophils in the blood. In this critical phase, Scott is somewhat isolated from normal contact with family and guests.

The drugs make Scott sick almost immediately with mouth and throat sores, nausea, headaches, loss of body hair, and intense pain. Bone marrow biopsies, taken with long needles through his pelvic bone, were also painful and left him sore, but he did not complain.

Significant weight loss is common, and Scott began to lose weight rapidly because of the medications, nausea, sores, and loss of appetite. His weight going into the hospital was about 190 lbs. At the end of the induction phase, he weighed 165 lbs.

A naturally picky eater, he disliked most of the hospital food offered him, chocolate shakes and ice cream excepted, with an occasional omelet with fries. Terry and Joan and I often brought him his favorite foods from outside, or at least ones he thought he could hold down, including pizza, thoroughly cooked chicken dishes, lots of fresh fruit, scones, muffins, and the strong coffee he loved.

Terry was with him from late morning until late in the evening, every day, often sleeping in his room ion a rollaway bed, monitoring his treatment, asking questions of staff, looking after Scott's needs, taking him for walks when he couldn't sleep. Joan or I or both were with him mornings until Terry came, and sometimes returned at night. Jack and Audrey were occupied with school during the day, and had restricted visits in any case due to his vulnerability to bacterial infection.

Doctors and nurses encouraged frequent walks, and if at all possible, daily time on the stationary bike in the visitors lounge. Exercise was essential, they said, even when he didn't feel like it. His devoted nurses went along with him on these walks.

Some nights were sleepless, and he tried to nap during the day in spite of multiple disruptions and tests. He stayed in touch with friends and associates at work during these times, using the room phone, his Blackberry, and his beloved iPad. His oldest pals called him often, and they chatted at length, laughing over some fun event they had shared. Jim Stern, his General Counsel at A.O. Smith, was a frequent visitor, and Jim briefed Scott on all the company happenings and made him feel a part of the team. Later, Scott would call his staff and offer guidance on cases in progress. He felt in touch, and fully believed he could make a contribution from his hospital bed, and from home in recovery.

All the while, his sense of humor, sometimes dark, never left him, and frequent laughter could be heard on the other end of his conversations.

Howard Roughan, Lance High, Dean Bordeaux, Ken Hurley, Steve Ely, his cousin Stan Cribbs, Jim Stern, his "Jimmy" friends, kept his spirits up. He loved getting calls from Jack and Audrey, telling him everything they were doing.

A tall multi-armed metal pole with four beeping screens held several clear plastic bags of chemo and fluids being pumped into his body. The device is a common hospital sight accompanying the patient wherever he goes. At her first sight of it, Audrey claimed naming rights. *Estevez*, as she tagged him , was physically and intrusively attached to Scott's body through the rest of his hospital stay, dispensing poisons, nutrients, antibiotics, steroids, and, ultimately, brand new bone marrow.

On June 16, Thursday, first phase chemo was completed, now tests will tell whether he is on trend to achieving remission. He had suffered humiliatingly but stoically and willingly through every day since treatment started nine days ago, seeing this as a necessary darkness leading to a good end result. Just the first step of going through hell!

Yet he also understood clearly that his suffering had only just begun. Daily transfusions of red blood and platelets continue, along with preventive antibiotics and other liquids, all flowing from transparent plastic bags, digital monitors forever beeping as they dispensed their life-sustaining fluids.

10. Phase One Test Results

"Enjoy the little things, for one day you may look back and realize they were the big things."

--Robert Brault, educator, opera singer

"Turn your face to the sun and the shadows fall behind you.

--Unknown

On June 17, the preliminary test results came back, indicating his progress along a spectrum of possibilities was in the "middle of the middle", neither bad nor great. The word was that bone marrow transplant preparations should be made in case needed, although complete remission was still expected.

The international bone marrow donor bank, with thirteen million pledged to donate marrow if needed, was talked about. But the best and most likely match would be from his sibling Jon. Jon volunteered to have his marrow tested through a simple blood test during his visit to Milwaukee on June 28.

On June 18, Scott talked frankly about his disease with me during our morning visit. He was optimistic, as always. He had ordered plans for a new wing addition to his home, which would house Joan and me and Terry's parents during our visits, and his own children's visits home during their college. He talked at length about planning his 50th birthday party at Pebble Beach, staying at the lodge, reprising the wonderful visit he and I shared many years ago when he graduated from college, before law school. He said he wanted the entire family to be there, and was budgeting $20 thousand dollars for the three or four day stay. He wanted nothing spared.

He talked about his life insurance, a recognition that significant risk lay ahead of him in fighting his disease. He was entering the most neutropenic stage, when he had the least ability to fight infection, and the need to take strong precautions, including restricting visitors. Terry became his gate-keeper in this regard. Very frequent hand washing and sanitizing, mask wearing during walks outside his room, some hospital staff wearing masks when doing tests or exams. He developed more mouth sores, rashes, and night fevers, which fortunately subsided, managing to avoided serious complication.

June 19, he called me in the early morning to wish me a happy Father's day, just one of the "little things", which, looking back, became a very big thing to me.

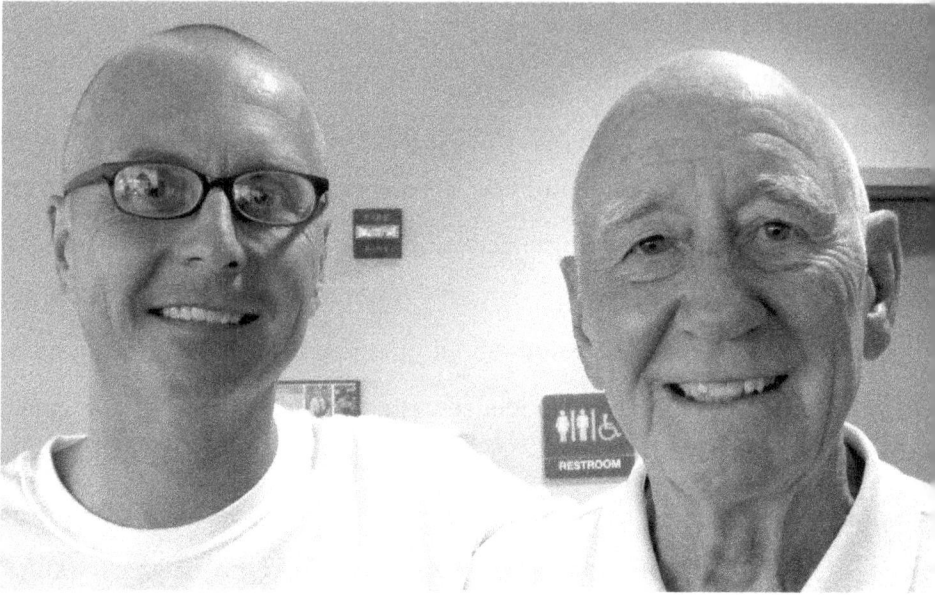

Scott and Dad, heads shaved

I went to his room at 3:30 PM to watch the end of the U.S. Open golf tournament with him. About this time, we shaved their heads together, in symbolic solidarity. Scott was now losing most of the hair on his head and body, so the time was right. An electric razor was used instead of a blade to make certain his skin was not nicked, opening possible infection.

THE DINNER TREE, A BIG THING

At home, Terry's and Scott's women friends has formed a remarkable "dinner tree", through which a number of them had volunteered to rotate in supplying complete dinners to the family every night as long as Scott was Scott was hospitalized, recognizing that Terry had neither the time or inclination to shop and cook meals. Most were their friends from Christ King Catholic school and Christ King church, who recognized a family in need and took initiative. Theirs was an unselfish, generous act, which spoke of the value and closeness in a church or school community or tribe devoted to each other in times of need. Whether religiously or secularly motivated, their deeds were acts of kindness and thoughtfulness never to be forgotten.

This dinner tree, which brought delicious and huge meals, continued throughout the year of 2011, and ended only when Terry asked that they stop.

BONE MARROW TALK, A VERY BIG THING

On June 20, Dr. Jeanne Palmer, head of Froedtert's bone marrow transplant unit, conferred with Scott and Terry, explaining that a marrow match was only about 25% probability with a sibling, 80% from the bone marrow worldwide registry, with an average 80% success rate, meaning a cure of at least five years, and with a 95% success rate at Froedtert hospital. She suggested a second opinion be obtained from BMT experts in Chicago, or in Madison, Wisconsin at the University medical school.

She said that the prospect of a relapse was greatly reduced with a transplant, provided a suitable donor could be found, and while the ratio of cure with remission with chemo alone was only 3 in 10, the cure rate with BMT was 6 in 10. In other words, the probability of lasting cure with transplant was double that of non-transplant. While doubling the odds of a cure, the failure rate with BMT was still a mind-boggling 40%.

She warned that post transplant, another month in the hospital would be required, followed by a year at home and out of work, then a lifetime of regular check ups and boosters as needed. Dr. Palmer felt strongly that Scott could not entertain working from home because of the inevitable stress that would accompany being involved with the office. This statement was met with some skepticism, noting that being excluded from office involvement would likely be more stressful than the opposite. The issue was not resolved, and not argued.

Covering all bases, Palmer noted that the millions of indicated donors did not necessarily indicate a computer match could be found in reality. Some registrants may have signed up long ago, perhaps as students, but may now be married with families, in the middle of careers, and may no longer be willing to donate . Other potential donors may now be contaminated and ineligible, or have children and unwilling to take the risk of donating marrow, however small. The attrition rate from all causes, including death of the potential donor, could be very high.

Palmer said that Scott is in perhaps the third step of a 15-18 step process, each fraught with risk. Getting a marrow match is but one hurdle, the next is getting the actual donated marrow hand carried from wherever the donor is to Froedtert, the big challenge to avoid rejection, then the extended period of time required to know if the transplant will hold and be successful for the long run..

The possibility, however slight of complications and infection post transplant also would have to be recognized. Palmer was pointing out worst case, but the overall effect of the conference was sobering and provocative for both Scott and Terry. They would have to weigh these risks carefully before deciding on the next move.

Scott is beginning to face reality in terms of his career goals, his likely position when he might return to the office, his restricted mobility with his family and his business activities. But immediately in front of him was the goal of getting to remission.

REMISSION EXPECTED:

Brother Jon and Scott visiting in the hospital.

The following week involved continued monitoring and infusions of red blood and platelets, but no more chemo. Coming out of neutropenia, his blood counts are rising, very good signs. He is anxious to get out of the hospital, says that he and brother Jon have renewed their relationship after been at odds for some years, says he plans to take an annual "brother" trip with Jon so that they can bond more closely. Their philosophical approaches to life have differed greatly since childhood, with Jon the free spirit not interested in working in a hierarchy, and Scott filled with career ambition and dedication to goals all his adult life. They now talk regularly on the phone. Their sibling rivalries of the past seem to have abated.

He also talks about wanting to compete in the Blue Mound Club Championship in late August if he can. He competed in 2010, reached the semi finals, and lost on the 20th hole to the gentleman who went on to win the championship the next day. So he felt capable, and wanted to get back to practicing as soon as possible. For now, the PICC line in his arm precluded any such activity. He decides 2012 is a more realistic possibility.

On June 28, Jon had his blood tested for a possible marrow match, with results to come later. He visited Scott in his hospital room, and, as always, humor prevailed.

Bone marrow biopsies were taken on June 23rd and June 30. On July 1, the doctors announced that his marrow appeared clean of detectable leukemic cells.

On July 3, he was released from the hospital, but with daily hospital appointments. He was welcomed home with great fanfare.

On July 4, my 78th birthday, optimistic that full remission would be confirmed through a bone marrow biopsy on July 7, the whole family had a joyful dinner at Scott's house, with him in his usual head of table chair. Everyone held hands and offered thanks. Scott thanked all of us for our support, and urged kindness, tolerance, and respect for each other.

We ate corn on the cob, the first of the season, and laughed our way through a very happy meal, each mindful of the long road ahead. We chalked up another "little thing", and were immensely grateful.

WE TURNED OUR FACES TO THE SUN, AND THE SHADOWS FELL BEHIND US.

11. Remission, Consolidation, and Happy 47th.

"Life is a song-sing it. Life is a game-play it. Life is love-enjoy it."

--Sai Baba, Indian Guru.

Scott at home in remission

The bone marrow biopsy on July 7 left Scott sore but hopeful. Two days later, the news came that, indeed, he was in full remission, and ready to enter the consolidation phase of treatment. The sickness and suffering of the past month had paid off, as Scott expected. But the harsh confinement and the chemistry of the drug cocktails had put him on edge, made his less patient, more worried, more critical and less tolerant of hospital staff and their by-the-book routines, yet he continued always to follow instructions to the letter, expecting the reward of remission, and now it had come....with strings.

The daily log I kept from today until his birthday on August 30 charts the ups and downs, the hopes and disappointments, the agony which he endured while awaiting the reward of life.

On July 8, word that his brother Jon was not a match, meaning total reliance of the Bone Marrow Computer Registry to find a donor, if a decision is made to go forward with the transplant.

With AML leukemia, if no further post remission therapy is given, almost all patients will relapse. More chemotherapy at this stage is intended to keep residual cancer cells at bay. Consolidation involves three to five additional courses of intensive chemo, each over five day periods. Most of these require hospitalization. For patients judged to be intermediate risks, Scott's category, a stem cell transplant (new bone marrow) is thought to be the best option for cure, depending on the age, overall health, and values of the individual.

Intermediate risk AML is curable, but with five-year survival rates of 48%, and a 50% relapse rate without new bone marrow, rising to 70% five-year survival with a transplant from a well-matched donor.

AML is rare, with only about ten thousand people in the United States developing the disease each year. It accounts for just 1.2 % of cancer deaths. The median age at diagnosis is 63, according to medical literature on the subject. Younger people have better survival rates due to better ability to withstand the harsh therapies required.

July 9, another luncheon reunion at Scott's house, this time with chicken enchiladas sent by a good neighbor as part of the dinner tree program.

July 11. Scott is back in the hospital for five days of chemo, part one of the consolidation. The same old hospital routine resumes, with around the clock nursing and testing and data gathering, and unwelcome hospital food. We bring him fruit and other foods as before, labeled and stored in a fridge in the nurses station. He is again made very sick by the chemo cocktail and other drugs. *In hell and going through it.*

July 16. He is home for three weeks, with alternate day visits back to the cancer clinic for tests and infusions, and will go back in the hospital on August 8 for another week of chemo. Before he leaves the hospital today, he is given an injection to boost his white cell count, a drug named Neulasta, which was to produce painful side-effects.

July 17. His check-up at the clinic indicates everything on track, with white cell count slightly elevated, thought to be the result of a white cell booster shot given him yesterday to help elevate his white count.

It is also revealed to him that just two computerized bone marrow donors seem to be a good match for Scott, and that only one of them has agreed to come in for additional testing. It is not known who or where the person is, information which will be kept confidential until at least a year after successful transplant. The news is good, but the hope was for 8 to 10 good matches, given the attrition rate of the donors, for a variety of reasons. There is much speculation about the potential donor, his home country, his family his occupation, and whether he will continue to be willing to donate if that is Scott's choice.

Scott's weight is back up to 177, but he will lose weight again as soon as the effects of the latest round of chemo kick in, expected to be about Friday, July 21st. He will also become neutropenic again, highly vulnerable to infection. He will be in semi-isolation for a few days, restricted from visitors, kids, or dogs.

His time at home is not idle, but plenty of rest is recommended. He makes calls to the office and friends from his upstairs bedroom and office, works through personal papers and bills, and has some contact with family, watching television a lot. He has the lumber, hardware, and supplies to begin work on his long planned Murphy bed project to fit the opening in the anti-room of their master bedroom, and is eager to get started with its construction. Prior to hospitalization, he had cut the lumber to size.

July 23. Sores erupt in Scott's mouth, expected as a result of infection fighting neutrophils in his blood, and a low white blood count.

July 24, At his cancer clinic appointment, tests showed that he needed two bags of red blood and platelets. These were infused during a four-hour stay, interrupted by the sudden side effects of hives, but continued after infusion of antibiotics through his picc line.

In the late evening, at home, he has sudden unbearable pain in his lower spine, the after effect, said Dr. Atallah, of the Neulasta shot given him a week ago to stimulate white cell growth. Unable to sleep, and tolerated pain only by resting on his knees, with his upper body resting on a pile of pillows or an ottoman. The pain subsided at 3 AM. He had no standby pain medication, and just suffered through it.

July 26, seven vials of blood drawn and analyzed, with blood counts good. No need for infusions of platelets to fight infection. Back home in an hour.

July 27. Today's appointment at the cancer clinic again showed good blood counts with no transfusions needed. If platelet counts are above 60 on Sunday, he and Terry and the kids can take a two-hour driving trip to Lake Waupaca, Wisconsin, where Terry's uncle and aunt live.

And news of a further breakthrough on the probability of a donor match. The second potential match has now come forward for additional testing and screening. A complete physical and blood analysis are required. This development means both potential donors have agreed to donate if their markers are a good match.

The logistics of donating and scheduling of infusion mean that a transplant might possibly take place in late October. If the donor is in a foreign country, somewhere in Europe for example, the extracted marrow would have to be picked up, protected and hand delivered to Froedtert by qualified courier, housed in a closed dry ice container. At Froedtert, the transplant team will do a final evaluation before drip infusion.

The next round of chemo, scheduled for August 8, can be done as a daily outpatient, from 6 to 8 AM each day, in the cancer clinic, a structure adjacent to the main hospital, where cubicles with recliners and TV are arranged around the perimeter of nursing stations. This arrangement is much easier and more comfortable for Scott and Terry. He can talk on the phone or work with his iPad while receiving chemo from an "Estevez" pole, while Terry reads or watches TV or talks with Scott. Doctors have agreed to this outpatient arrangement only because Scott lives so near the hospital and come back in a few minutes should problems arise. With chemo, there is always that potential.

July 31, Scott's first day trip, by car, to Lake Waupaca. He talks of partnering with Terry's Dad, Dr. Jim Bowers, to buy a lake house there as a second home. They came home in time for a dinner of tacos, ice cream and angel food cake, which Joan had put together.

Scott talked about his impaired memory, a side effect of powerful drugs. Cancer literature has named this effect "chemo brain". He says his long-term memory is shot. Cannot remember much of anything since the disease hit except the treatment details. He is concerned about work, and his effectiveness on the job when he goes back. He is anxious to get all treatments behind him so he can concentrate on the future with his family and his work.

He has had a sore throat for several days, but the doctors have said not to worry so long as he has no fever. Scott worries that the throat pain might be an infection or tumor. The doctors say no.

August 1. Scott and Terry keep a date at the cancer clinic at 11:20 AM. Audrey and Jack are to have lunch with Joan and me. Audrey has a meltdown, acting out, and crying hysterically. Scott believes that these outbursts are her reaction to his illness, the source of her bad dreams and her anxieties, and the disease as the center of attention taking parental focus away from her and Jack. Both Jack and Aud have had dates with a child counselor. Both seem OK except for rare flare- ups, like Audrey's today.

Scott says headaches and sore throat continue, with stomach upsets, but goes on to talk about the new mother-in-law addition he is planning.

August 5. Scott and I begin assembling the Murphy bed kit, which is quite involved. We had six good hours together deciphering the project and making some progress before he ended the session, exhausted. We continued working the project the next day after his visits to the clinic for blood checks and a cat scan to determine the cause of his persistent sore throat. Scan came back negative, with "nothing to worry about."

August 6, Terry's 43rd birthday, but the kid's daytime activities postponed the party until tomorrow, at Blue Mound Club. We expect to resume work on the Murphy bed Saturday morning, maybe finishing the assembly on Sunday.

Jack and Aud spent the night with us. Jack famously said, *"Dad has a half lucky side to his sickness. He can have all the milkshakes and sweets he wants."* "Half Lucky" stuck with us as a decent way of looking for the bright side of every down situation. Both kids begin a week-long volleyball camp on Monday.

August 8. Scott and Terry now go to the cancer clinic for two sessions a day, 6-8 AM and 6-8 PM, Monday, Wednesday, and Friday. Still no further word about a bone marrow donor match.

Some hours in between the dates, Scott and his I work on the Murphy bed, finishing the assembly, and installing the bed into the existing opening. The mechanics work perfectly, with some tweaking. Cosmetic moulding will finish it off aesthetically, followed by Joan's painting. Then a large 46" flat screen TV is to be fitted on the bed's underside, visible only when the bed is closed. This is tricky, and requires scoping out the hardware needed, and hiding the wiring. Not since our father/on duo jointly assembled a large slide/swing set for the kids in Springfield, MO., have we worked together to complete such a project. *Another small thing to remember.*

Start to finish, the project allowed gabbing back and forth about procedure, measurements, and techniques. We were delighted with the product of our collaboration, and the memories it created. The conversations, the laughter, the work, the effort, will always be treasured.

Jack and Aud spent the night with us tonight, and played Fan Tan, a game of sequential placement of cards beginning with the seven of clubs. They got it instantly. The kids are smart academically and have good bearing and quality parenting which many kids lack.

August 9. Scott stopped by the house with sweets from Alterra coffee shop. He has been up since 5 AM, the effect of steroids administered to offset strong chemo. He talks loud, is lecturing, opinionated, had trouble remembering his own cell phone number. Seems actually on a high from meds, the side-effects of which he has no doubt. Today, he and Terry have his first lunch out with friends, which was *another one of the little things* he enjoyed

August 12, Official word that a single donor match has been qualified from the bank of 13 million worldwide. The match is good, with five major and five secondary points of matching, in other words, said Dr. Atallah, "a perfect match."   October 1 is the tentative date set for transplant.   Now, Scott and Terry must make a final decision about whether to go forward, a critical choice to be made only after second expert opinions are sought.   A date is set at the University School of medicine in Madison, WI, for meeting with a recognized expert to discuss all pros, cons, and risks, leading to a decision.   Scott thinks that he probably has no real choice but to go for it because he wants a permanent cure, and this route offers the only solid chance to achieve it.

August 14, Sunday morning.   Scott and I are at the clinic at 9 AM for his shots, blood tests, nulasta shot, and PICC line flushing.   The nurse advised that he is neutropenic, but no transfusions or platelets needed at this time, but would likely be required on Tuesday, the 16th.   In the afternoon, we watched the finals of the PGA championship tournament, won by Keegan Bradley in a three-hole playoff. *A little thing.*

August 16, Scott and Terry at the clinic for seven hours today, for two bags of red blood and a range of tests.   Keeping the proper balance of red, white, and platelet cells seems always a challenge.   One or the other is always thrown out of whack by various medications being infused.   Scott is weary of the process, tired of the PICC line in his arm and how it restricts him, eager to get to the finish line of treatment, but knows much more patience will be needed.

Scott drives his Porsche Carrera to and from the clinic, top down, waving and honking through his neighborhood at friends as he goes. Great that he can enjoy the car he loves this summer, but no golf allowed yet, which he misses greatly.   We go to the club for some lunches, and do some putting, but nothing strenuous.

August 18. A bag of platelets required after his week of chemo last week and his neutropenia kicked back in.   Jim Stern visits often, keeping Scott up to date on office matters, but he is still anxious about his future.

He tries to be philosophical, saying he must look at this year as a sabbatical, a chance to develop new perspectives, to reflect on the meaning of work and career, and set new career and family goals.

Today is the first day of true depression, largely dictated by meds and neutropenia. Kids forbidden to have friends over today, especially not in the house, where he wants quiet. All shoes off for everyone before entering the house. Frequent use of hand antiseptic cleaners, which are stationed in every room of the house.

August 19.   Scott at a low point and neutropenic, but mobile. Stopped by the house with drawings of his home addition.   Feels sick. Slept four hours during the day yesterday.   Expects harsh pain from a neulasta shot to kick in at any time. *In hell and going through it.*

Firm decision about the transplant.

Scott and Terry have been to Madison, finished their second opinion consultation with the medical expert, and have made a firm decision to go forward with the transplant.   The most important and difficult decision he has ever had to make, with huge implications, positive and negative.

With the decision, news that his gall bladder will have to be surgically removed very soon.   This will assure that another source of potential infection after transplant is taken out of the equation. No date set for the surgery.

Jack is off to a friend's lake house for the weekend, a good distraction for him. I am eager to get to work finishing minor details of the Murphy bed, but Scott will not hear of it. With this project, he wants to control every decision, which is good, but suspect that medicines and steroids make him more assertive this way, and argumentative. The Murphy bed details are put on hold.

August 20.   Gets another bag of platelets, and another one scheduled for tomorrow, to aid blood clotting. White counts low. Pain from neulasta expected any time. He is prepared for it. Leaving the clinic today, he said, *"This is like living in a dream."*

August 21.   More platelets infused. Blood counts lower than yesterday. Mouth sores, shrinking gums, hyper sensitive teeth. Headaches persistent. Lots of sleeping in the daytime.. Cranky, irritable, content to be alone all day. Small rashes on feet, legs, and forehead. A difficult, foreboding day. *In hell and going through it.*

   In the evening, a fever of 100.4 erupts suddenly, and the duty doctor, Shu, gives him the option of being hospitalized immediately or monitoring the fever for an hour, and, if not more elevated, keeping his regular appointment tomorrow, when he is already scheduled for blood work. Fever holds steady, and he decides to wait till morning before going in. Terry is worried.

August 22.   On arrival at the clinic, Dr. Atallah hospitalizes him immediately, concerned over low blood counts and his weakened immune system. Coupled with symptoms of the previous night, a serious infection could be in the making. Runaway infection could be fatal at this time, and Atallah wants no chances taken.   Simple infections can now be life threatening.

   He is put on intravenous antibiotics immediately, given two bags of red blood, and morphine for severe headache. Assigned to room 9 on the 4th floor. Since he was an unexpected patient, he has different nurses and is in a different corridor than before.   Fever spiked again in the evening at 101.9, and then started back down.

Unpredictable hell and going through it.

August 23, 8 AM, in his hospital room, I brought scones and coffee, to find him beet red, like he had come from a day at the beach without sunscreen.   Overnight, red blood infusions had to be stopped because of the fever, and more antibiotics were infused. Fever normal this morning, but with severe headache. Named, "red man's syndrome" by doctors, the color is from strong antibiotics. Eyelids and throat swollen, eating, drinking, swallowing difficult, but appetite good.   Said he was awake most of the night as doctors and nurses swarmed about him. Hardly any sleep.

He is sick and helpless, not in control, totally dependent on others who presumably know what is best for him. He is totally at the mercy of the disease and treatment administered by strangers, but he has to trust them.

I am angry and see the situation as completely surreal, unbelievable that our son has a potentially fatal disease, and there is nothing he or others can do except place blind faith in his caregivers, the "experts", who we know are human and fallible. Humans err! What is happening is unfair, unjust, inhumane, that he should be singled out for this disease and prolonged pain and suffering, and entirely by chance. It seems clear that no higher power assigned this malady to Scott. It is just an unlucky draw, a random pick of his name, a mistaken hell inflicted on so needed a father and husband.

When the young lose their dreams, the tragedy is far greater than dreams lost by those nearing their mortality, who, having had their turn at life, have at least had a try at realizing most of their goals. Senescence impinges imagination, reduces dreams to fit the remaining horizon. The old may have an overhanging bucket list of wishes, but no one is really devastated if death leaves some boxes unchecked. It is natural.

But the dreams and desires of the young are different. The parents sign on to them, invest in them, identify with them, and work in parallel to achieve them, perhaps with the unconscious purpose of advancing their own selfish genes. True to this paradigm, we, his parents, are totally invested in the dreams of Scott and Terry and their children. This interdependent relationship has happened so gradually that we were unaware of the totally transformative nature of parenthood, and the depth of our investment and commitment. Our narcissistic, carefree years before his birth carried no such heavy thoughts. The years since the births of our sons have made us less self-concerned and more focused on their lives and their futures. Call it altruism, at least within the family unit. With the coming of our boys, they instantly became the centerpiece of every plan. Both generations are now aligned, so the loss is doubly shattering when the children's and grandchildren's dreams are interrupted and denied, taken away by fate.

Scott's hospital room conversation now moves to golf, the golf swing, about how he intended to perfect his game once out of the hospital and well again. He talked about the Murphy bed, and he agreed to let me sand the bed and get it ready for painting, and to shop for a 1 and ¾ inch thick mantle, on which the bed will rest when in the down position. But he wants final approval of the look and the mounting. *He mentions again that he wants to become Catholic when out of the hospital so that he can be in step with his wife and children.*

August 24, Joan and Terry visited early, finding a red blood transfusion underway and Scott also receiving morphine, but he is requesting a change in the medicine because the morphine was giving only short-term relief. He undergoes a CT scan of his head to make sure there are no blockages or bleeding. None were shown.

He cannot leave the hospital until his neutrophil count is 500 or greater, and he is free of fever. This likely means he will be there through the weekend and beyond, when his immune system is partially restored.

He will not be home for Jack's 12th birthday on the 26th, so a party for Jack is planned in Scott's room. Scott shows increasing signs of weariness in fighting the disease, realizing the long and painful slog ahead of him. More than a month and a half into treatment, during which he has been effectively hospitalized most of the time, with huge up and down swings in his condition, have cracked his resolve on some days, but he is determined, as only Scott can be. The chemo combinations have hurt him badly, physically and psychically. *In hell and going through it.*

August 25, coffee and scones at 8:30 AM in Scott's room. He has been awake most of the night, on morphine again for continuous headaches. No fever overnight, blood counts trending in the right direction now. Starts directing how he wants the Murphy bed finished and painted. A much better day overall.

August 26, Jack's 12th birthday party in Scott's room at Froedtert Hospital.

What little stubble he had grown back from the initial shaving has now fallen out.   He is hairless.....and a handsome guy, but needs to gain weight.   Still no fever, good counts, and no infections.   Infectious disease team says small leg sores are caused by hair follicles, not infections. May get to come home tomorrow. He laughs easily during the party, hugs Jack and Audrey in his bed, glad to have this moment with both of them.

Joan wanted to go back and visit him tonight, but he preferred to rest and take it easy rather than visit.

August 27.   Joan and I visited early and found him asleep.   His neutrophil count is now 380, but rising toward 500. No fever. Nurse gave thumbs up. With scones and coffee, and, while talking, he fell asleep for a good half hour, even though he had slept most of the night. Very depleted by the hospital stay. Wants badly to come home.

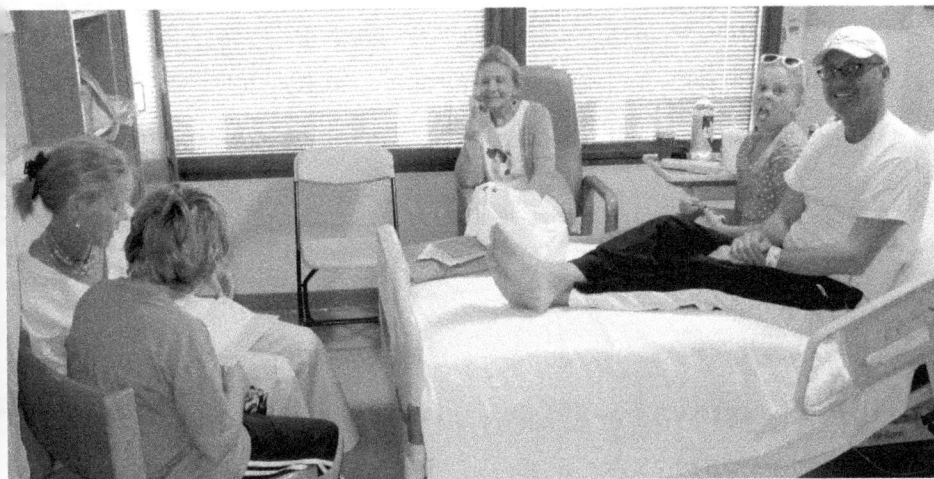

Jack's 12th birthday party in Scott's room

Joan sheds many tears watching him sleep, a frail, helpless figure, tough for his mother to see. The gravity of his situation and the long road he has to recovery, his questionable path to a normal family and work life, and the uncertainty of all outcomes, are suddenly in focus, and are breathtaking to consider and live with. Seeing his kids without him every day, his desire but inability to be involved in their day-to-day lives, his isolation from work and associations there, is difficult to watch, but he knows he cannot give up, and he is not about to.

Terry stayed until 10 PM, and said he may be discharged Sunday afternoon, but his blood pressure at one point this evening was 150 over 100, later near normal. He may have to stay an extra day to measure the impacts of all medications. Still no fever, but backs of legs cramping, a possible side effect of muscle relaxants he has been given. Slept a lot today.

Today marks the 80th day since his diagnosis and hospitalization, and the fortieth day in his hospital room. Constant hook-ups to IV dispensing, beeping machines forcing saline solution, antibiotics, chemo, pain meds, the extremes of pain and intrusive medical procedures, all daunting examples of how sickness in hospitals can easily happen even if the patient came in relatively healthy.

There can be no escaping the conclusion that prolonged hospital stays while undergoing continuous, often painful invasions of the body, and constant interruptions of any semblance of ordinary life, make a perfect venue for illness. The mere volumes of pumped fluids going into his body for the last eighty days, with possible conflicting effects on his brain and other organs, have had huge, sometimes grave impact on him.

He is the one constant. Skilled and dedicated nurses and doctors work their shifts. Specialists come and go, taking time off from the stress of caring for the very sick, and go home to their families with seven days off after seven on. They get relief and recovery time. But there is no relief for the harried patient, only the hourly indignity of being punctured, probed, drugged, and handled as a subject needing care, by the book. It is an inhuman setting, in spite of his comfortably equipped hospital room with picture window view of verdant forests and seemingly normal life outside. From his room, he can look north and see the spire of Mount Mary College, two blocks from his home. He longs to be there with his wife and children.

To lay people, treating leukemia seems analogous to a high wire act, with constant tweaking to keep the blood mix in balance. For every dosage, an unwanted side effect, for each step forward, half a step back, for every yen, a yang. There are good and bad reactions to each hook-up of each chemo type, each transfusion of blood, each antibiotic, each steroid, each biopsy, each pain killer, each invasive test. The patient's blood is a raging bull, turning left one day, twisting right the next, with no real idea what the next turn might bring. And unlike many types of cancer, leukemia has to be monitored and medicated so closely that hospitalization is necessary and prolonged. The history of leukemia treatments is documented as one of promise and disappointment, of seeming magic bullets followed by abject failure, of fits and starts, of experimental drugs and new chemo cocktails. Still, each type and case responds differently, and the mortality rate is alarmingly high.

FINALLY, his remission brings a great sigh of relief, and a deceptive, wishful sensation that he is cured, that he is healthy. In reality, remission is only a brief respite. The road to cure is only at its beginning, with miles of mine fields to go.

In mid June, Terry had arranged a Caring Bridge Post in order to communicate with the great number of friends and relatives who wanted to keep up with Scott's condition. Her weekly postings to this site proved to be an important conduit for both keeping everyone up to date and receiving hundreds of postings back, offering prayers and good wishes from all over the country, and, in fact, the world. These good wishes were read and appreciated by Scott and Terry and by their extended families.

Many old friends and fellow lawyers expressed their joy and continued prayers at the news of remission. All offered encouragement, and some formed prayer chains at their churches, and held vigils and rosaries asking for full health to be restored. If the grantor of prayers is impressed by sheer numbers, surely those for Scott will be acknowledged. Yet based on what we are seeing Scott go through, there is no hint that the prayers were received, much less answered.

His 47th birthday on August 30, was celebrated at his home, with a special marzipan cake he had insisted upon for himself, decorated with a single candle and the words, *"happy birthday to me."* His children, Terry, and Joan and me, and the family of Bressanelli's shared the moment, and the great joy was in having him home again, and smiling.

"Life is a song-sing it. Life is love-enjoy it."

We celebrated this precious moment with songs and laughter…..and love. No one had a clear, realistic idea of the trials ahead.

Scott chose his own cake for his 47th birthday, decorated with "Happy Birthday to me."

12. Back Home To Connecticut

"Travel is fatal to prejudice, bigotry, and narrow mindedness."

--Mark Twain

"No one realizes how beautiful it is to travel until he comes home and rests his head on his old, familiar pillow."

--Lin Yutang, Chinese writer

Returning to Connecticut, in June, 1977, was like resting our heads on our old, familiar pillows. We had come to regard Connecticut as our real home, precisely because it was our first house, and the place where our children first had memories. Five years in Atlanta had been food for all our minds, especially enlarging the boy's views of the world and humanity. They had grown in many ways, but significantly, we thought, in understanding a culture quite different from that in New York and New England. The historical artifacts of old slavery-segregated/civil war south could still be seen in Atlanta, now a thoroughly modern city proudly displaying its past in various exhibits.

Monsanto transferred us back to familiar turf, surrounded by old friends. I was back in the New York regional office. Scott and Jon went immediately into the summer programs at Riverside Yacht club, swimming, sailing, and fishing, and resumed their earlier friendships.

This time, their home was in nearby Old Greenwich, on a spit of land bordered by ocean on three sides and jutting into the large, protected harbor at Greenwich Point. The area was known as Lucas Point, after its developer, George Lucas, who had years earlier managed to get town permission to build the neighborhood on dirt and rock hauled from the excavation of Manhattan's Lexington Avenue subway line.

The home, at 21 Cove Road, was near the association's private beach, and a short distance from Tod's Point, also known as Greenwich Point, one of the premier public parks anywhere. Tod's had its own wide, flat beaches, hiking trails, picnic facilities, boat storage and rentals, and some of the best fishing on Long Island Sound.

Living within the smell of salt water brought to mind the thought I had read somewhere, " *the mind moves more freely in the presence of the ocean. Living next to the ocean seems to give rise to thoughts of the infinite and ideal.* "

On weekends, the park was filled with runners, bikers, hikers, family gatherings, and children building sand castles. The harbor was brimming with moored and underway boats of all sizes. Yachts were coming and going from the harbor at all hours, many under full sail. Others, mainly Long Islanders, rafted to each other for group parties lasting the weekend.   Admission to the park was through a gatehouse where residents showed town passes.   Non-residents were not allowed, except by boat.

From Tod's Point, a clear view of Manhattan and the Twin Towers thirty miles away.   Twenty-four years later, my good friend Verne Westerberg and I sat on the deck of the Riverside Yacht Club and watched the twin towers burn on 9/11/01.

Looking South across the Sound from Tod's Point, there were views of the coast line of Long Island all the way east to Port Jefferson, New York, and beyond.   Long Island Sound is one of the world's best venues for sailing, and is filled with hundreds of recreational sailors, motor cruisers, and club racing regattas every summer and fall weekend.

A mile east of Tod's was the quaint little colonial village of Old Greenwich, dating to 1640, with landmark churches, traditional small shops, small restaurants, a grocer, a deli, and an old fashioned hardware store. Two blocks farther east was the community center where the boys had first learned organized sports, and the Ennis Arden golf club, a tract seeded on the natural contour of the land.   The setting was, as before, picturesque New England, but this time, we were living virtually on the water, which lured the boys from day one. Both Scott and Jon loved being near and on the ocean, and the beaches just out our door.

East beyond Old Greenwich was the much larger city of Stamford, a business center, good enough but with nowhere the residential cache of Greenwich.

Scott was just turning thirteen and entering eighth grade at Eastern Junior High School, a stone's throw from his old elementary school. He was also starting three of his most important formative years, during which he grew in stature and personality, self-reliance, and sense of adventure. He shed his braces, began paying attention to grooming and clothes, broadened his circle of friends, and began loosening his parental constraints.... finding out about life on his own. His voice deepened. His feet grew. His very blond hair flew every which way.

His interests tended to those of the typical Greenwich teenager, dominated by water sports because of proximity, windsurfing, water skiing, tubing, fishing, and exploring. Next came tennis and swimming at the yacht club, some soccer, and hanging out with other teenagers. Golf at the Greenwich municipal course filled in only occasionally. Distance to the course was close to ten miles, and inconvenient.

All his life, in whatever he did, he aimed high. He went for the high dive, the no hitter, the gold medal, the high jump to other's jog, the brass ring, the best team, the knockout, the high end. He never wanted to finish second....never saw the point. No to short yardage or a clean double, when a hail Mary or a home run was what was needed. He did not lay up in golf or in life...daring the hazards as he went for the green. In Gretsky's hockey vernacular, he took all the shots available to him, missing very few.

He lived next door to Roger Haney, a young man his own age, and the two formed a sometimes contentious but good friendship. He resumed his friendship with Nick Mark, whose family still lived in Riverside, and with Todd Kitchen, who lived on Club road, on the way to the Yacht club. John Harris of Old Greenwich was a frequent visitor to our house, as were

Mark and Chris Hellman, who lived on Lucas Point. Scott and Mark soon became pals eager to broaden their horizons in any direction.

Great family friends, John and Harriet Roughan, continued living in Riverside, and their son Howard, a contributor to this book and later a well-known author, became a friend of Scott's. It would be some years later when they started to "hang" together, and laugh their hearts out.

We brought the BIG ORANGE powerboat with us from Atlanta, and moored it at the Riverside Yacht club, where it seemed out of character among the serious sailing yachts moored and birthed there. It was used sparingly the next three years and was finally sold to a Swiss expat who paid in Swiss francs. The boys favored a much more agile 13 ft Boston Whaler with a 25 horsepower outboard, which they named SPRINT, used for fishing, skiing, tubing, and roaming Greenwich Cove Harbor. Both boys took tests and got their boating licenses.

The boys came into possession of a Windsurfer, which requires some description. It is basically an eight-foot long fiberglass surfboard with a two foot removable dagger board keel thrust down through its center. The keel was necessary for stability and avoiding sideways drift. Attached to the board by a rotating universal joint was a single vertical fiberglass eight-foot high, two-inch diameter round mast. The triangular sail was threaded over the mast like a shirt sleeve over an arm, and hung within the confines of two horizontal struts of a seven-foot teak wishbone boom suspended at it's fore end from the mast. The sail was technically an isosceles equilateral right triangle, attached at points A and C to the mast, and at point B to the aft end of the boom. It was a neat and efficient wind powered machine requiring practice and good balance to master. For the non-sailor, a less complicated image is that of a surfboard with a sail.

The sailor stood upright on the board, behind the mast, and trimmed the sail by pulling the boom towards him for a beat to windward, or easing it away from him for a broad reach or a run before the wind. The heavier the wind, the more he used his body weight to manage the sail. When coming about, the sailor would step around the front of the mast during the tack, and grab the boom strut on the opposite side of the board. These boards could fly under heavy breezes, and move quickly even in light breezes. The Windsurfer was a great way to quickly learn the fundamentals of sailing and sail handling, and Scott took to it immediately. He became skillful in a short time.

One summer day, Scott and Mark Hellman decided to windsurf across Long Island sound, a distance of some five miles. They departed from Lucas Point beach in decent weather and a good breeze with the expectation that the round trip would take about two hours. Fortunately, they each wore life jackets, which were standard safety gear. Four hours later, sailing in dangerous lightning and blowing rain and fog, they appeared out of the gloom back at the same beach, safe but wiser, hardly aware of the scare they gave those of us who waited anxiously on shore for sight of them. They could easily have been lost in the sudden and violent storm.

Jon, meanwhile, enrolled in fifth grade at Old Greenwich Elementary, and soon became very active in Pop Warner league football, which he loved. Jon and Mike Moran and Matt Heist became joined at the

The family in Connecticut, 1977. Scott is in 8th grade

hip, with frequent sleepovers, and brought home a variety of animals like chickens, mice, and snakes.

Nighttime skunk hunting was a hit on Lucas Point, with Scott, Roger, Mark, Jon, Mike, Matt, and another kid named Dougie Kindle. Crab Apple trees were thick on the point, so the boys used the fallen apples as weapons to stone the skunks, chasing them up and down the narrow Lucas Point streets, with the aid of Pointer, the Moran dog. Skunk spray eventually saturated all of them. Some clothes simply had to be thrown out, and the boys washed down with tomato juice, which seemed to dispel the odor.

According to Jon's account, if they killed one or more skunks, they sometimes tied a rope around it, slung it over the cable or electric overheads, and lowered the animal to eye level of cars passing by. They hid in the bushes to watch reactions.

This mischievous group chose teams, chased opponents around houses at night, throwing lighted Roman candles at unlucky opponents when caught, oblivious to the danger.

In the Junior diving competition at the yacht club, Scott was awarded the "most improved diver" trophy, and his name is inscribed on the trophy displayed in the RYC trophy room. Jon swam but preferred fishing from the boat ramps.

TO SWEDEN:

The summer before his freshman high school year, Nick Mark and his parents, Arnie and Gund, invited Scott to go with them to their native Sweden for a couple of months, their standard home leave. Arnie headed the American arm of ABB Engineering, a large Swedish firm with significant operations in the U.S.. Scott jumped at the chance, and with appropriate vaccinations and a passport, off he flew with them to the land of his maternal great-grandparents, Ben and Sophie Johnson.

The Mark's vacation home base was a smaller city on the coast, but they did manage to visit several other cities, including Stockholm, and, attended a pro tennis tournament in a seaside village with a name translating to Boattown, where Scott and Nick managed to meet and get the autograph of Bjorn Borg, then the number one ranked tennis player in the world.

Joan had no idea which part of Sweden her ancestors came from, so no attempt was made to track down surviving relatives there, of which there were certainly many named Johnson (Jonsson).

Almost 14 now, the boys roamed parts of the country by rail, and the family went by car on some excursions, so Scott was exposed to a good part of the small country, where English is so prevalent he had no problem getting around, ordering food, or asking directions.

He wrote letters home only a few times, and there were no more than two phone calls. International phone calls were still expensive and sometimes difficult, and the internet was yet to come, so communications back and forth were scarce.

The trip was broadening and fascinating for Scott. He returned home looking European, with a bleached blonde look, tan, and with many stories to tell. To Scott, international travel in the jet age was no big deal. His attitude was, "of course, this is just another place", much like Atlanta or his summer in Texas had been, and perhaps Sweden was less different from Connecticut and New York than Atlanta had been, culturally and climatically.

His good friend, Nick Mark, has more to say about this trip in the next chapter.

In back-country Greenwich, he and Nick also went Quarry jumping, not a recommended sport. It involves sneaking to an obscure hallowed out stone quarry, its holes now filled with water of unknown depth, climbing to a nearby rock overhang, some 50 feet above the pool, and jumping into the pool below. It's daring and dangerous, and involves pure speculation on the depth of water below. Of course, the boys had done a reasonable exploration of the depth, but it was not uniform and still high risk.

Nick Mark now lives in Maine and heads a company based in New Hampshire. Better that Nick himself tells the story of their times together.

13. Memories of A Boyhood Friend

By Nick Mark

Scott was a dear a dear friend from my childhood. We grew up in Greenwich Connecticut and were close friends from grade school through High School at which time his family moved to St. Louis. We saw each other once while he was in St. Louis, an amusing tale all itself.

Scott was a popular kid who had a lot of friends. We were on again off again best friends in the way kids can be but we were always in each other's circle. I was, and to some degree still am a cautious sort who would not venture unbridled into the unknown. Scott wasn't. I am not sure I could call him fearless, but I can definitely say he was unafraid. Whether it was boot hitching behind a car in the snow, lighting something on fire, running through the back of a neighbor's yard or shooting each other with a BB gun (really), he was the first to go. And he was borderline cocky about it. No, he was cocky about it. To this day I am not sure if that was bravado to cover up the fear or if he indeed just felt a bit cocky. Either way, I followed him into many an adventure simply because I couldn't stand down to his pertinacious attitude towards doing it.

When we were in grade school we spent a lot of our boyish time dismantling things. We would take apart our GI Joe's by pulling their arms and head out of their sockets. I still remember the distinctive popping sound. We would float little boats down a brook I had in my yard and hurl large rocks at them. We broke my parents motorized garage door by running it so much that the motor started smoking. In fall we would smash pumpkins. In winter we would throw snowballs at windows. Truthfully, this was great stuff. No one ever got hurt and we always learned a lesson. Whether it was our parents getting mad or the neighbor yelling or the fish that we killed in the brook, we came away with some sort of new knowledge, a boundary to use an adult term, which kept us in check.

In middle school the more interesting things started to happen. BB guns, fireworks, Estes rockets, sling shots. It is truly a wonder we did not get hurt or end up in Shriner's burn institute. We did some really stupid stuff. Once we soaked a tennis ball in gasoline, lit it on fire and played catch with it. It was kind of cool and funny until the ball rolled under my Dad's Mercedes. Lucky it was a diesel. Other times, we would just pour a puddle of gas down my driveway, set it afire, and reveled at how much it looked like something from a James Bond movie. Once we stuffed a mouse into a model rocket and shot it 1000 feet into the air. Poor thing.

Back then Scott had braces and in those days braces were not camouflaged as they are today. Combined with the mischievous grin, his braces shone like a full grill on a car. I remember it so well.

My parents were first generation Swedish immigrants and had a home in Sweden that the family would travel to each summer for 6 weeks or so. Scott came with us during one of those summers and we had a really good time. You could say that our mischievous ways went International.

The summer house we rented in Sweden was a shared "row style" matter that had narrow hallways, a sit in the tub shower and a tiny kitchen. In the connected unit lived a senile 90+ year old woman with impossibly long hair and leathery skin. She would sit outside during the day and listen to the birds and although she was harmless and sweet, she kind of spooked Scott and me. Scott's favorite thing to do was to hide in the nearby bushes or behind a wall and make funny sounds to draw her attention. It's such a goofy memory, but I can see it just like it was yesterday; his head popping up out of a shrubbery and saying "boup", flashing me that shiny grin of his and disappearing again behind the leaves. She never figured it out.

Scott and I were avid tennis players then and the town we vacationed in was hosting the Swedish open tennis tournament. We met some of the professional players from the US but the coolest thing we did was push our way to the front of the mob and meet Bjorn Borg. He was in his prime then. He shook our hands and signed our tennis racket covers. We invited him over for dinner but he never came. It didn't matter though because the racket covers were like gold to us.

The shoreline of Sweden is littered with old military bunkers from WWII. They are tightly sealed up with locks, barbed wire and wooden barricades but that did not stop Scott and me. We found one in particular that looked more breech-able than the others and set to work. We would ride our bikes out to the bunker each day with some sort of tool that we scoffed from the shed at home. One of us would keep vigil for passersby while the other worked. We got past the barbed wire. With a lot of work we got past a wooden barricade. And after even more work, we busted open the lock that held the steel door. We were in. It was dark, musty, and smelly but darn was it cool. We would put our heads up in old turrets and poke sticks out of the gun holes. We made machine gun sounds, called for air support and took turns manning the turret. Our adventure came to a halt one day when an elderly Swedish man saw us going in and started yelling at us. I think he even waved his cane. We bolted on our bikes and didn't come back for a few days. When we did return we found a brand new barricade, lots more barbed wire and a sign saying keep out. To our amusement, all of the other bunkers were given a fresh coat of repellent as well. Although we lost battle, we had won the war.

In High School our adventures took a decidedly more mature course. In fact, beyond all the teenage dramas, discovery of girls and chemical experimentation, we embarked on one of the most memorable adventures of my life; a nearly 500 mile bicycle trip.

During our sophomore year we became enthralled with biking (we hadn't started driving yet). We had nice road bikes and we rode them everywhere and we rode them hard. During that spring we decided that we wanted to take a bike tour and started planning. We saved money and bought a tent, sleeping bags and panniers for the bikes (I still have mine). We taught ourselves how to do basic maintenance. On weekends we took long rides for training. We spent weeks figuring out the route and where we would stay along the way. I'm not sure our parents even really believed us. But alas, on 4:00 am one day in early August we departed from

Riverside, CT.. I remember it so well. It was dark and cool. Our bikes were shiny and loaded up with gear. Our map was marked out. We were charged. I don't recall either of us having even an ounce of fear.

At approximately 5:30 am, we rode through downtown Bridgeport on route 1. Now in case you don't know, route 1 in downtown Bridgeport is not a particularly friendly environment – especially for a couple of skinny white kids on shiny bikes loaded with equipment. To this day, I remember the looks of people. They actually came out on their front porches and just stared at us as if we were from another planet. Even at that hour of the morning, we drew a bit of interest from the neighborhood. We picked up the pace a little and decided that we needed to reconsider riding through a city again.

For the next 4 days we rode and camped all the way into Vermont. Some days were rainy and while others were beautiful and sunny. We stayed in our tent each night except for one night where we stayed in a small cabin. It was heaven. We cooked all our meals at night and ate gorp during the day. We fixed many a tire and drank gallons of water. We tried drafting trucks like in the movie "Breaking Away" and we climbed more hills then we glided down. We always kept pace with one another and respected the need for either to rest.

On one section of the journey we rode this tiny ferry across a river. It was somewhere in Massachusetts and it was just beautiful. We had to wait for the ferry and we ended up being the only ones on the ride. I remember both of us leaning on the railing just watching the calm water. The ferry driver gave us a warm smile and waved us off.

Near the end of the ride, we were running out of money and food. For some reason though, we decided to spend our last few dollars at McDonalds. Poor Scott was hungry and cranky. He ordered a hamburger and specifically asked for ketchup and no mustard. We received our food and went outside. Scott unveiled his burger from the wrapper only to discover that it had mustard. Instead of going back in, he threw the whole meal at the wall yelled "I hate mustard" and hoped back on his bike. I scrambled to stay with him, my mouth jammed with burger and fries, and knew the fun part of our trip was over.

In fact, that night, somewhere in Rhode Island and in the pouring rain, we decided that it was time. Making collect calls from a payphone, Scott arranged for what I remember as his older cousins (The Connett's) to come pick us up. We were tired and ready to be back in the safety of adults. In fact, I remember both of us feeling like we had used up our good luck. We were both scared and knew that the odds were against us staying safe.

God I wish we had taken pictures during that trip. I'm not sure why we didn't. Best I can figure is that we had no more room in our packs. My memories are still in vivid color though and remain as some of the best from my childhood.

Sometime the following year Scott and his family moved to St. Louis. I was sad to see my friend go. The one time I went to visit him was the summer of our junior year. We embarked on another memorable albeit more brief and much less wholesome adventure. Scott came up with the idea to rent a canoe and go down this long river for a couple of days and camp along the way. 2 nights if I recall. It took a couple of hours to drive there in his silver Toyota Celica which was packed to the gills with stuff. Somehow we got the bright idea to bring booze. We flashed a fake ID at the grocery store and bought a case of generic beer. And by generic I mean a white can with black lettering that said "BEER". We anchored the case of beer in the center of the canoe and it didn't take long to crack a few warm ones. By nighttime it was pouring rain and we had poured ourselves into a stupor. Rounding one corner, we tipped the canoe and out came everything including the beer cans. Of course we saved those first and then "set up" the tent on some tiny island. Wet clothes. Wet sleeping bag. Soggy bread. No flashlight and no fire.

But you know what, we laughed and howled throughout the night telling stories and doing what tipsy teenagers do. The next morning was an entirely different matter. Everything was soggy, cold and muddy. White beer cans were everywhere. An atomic headache and nausea ruled my body. A few hours later we emerged into the sunshine and regained our sense of humor.

After high school we both went our separate paths and sadly lost touch. Scott was a precious friend and daring friend. I miss him so much as an adult but am honored to have had him as my childhood best friend.

--NICK.

14. Greenwich High

Greenwich High School in 1978 was considered the academic equal to the many private college prep schools. Graduates had a good record of acceptance in the Ivy League colleges, and in prestigious universities in the South and West, such as Vanderbilt, and Stanford, as well as leading state universities around the country. The sprawling campus in central Greenwich, with its well-equipped classrooms and libraries and athletic facilities, was a crowning achievement reflecting the financial heft of Greenwich's highly educated populace. The great majority of Greenwich parents were well satisfied with the preparation for higher academic experience the school afforded their teenagers.

Scott began ninth grade in the fall of 1978, and was assigned to Sheldon House, one of several fraternal designations intended to acclimate students to similarly structured college life. There was some team building within the different houses, and academic and intramural sports competition.   Segmentation of the student body into smaller, more manageable groups permitted students to identify with a group, or tribe, to have a sense of belonging to something special rather than simply being thrown in with the large, amorphous student body.

Scott got by in this challenging environment, expanding his friendships and finding expression for his personality. He adjusted easily, but had not yet committed himself academically.

His value system was forming. For the first time, he began to realize that self-management, self-control, setting borders and limits on his own behavior, would be the right approach for managing his life. We were not a religious family, so his development was not ruled by external dogmas. He was not guided by membership in a special ethnic group or clubs. He was guided by his own intelligence and common sense principles learned through associations with many friends.   His deportment was built on day-to-day conduct with fellow humans and his own introspection.   Joan and I thought this the best way for values of decency, caring, ambition, and life goals to evolve.

While realizing the need for self-regulation as the route to character building, awareness did not always translate to positive action. He and friends experimented with substances they shouldn't have, which teenagers always do. His friend Nick Mark alluded to this a few pages earlier. They shared a love of leading edge rock music, and relished expanding the English language with original expressions and jokes. Their dress was conventional for the time, enforced by the day's fairly strict codes of Greenwich High. Such were the rites of passage of youth, trying every vice until it is adopted or discarded.

He was too slight for football and had no interest in it, but tennis appealed, and he continued playing at the yacht club. Ice-skating and hockey were in his head, but not in organized participation until later. Individual water sports occupied most of his athletic interest.

In the Fall of 1979, I attended Harvard Business School's Advanced Management program, living on the Business school campus for the entire Fall term. Scott took the New Haven railroad to Boston for an October weekend and stayed with me in the dorm. We attended a movie, BREAKING AWAY, about a young teenager and his bike in racing competition with touring pros coming through his town. Scott was inspired by the movie, talked about it incessantly, and used it as the template for the wonderful adventure Nick just chronicled about biking from Greenwich to Cape Cod. Nick has already provided vivid details of their journey.

Suffice to say that neither the Marks nor the Garrett's ever got the full true story of all that happened on the trip, but they made it through safely, thanks to the largesse of strangers.

As resources and energy became totally depleted on their way home, near Stonington, Ct., our friends Effie and Gene Connett drove out to route 1 and picked up the boys and their bikes, sparing them from a hungry night on the road. Dear Effie fed them a big dinner, they had showers, and collapsed into bed. Next morning, they kindly drove the boys to Greenwich, ending a memorable adventure. They kept no journal of the trip, probably happily so. There could very well have been information therein which parents would not want to know...

15. Decision Time...September

"Necessity is the Mother of taking chances."

--Mark Twain

September was a month of anticipation, hope, relative freedom, and a time for consolidating remission. September was also a month of waiting to see if a bone marrow match could be found from the computer registry, and days of emotional extremes as optimism crested and ebbed.

For the patient in need of the new marrow, the time was like waiting to be thrown a lifeline, with survival totally dependent on the willingness and kindness of a complete stranger, an unknown human willing to take the risk of giving part of him or her self to a person on another continent who most likely would forever remain anonymous.

Without the altruistic act of donating marrow, the gamblers odds are against patient survival. With it, a chance for survival and a semblance of normal life, of narrowly avoiding what might have been a fatal crash.

Some good news comes early in the month in a cancer clinic meeting with Dr. Ahab Atallah. He reveals that the potential donor match is five major and five minor, translating, he says, to a perfect match. Now the issue is whether the donor is still healthy and still committed. This won't be known for some time.

Scott's gall bladder removal surgery is set for September 13. Tests indicate a straightforward laparoscopic removal, and, without complications, an overnight stay in the hospital. At least a month must elapse between gall bladder surgery and bone marrow implant.

September 2, Scott and I shopped for small hardware to complete the Murphy bed project and mount his new 46" flat screen TV. He is animated and seems to feel good. He and Terry will drive up to the Stern's lake house tomorrow for lunch and to pick up Jack and Audrey, who went with the Sterns a day earlier.

September 4. Jon arrived for Labor Day weekend, and he and Scott and Terry attended a neighborhood block party, seemingly unique to Wauwatosa, during which the street is blocked off, picnic tables set up, and a party goes on until wee hours. The boys laughed and had a good time together, *another little thing.* Next day, Scott, Jon, and I had a putting contest at Blue Mound, then to Scott's for family dinner. Scott continues to feel good, happy at being with his kids and with his new mobility and energy.

September 8. Scott and Terry spent a long day undergoing gall bladder tests and talking with the surgical team. They want to do the surgery soon while his immune system is strong to aid a quick recovery. It must be completely healed before the BMT conditioning chemo takes down his immunity in preparation for new marrow, so his body won't reject the foreign matter.

There will be attempts by the body to reject the new bone marrow in any case. It's called GRAFT/HOST disease, and the medical team explains that every implant patient has it to some degree. The goal is to minimize and control it.

On the 9th, we all went to Jack's volleyball game at Christ King School, a little highlight of family time together today.

On the 10th, mounted the mantle on the Murphy bed, and scoped out the hardware for mounting the new TV. This Father/Son effort is taking a long time, but it is a little thing we very much like doing together. Scott wants to submit photos of the finished product to the manufacturer as "Murphy Bed of the Month." On the 11th, the project is officially finished, and now Joan will do final caulking and painting before pictures are taken.

September 12 was devoted to extensive testing at the hospital before gall bladder surgery tomorrow.

September 13. Gall bladder surgery took place at 2:30 PM, he was awake at 5 PM and eating pizza, and came walking through the door at home at 9 PM, much to our surprise and delight. He had just four small puncture wounds, and no stitches.

September 14. He is well enough to walk to our house for coffee at 9:30 AM, saying he slept well but was careful not to turn over. The next day, he dressed and went to his A.O. Smith office, spending two hours there with the staff and Jim Stern. Paul Jones, the CEO, same in to say hello and wish him well. This was just his second brief visit since diagnosis on June 7, and a tonic for his spirits.

Scott and Dad working to complete the Murphy bed project.

It was agreed that he would spend time on a special legal project, working at home. Good psychology on Stern's part, and just what Scott needed to make him feel relevant. Scott and Jim have swapped cars for a few days, with Jim taking the Porsche and Scott's taking the Lexus SUV. Jim is interested in owning a Porsche.

Scott's oldest high school friend, Ken Hurley, now head of human resources at Penske U.S, is paying him a two-day visit starting today. This will be a morale booster for Scott, who was inspired by Ken to go to law school after Ken announced his intention to do so. The two backpacked in Europe together and have much to share.

On September 19, Dr. Atallah signed off on Scott and turned his care over to Dr. Jeanne Palmer, head of Froedtert's transplant unit. His blood counts remain perfect. No conference with Palmer today.

The next morning, Scott and Terry drove to Madison for the final second opinion with the bone marrow transplant specialist there. The doctor gave them "scientific and educational information" according to Scott, but outlined pros and cons without offering a recommendation. He told them that Scott's good health and age were in his favor, plus having a perfect donor match. He also pointed out risks of complications and made clear that some could be fatal.

He noted that the blood type of the donor could change the recipient's blood type, from O to A for example, saying the new marrow is a new factory installed, and the new factory can bring with it some of the donor's characteristics. Because of a severely weakened immune system, recovery at home will be in semi-isolation, with his exclusive use of a designated bathroom, no visitors with any signs of cough or cold or infection, sanitized hands at all times. His body will have no ability to fight infection for an extended period of time.

The transplant itself is simply a precious bag of marrow diluted in liquid, dripped through his port line. There is no surgery. The procedure is far simpler than a marrow biopsy or liver biopsy, as examples.

Scott and Terry talked and made a firm decision to proceed with the transplant. It was a decision made after thoughtful and prolonged deliberation.

The next day, at lunch, Scott was quiet, and seemed worried, possibly allowing negative thoughts to creep in because of the long wait to get the transplant. Dr. Jeanne Palmer had told them that October 26 would be the first possible date, but that there could easily be slippage due to logistics. Once the date is finalized, intensive chemo with a drug named

Busulfan will begin seven days earlier, followed by the chemo clean-out drug Cytoxin, then a day of rest and tests, then infusion of the marrow. He will have essentially no immune system for the month to follow, while the marrow implants itself and starts producing. He will not be able to see his children for the entire month. Any visitors must be over 16 and healthy.

Next day, with the next month basically free of doctors, his Picc line is removed, the first time in three and a half months that he has not had the line threading through his arm and across his chest and into his vascular system. He now will have much greater freedom of movement, and can shower without putting his arm in a plastic bag.

Dr. Palmer confirms again that he will lose all of his newly grown stubble about ten days after resumption of chemo, and will get a double PICC or Port line when he reenters the hospital. Scott seems at ease with the plan, relieved to have some time off before confronting another life or death medical issue. He is determined to take advantage of the time with his wife and family.

He and Terry do so tonight by attending a Brewer's game, staying within the confines of the luxurious A.O. Smith enclosed box, with its own TV's and food and drink service. He avoids going into crowds and they leave the game early. Tonight, the Brewer's clinched the National League title when they won against the Mariners, and St. Louis lost to the Chicago Cubs.

Weather in Milwaukee now turning to fall, with a high of 62 and a low in the 40's. Joan and I decide to extend our rental stay through October at least, until Scott gets home from the hospital and appears on the road to recovery.

Audrey's 11th birthday party is staged at Blue Mound club in a private room, with several deer ambling across the fairway outside. Scott is front and center in helping orchestrate everything. Her actual birthday is on the 26th, and her grandmother is making her favorite, a chicken pot-pie. The party is attended by most of Audrey's girl friends, her brother Jack, and Jake, the boy down the street. There are lots of presents and songs, and lots of pictures.

Scott treasured the party, no doubt assigning new importance to these seemingly routine family events. Every one of his children's birthdays from now on would be a treasure to him, he said.

On September 27th and 28th, Scott went to the office two hours each day, keeping a presence there among many well wishers. He already knows that effective January 1, 2012, his base salary will be reduced to two-thirds of present level because of long-term disability rules, and will go back to full salary when he returns to work with regular hours. His eligibility for bonuses will not be affected. He says that his family can get by fine with this arrangement, and thinks A.O. Smith has been very generous in administering his benefits.

The entire family had lunch at Blue Mound Club, and were all treated to SKINNY COWS afterward, which Scott bought on his way home. The next morning, he Skyped from his iPad to try out a new system his office had set up for him so he could communicate better from home. It worked perfectly.

On the morning of September 29, word is received that Scott will reenter the hospital November 2 to begin prepping for the transplant on November 8. If all goes as expected, he will be home from the hospital on December 15, about a month after the new marrow takes hold and activates, and his immune system rebuilds itself. This means a month and a half in a hospital bed in the transplant wing at Froedtert,

He and Terry know that this stay and this treatment will be life threatening and trying for them. It will test all their resolve. It will often be tearful and painful and suffering surely will follow the invasions of his body, the effects of the toxic medications, and his immune system's inability to ward off fevers and infections.

Another hell to go through.

With this picture clearly in front of him, they both insist on staying positive and enduring the worst, expecting all will be good in the end.

He feels good for now, still taking afternoon naps. Late in the day, he and I shop for his Alan Edmonds shoes, the only brand he buys. And they talk about his new online order of custom shirts made in England, the only shirt he buys. He talks about simplifying his wardrobe when he is healthy again. And we talk about the Murphy bed and the satisfaction it gave both of us. He talks about wanting a new circular driveway in front of his house, of his possible new addition, of a new design to replace the existing red brick on his back patio, of future trips with his family. He again reviews his plans for his fiftieth birthday gala at Pebble Beach.

He is very much thinking about the future.

16. Scott Through My Eyes

By: Stan Cribs, Cousin and Friend

"Cotton Pickers!! Cotton Pickers!! Look, it's a bunch of Cotton Pickers."

Those shouts from Scott are some of my first memories of him. I assumed that was the first time Scott had ever seen a mechanical cotton picker or stripper out in a field. We were six or seven at the time, and to kids of our age, these really were funny looking machines that crawl slowly along, picking the cotton from the bolls of the plant.

It was a cold and sunny fall day, and Scott and I, along with his brother Jon and our cousin Brad were riding in the open bed of uncle Raby's Dodge pickup truck. We were headed out to Raby's horse farm to feed his horses. I'm sure Scott had heard of these lumbering picking machines, but it was the first one he had seen, and, to a city boy new to farm country, it was as exciting as seeing some strange animal or dinosaur on the loose. There were many such "sightings" over the years as Scott and Jon came to visit from Atlanta, or Old Greenwich, or St. Louis. These two were my "cousins from afar." For us, it was a big event for our whole family when they came to visit in the Summers, or at Thanksgiving or Christmas.

After feeding the horses, it was back to Grandmother Garrett's house for a warm up over the living room floor furnace, then good eats, then some touch football at the high school grounds across the street. Scott was always the one calling plays and planning the passing routes. The same was true whether we were climbing trees, pelting each other with grapes off the backyard vines, dipping snuff, or learning to smoke the grapevines. Scott was always "full throttle", leading the charge and making our games interesting and exciting.

As we grew a little older and the family get-togethers continued, Scott showed up wearing Sperry Topsider boat shoes and khakis, while I was still in cut-offs and tennis shoes. My next pair of shoes had to be Topsiders. Scott also brought with him his Eastern accent, so different from our families West Texas drawl. His spit-fire personality put a fun spin on whatever activity we chose, and I was always glad to hear that they were coming for a visit. Scott liked the visits, too. He got a kick out of seeing farm machinery do its job, feeding horses, hanging out at Grandmother's house, playing with "Bitsie", her one-eyed toy poodle, and games we invented.

High school and college years passed in a few blinks, and the next thing I knew, Scott and Terry were getting married in St. Louis, which is where Uncle Joe and Aunt Joan moved the family when Monsanto transferred them to their headquarters there. Kerrie and I had married just a year before, and here we both were, embarking on families of our own. Several aunts and uncles and cousins made the trip to St. Louis and to a great weekend at the Hyatt at Union station, where accommodations and arrangements were great. The big Catholic wedding was at St. Clement's Church, and the unforgettable wedding reception and dinner were at the Missouri Athletic club downtown. I remember Scott taking the microphone and thanking everyone for being there. His sincerity and polish made a big impression on me, causing me to realize we were really adults now.

Scott also showed really good judgment in marrying Terry, who we love very much. After a few years of marriage, Jack and Audrey came along, and we are very proud of both of them.

Scott and Terry moved to White Plains, New York, just north of the big city, where he began practicing law. Kerrie and I visited Scott's Dad and Mom in nearby Old Greenwich, Ct., and Scott and Terry and Jon all joined us there. Scott was in charge of grilling steaks and mussels as part of celebrating Joe's hole-in-one that day at Bruce Golf Course. He gave us a comedic play-by-play on how to rub the filets with just the right amount of olive oil while not over-cooking them, and the exact time to pull the mussels off the grill as they popped open. In his white linen slacks, brown loafers and slicked hair, looking very GQ, he never failed to add to the sense of a good time, while being very casual in his attitude....a good combo of Scott's traits that I always liked.

The next day, after golf, we saw the movie, "The Spy Who Shagged Me", and for the rest of our stay, Scott was "on" in the role of Mike Myers' Mr. Evil, reciting the one liners with just the right sneer and

English humor , while biting the end of his pinky finger. OK! You had to be there!

Scott could make you laugh, no matter the situation. Whether a serious matter or just having fun, he had the gift of putting a layer of humor in just the right place, while still addressing the reality of whatever was at hand..   I noticed him doing so several times even when he was very sick, and admired his attitude greatly.   It's an attitude I try to copy, and I think we would all be better off in life by taking that approach.

Before long, Scott and Terry moved to Springfield, Missouri, where he worked for a large law firm. Springfield was not too far from Terry's family in St. Louis.   Kerrie and I visited them there before our son Sam was born. As we grew

With Joan in front of his beloved Porsche

older and had more responsibility with career and family, Scott and I had many things in common and much more to talk about, which we did, and I am thankful for the bond we developed.

After he worked several years as a lawyer for Caterpillar in Peoria and moved on to A.O. Smith in Milwaukee as head of their litigation department, we both had a sort of obsession to own a Porsche 911. When the hunt was on, he sent me a listing of one he thought I should buy. He would say, "Just go get it! There is no substitute for a Porsche. Life is short."

I'm really glad we both got our Porsches before Scott passed.

We were born cousins, but Scott and I became primarily friends, even though our first contact was through family bloodlines. The gifts of texts and emails made up for our infrequent face-to-face visits and kept us in touch on a regular basis. I would love to have saved some of the funny voicemails Scott left on my phone, but thank goodness I have the memories.

Here are some other things I admired about Scott.

He loved his family and showed it.

He loved and enjoyed life.

He was a good golfer. I could never beat him, even when he was using my old set of clubs during his visits.

He was an explorer and never feared improving himself.

He kept a clean car, but was not obsessive.

He was a sharp dresser with good hair, but a man's man while doing it.

He was confident without being arrogant.

He knew when to be a joker, and when to be a gentleman.

He stood firm in whatever he did.

He was a difference maker in a humble way.

He seemed to know that to have good friends, you have to be a good friend.

He was a good Father, good husband, son, brother, and cousin.

Every once in awhile, some like Scott Garrett comes along. I am proud to have had him as part of my life and family. Thanks, my good cousin, for the mark you made on me. STAN

17. St. Louis and College

*"There is only one corner of the universe you can be
certain of improving, and that's your own self."*

--Aldous Huxley

St. Louis in late 1980 was, like the rest of the country, in recession, having survived the disastrous Presidency of Jimmy Carter, arguably the least effective chief executive in the history of the country.

Inflation rates were off the charts, and had to be curbed by the Federal Reserve and the Treasury with 18% mortgage rates, effectively killing the housing market and slowing the overall economy. Business borrowing costs precluded expansion and hiring. For Fed chief Volker and President Ronald Reagan, job one for the country was to kill out-of-control inflation.

In this environment, I was transferred by Monsanto to their world headquarters in St. Louis. Scott had entered his second year at Greenwich High, and was uprooted in early November, two months into the term, to transfer to Horton Watkins High School, in Ladue, Missouri. He never considered the move a problem. In hindsight, his attitude was remarkable. Transferring to a new school in a new city during high school years has to be one of the most difficult adjustments for any young person to make. Scott never looked back.

Ladue is small wealthy suburban community some 10 miles west of downtown St. Louis. Its public schools are highly regarded, one of the reasons the reasons we chose to locate there. Another was Ladue's close proximity to the large Monsanto headquarters campus, just two miles North.

7 Conway Lane in Ladue would be our home for the next decade, during which key events in his life changed Scott's course. He would complete his university degree there, meet the lovely Terry Bowers, his future wife, and survive his growing-up days of self-discovery, while evolving the values and convictions he knew to be correct.

He immersed himself into the school culture by making new friends, joining the school hockey team, and becoming the sports editor of his school newspaper. He low-profiled this honor, but his yearbook gave him proper credit. We heard about it only later. He met the challenge of adapting himself to new people in already established and insular friendship circles, a new curriculum with new teachers and rules. He had already formed the belief that the challenge of change brought new thinking, a mature attitude for a sixteen year old.

A key and lasting early friendship was with Ken Hurley, whose large Catholic family lived nearby. The two spent large amounts of time together, later backpacked through Europe together, and both chose legal careers. Scott's career choice was no doubt influenced by Ken's. Scott and Ken remained close from that time onward.

He held summer jobs during high school, first at McDonald's, and later as a bicycle messenger, graduating to a Dodge Dart as his delivery vehicle when he obtained his driver's license. The Dodge became known as his "trainer" car, starting new but hardly recognizable after a year of bashing on all sides. He felt the McDonald's job was OK, not at all beneath him, consistent with his feeling that all teenagers should hold some of these types of entry jobs as part of their life experience.

An avid hockey fan of the St. Louis Blues, and a decent ice skater from his Connecticut years, he earned two letters on his high school hockey team. He was tall now, and willowy, a high-profile target on the ice, competing against stout low-profile players. He got playing time, but after two seasons, had to have orthoscopic surgery on both knees to repair torn cartilage.

One of his greatest pleasures was skiing with the family during multiple winter vacations at various Colorado ski resorts, usually Breckenridge and Steamboat Springs. We caravanned there from St. Louis with the Bruce English (now also in St Louis) and Don McKinley families. They had sons and daughters the same ages as Scott and Jon, with built in fun for teens. Jim and Anne Mckinley, and Rob and Patricia English and the boys, made a good, fun loving cadre of teens capable of entertaining each other and spicing up any gathering.

Scott and Jon became expert on the most difficult slopes, including the daunting bowls. They left the ski in/ski out condo immediately after breakfast and were not seen again until dinner, choosing slopes the parents wouldn't dare.   This was classic Scott and Jon, consistent with their tendency to chose life on the edge.

Jon tells how they would take the chairlift to its top, switch to the rope lift there, and rise to over eleven thousand feet, above the tree line. There, they strapped on skis and had races down the bowls to see who could finish first. They reached dangerous speeds on the nearly vertical slopes. They repeated this same routine all day, or at least until their leg strength was totally depleted and they thought they would melt. Coming down in the tuck position wore down the legs quickly.

Jon remembers them taking few breaks for food. They were too innervated to stop for nourishment. They wiped out a few times, but learned to fall and roll in the fresh powder, undisturbed because not many skiers attempted the bowls.

Evenings around a roaring fire in the condo were for eating pasta and laughing about the day's thrills and spills, of which there were many.

For the adults, the unaccustomed high altitude was short of oxygen, and our energy was used up quickly. Not so for the young people, who wanted to go out after dinner to find excitement.

The Colorado experience had great influence on both Scott and Jon.   When Scott graduated high school in 1983, his first college application was to the University of Colorado, in Boulder, where he was accepted. He also applied to and was accepted at Dennison University, a fine private college near Columbus, Ohio. He and I visited the campus there and found it very appealing, almost Ivy League in its setting, but Scott's heart was already fixed on Boulder.

In the fall of 83, I delivered him to the Boulder campus and he was assigned a coed dorm, populated, it seemed, with the prettiest young women anywhere. There was a clearly recognizable party atmosphere there even before classes began. His assigned roommate became his well-suited party mate from day one.

True to prediction, parties won over academics, and after two fun filled years, he left Colorado with few transferable credits and returned to family in St. Louis, where he started work to repair a less than sterling transcript. With remedial work at a local community college, he managed to get himself into St. Louis University, a respected Catholic institution, and got his degree there in the fall of 1989, six years after graduating high school.

In 1988, we took a winter family vacation in Virgin Gorda, British Virgin Islands, where Scott and Jon did deep-sea scuba diving on old ship-wrecks near the islands, with one

Scott on the 18th tee at Pebble Beach

day of instruction. Another adventure to remember..

On his college graduation, Scott and I took a ten day father/son golfing trip to the West Coast to celebrate, attacking courses in San Diego, Indian Wells, Carmel/Monterrey, San Francisco, and Las Vegas. Scott would relish every minute on every one of ten different golf courses, the highlight of which was Pebble Beach. We stayed in luxury in the main lodge, dined well, played different courses each day with caddies. Scott thought it the most fulfilling sports experience of his life. From that day forward, he dreamed of repeating the experience.

This father/son trip inspired his plan to spend his 50th birthday at the lodge, in the company of his wife and children, his parents, and his brother, and spare no expense. He did go back to Pebble in 2007 when the Caterpillar legal department staged its annual outing there, and he was fortunate to be the event planner. (His CAT friend and fellow attorney Lance High will write more about this a little later).

We celebrated New Year's Eve, and New Year's day, 1990 hopping between nightspots in nearby Monterrey, with my cousin Ed Garrett and his wife Nancy, who just happened to be in the area.

Back in St. Louis, a narrowly averted disaster when he drove his Datsun 280Z sports car off the road late at night, and tumbled it end over end, crawling out from underneath it as gasoline leaked into the car from the inverted tank. An Ambulance picked him up, checked him out, and took him to the local constable's office, where he spent a tough night. Joan and I were called and went to pick him up, and found him with only minor scratches. The car was totally destroyed.

With Ken Hurley, backpacking through Europe

He was employed at the time by Geo Technology, a soil-testing firm in St. Louis. He was trained in operating equipment for analyzing soil. His undergrad major was geology, so it seemed a fit for part time work while in college. It was here that he met and fell in love with the beautiful young Terry Bowers, also an employee at Geo, who had recently graduated St. Mary's, Notre Dame. Terry would become his loving and supportive wife four years later, and mother of Jack and Audrey.

In April 1990, we trekked back to Old Greenwich, Connecticut, and our home on Lucas Point, which we had kept during the St. Louis decade. Scott and Jon picked up with old friends, many now scattered. Scott had his eye on going to law school, but was not quite ready to firmly commit. He secured a job as a paralegal at Cravath, Swain, and Moore, the highly regarded international law firm in Manhattan, and gained two years hands on practical experience in the legal environment. This stint was invaluable in allowing him to witness and study world-class lawyers at work on real cases, information which would give him a head start in law school.

In early 91, he accompanied me to Asia on a business trip. The two - week trip took us to Japan, Taiwan, Korea, and Hong Kong. In Tokyo, he went to the Sumo matches, finding his way by train in this very complex city. On his own during business hours, he explored a variety of districts in each city, fell in love with tasty indigenous foods and absorbed the cultures. Together, we went to the giant open air fish market, Tsukiji, in Tokyo, witnessed the huge blue fin tuna being carved into sushi, and ate some at the market restaurant, all at 5 AM. Scott was a sushi and asian noodles fan from that day forward. His favorite Manhattan eatery became a small inexpensive noodle shop on 9th avenue, where he always took family and friends for a "special treat."

Later, on an anniversary, Scott and Terry went back to Asia, this time to Singapore, where her older brother Jim was stationed with his company. Terry moved to Connecticut in 1991 to be with Scott. She was employed as a legal recruiter at a major Manhattan firm, and the romance continued. Terry shared an apartment with a roommate, and Scott did also, for a time on Greenwich Avenue above a French restaurant, in a 4th floor walkup. His apartment mate was Mark Musselman, an eccentric but likable young man, also a paralegal. Years later, at age 33, Mark was tragically killed when hit by a car while walking across an intersection. While at Cravath, Scott also lived in Manhattan for a time, renting a small apartment on the West side near Cravath's offices. He was now back living on the island of his birth.

18. Law School...And Marriage

"Most people can look back over the years and identify a time and place at which their lives changed significantly. These are moments when because of a readiness within us, we reappraise ourselves and make certain choices affecting the rest of our lives".

--Frederick Flack, writer

Having now made the certain choices of Terry as his life partner and of law as his profession, Scott and Terry moved to Washington in 92, and George Washington University School of Law.

Scott devoted himself to the books while Terry continued working as a legal recruiter. Scott moved first, living in a cubby near Dupont Circle. After Terry arrived, they rented a lovely apartment in a high rise in Crystal City, Maryland, near the Pentagon, across the river from D.C.,with views of Ronald Reagan airport. Joan visited and helped them unpack.

While in law school, Scott worked a summer internship at the Department of Commerce, and co-founded a magazine, THE

ENVIRONMENTAL LAWYER, in September 1994, serving as its first book editor. The magazine is still being published.

One of his study mates was Kathryn McHugh, the wife of John M. McHugh, a congressman from upstate New York. This gentleman in 2009 became secretary of the army in the Obama administration.

Scott formed close and lasting friendships in Washington with Steve Ely, later to become his son's Godfather, with Jack Cline, who was like a brother, and with Greg Wesner, all law school classmates. The four shared great times, ate, drank, and sailed together, and loved each other's humor. Their relationships never diminished.

A very proud day for Scott and his family was when he was awarded his JD degree in Washington, D.C. on January 13, 1995. Joan and I and his brother Jon were there, as were his soon-to-be in-laws, Dr. Jim Bowers and Joan Bowers.

His path through academia had been arduous and atypical. College and law school, with time off for work in between, had taken eleven and a half years. His first run at higher education was fitful, interrupted by multiple diversions in which he explored all facets of life, some to excess, postponing those achievements defined as traditional. Once through that phase, and committed to a goal, inspired by his love of Terry and their future together, he began to realize his talents and dreams. He became a high achiever in law, some describing him as a star, and quickly moved up the ladder.

Scott and Terry were married June 11, of 94 in a lovely ceremony in St. Clement church, in St. Louis, Terry's home parish, followed by a grand reception and dinner at the Missouri Athletic Club for hundreds of guests. Ken Hurley and younger brother Jon were both best men.

Scott and Terry on their wedding Day

Terry's sisters, Beth and Kathy, were her bridesmaids. A host of friends from Connecticut and family from Texas made the trip to attend, and had a ball. The rehearsal dinner the night before the wedding was at Old Warson Country Club. Many relatives and out of town guests held their own dinner in a private room at the Grand Hyatt, where everyone was staying.

Law school and work forced postponement of the honeymoon until early 1995, when they had enjoyed a week in Bermuda. They would return to the same resort in Bermuda for their tenth anniversary.

After graduation, the young couple moved to Westchester County, White Plains, New York, a few miles south of our home in Connecticut. Scott passed the New York and Connecticut Bars, and accepted an associate position at the law firm of Cerrusi and Spring, in White Plains. A new life had begun for the young newlyweds, making their way in the real workplace.

In quick succession in 95, Scott was admitted to practice in the following venues.

*Supreme Court, Appellate division, State of New York, July 7.
*State of Connecticut Bar, Superior Court, June 9.
 *Southern District, State of New York, July 28.
*U.S. Court of Appeals, second circuit, October 17, 1996.
*Supreme Court, Connecticut, July 3, 1997.
*U.S. Court of Appeals, First circuit, February 3, 1998.
*U.S. Court of Appeals, 8th circuit, January 26, 2001.
*U.S. Supreme Court, March 29, 1999.
 *Illinois Supreme Court, July 11, 2005.

Graduation day from law school 1995

At Cerrusi and Spring, he met Gina Von Oehsen, a capable fellow attorney. The two formed a close friendship, and three years later formed Garrett and Von Oehsen, their own firm, in Stamford, Ct., emphasizing environmental law. Scott and Terry's first apartment in White Plains was a short distance from his office, and just a short drive to our Old Greenwich home. There were many good times as we shared family meals at home and on our sail-boat. Brother Jon was back in Greenwich in his own apartment for some of this time, so the family was reunited.

They then bought a small house in White Plains on Stratford Avenue, their first family home. Joan pitched in to help Terry with the decorating, while she commuted to New York City for work as a legal recruiter. Scott and Terry scouted out good restaurants nearby, including Japanese, where the family gathered often. The small home would hold special memories as the birthplace of John Scott Garrett, born August 26, 1999. Thirteen months later, Audrey Joan Garrett, born September 26,

With his proud family at law school graduation, George Washington University, 1995

2000. Five years passed after their marriage before they started a family, five years of hard work and dedication. At Cerrusi, Scott had learned the fundamentals of working with clients and courtroom procedures. At Cravath, he rubbed shoulders with great lawyers and learned from them how to get along in the political atmosphere found in any hierarchy. He was well grounded by the rigor and quality of instruction and research at George Washington law. The time was right to take the big step and hang out his own shingle.

19. The Scott I knew

By Greg Wesner, Law School Friend

"Scott's dead."
This is the least probable combination of words I've yet to contemplate.
But the evidence is compelling. Scott's dead.

Why is that so improbable? Because Scott Garrett was one of the most alive, vital human beings I have ever known. This manifested in countless ways, some too direct and visceral for wide consumption. But, in ways that deserve sharing, Scott's vitality fed us. No matter where we were in our lives, Scott could supply energy and enthusiasm to overcome any obstacles. He could also bring enthusiasm and energy to the most unlikely subjects. My favorite being the giant turd he deposited in an airport stall, which he preserved intact and then ran to find his brother to show it to him. Scott moved me to tell the story in verse, as "The Airporter." See attached.

But the greatest gift of Scott's boundless energy and enthusiasm was his encouragement for us to seek excellence in our own lives. This manifested in his repeated directive that we should "go down into the basement." This was Scott's shorthand for an important process of self examination. Scott had hundreds of these shorthand references, in the way that "airporter" came to mean a particularly large stool. One of Scott's great legacies was imprinting these shorthand references on his friends. I will attempt a partial list, with definitions, at the end of this note. In this case, the "basement" reference was to a place in the first house Scott and Terry bought together, in White Plains. It was a small house, and brown, and so Scott shorthanded it as the "SBH." In the basement of the SBH was a tiny room that Scott devoted to himself. It had a desk, a small stereo, Scott's computer, and various Oriental trappings that Scott favored. Scott painted it a deep red, so that the room resembled the inside of an animal. This is where Scott would go to plot his life.

Scott was an impulsive guy in some respects - locked down in others. "The basement" was where he imagined major changes to his life, and developed organizing principals to guide the more unstructured aspects of his behavior. It was in the basement that he concocted opening his own law firm, where he had the crazy notion of calling up the Mayor of Stamford and declaring himself a citizen to be reckoned with. It was where he decided to join the Hibernian Society. Once concocted in the basement, Scott pursued his ideas with unbridled zeal. For example he didn't let a complete lack of Irish ancestry interfere with his designs on the Hibernians.

His enthusiasm overcame that minor obstacle, and the Hibernians reflected that enthusiasm by making him the Grand Marshall of the Stamford Saint Patrick's Day parade.

The basement was also where Scott dreamed of "Pepe." This requires some explanation. Somewhere near where Scott lived in White Plains was a Porsche dealer with a name that sounded like "Pape" or "Pepe," but to Scott it was "Pepe," like the Spanish name. The Porsche that Scott dreamed of owning was, therefore, given the shorthand name of "Pepe." Pepe would be sleek and black and have a killer stereo. It is very important to note here that Scott's Pepe ambition was wildly different from the ambitions of other wanna-be Porsche owners. Those guys want the brand and the status and the whatever else. Scott wanted to *be* Pepe.

Scott called me from the cockpit of Pepe the day he bought it. He was a man aligned with himself. Pepe was above all else sleek and fast, and it cut through space and time just like Scott did. Scott *inhabited* Pepe. Pepe was Scott's alter ego. Folks who didn't understand Scott might have thought he bought Pepe for all the typical reasons. But Scott just moved forward, as fast as Pepe would take him.

There are more Scott stories. Scott's whole life deserves to be told. Not because he climbed a mountain or flew to the moon, but because Scott improved the lives of the people around him Scott's spirit deserves to propagate, like waves from a passing ship, so that more people can learn from his life well led.

I really miss Scott. But at least I have these nuggets of Scottness to carry with me. This is only a small sampling:

Term	Definition / Explanation
Airporter	A particularly large stool, and especially applied to those that break the water's surface.
ANGCOMA	Scott's operating principle: Ain't Nobody Gonna Cool Out My Action. I bought him a plaque with this engraved on it, and Scott returned the favor. *See* "Dirtleg."
AZBEPY	[VOLUNTARILY CENSORED]
Basement	Shorthand for Scott's idea that we should all, from time to time, "go down into the basement;" to go into a quiet place, and reflect on our life. The term refers to the basement office in Scott and Terry's first house in White Plains.
Bon le bon bon	Something good. I have no idea where this came from.

Term	Definition / Explanation
Cone	(1) Invoking the cone of silence. Something to be kept secret. (2) The twisted paper towel products that Scott would insert into his nostrils in the morning, to completely clean them of any unwanted debris.
Dirtleg	An uncouth person. Scott used this term all the time. On one occasion, when he and I had just finished a round of golf, we entered the clubhouse for a drink. There were some uncouth persons in line in front of us, and I turned to Scott, and very loudly said, "Scott - excuse me while I wipe this DIRT off my LEG." This nearly killed Scott and he made me a plaque with this phrase written on it. *See* "ANGCOMA."
Fissure	Scott was obsessed with the health of his bowels. He read a risk profile for a colonoscopy, which included, among other things, the risk of a "fissure." Scott loved this word / idea. So he would call sometimes and just say the word "fissure." *See* "Stuck."

Term	Definition / Explanation
Jimmy	Scott might call any friend of his "Jimmy." It was a term of affection. Now we all refer to each other as "Jimmy."
Nectar	Something delicious - food or beverage. Sometimes applied to other things, as an alternative to "product." *See* "Product."
Pepe	A black Porsche 911.
Product	A good or service of superior quality. Not used in association with the good or service, necessarily, just spoken aloud (and repeatedly) in the presence of the good or service. *See* "Nectar."
Sphere	One New Year's Day we all went to see a terrible thriller / sci-fi movie called "The Sphere." Scott loved to say this word, pronouncing it "s" "f" "eer." Like they were distinct syllables. *See* "Stuck."

Term	Definition / Explanation
Stuck	Scott's habit of sometimes engaging in repetitive behavior or patterns of speech. I.e. "he's stuck." *See, e.g.* "Product." *See also* "Nectar," *et al., et al.*
Tarpola	He once described my ex-wife, Julian, of having breasts that looked like "two cubby bears wrestling under a tarpola." The term "Tarpola" became shorthand for her boobs.

20. Garrett & Von Oehsen

He formed a partnership with his good friend Gina Von Oehsen, at Garrett and Von Oehsen, 2777 Summer Street, Stamford, CT, in early 1998. Their first office was cramped, but within a year they had moved up to spacious offices, well decorated, with room for expansion. They soon hired an associate and enough business was built to sustain them, but budgets were tight. They sought environmental and civil cases, but wanted nothing to do with criminal cases, which had the potential to eat up large swaths of time and money.

One case which they considered was a class action against a major oil company for chemical contamination of ground water in a nearby Connecticut community. The case appeared sound on its merits, but the energy company's unlimited resources and the ability to force interminable legal delays, meant that the cost of pursuing the case through the courts became overwhelming. They decided, wisely, not to proceed.

Three years with their own firm grounded both in the fundamentals of business in addition to the specific economics of law firm management and monthly lease and payroll requirements. They assessed their situation and decided to go their separate ways as good friends. Scott had an offer from a large midwestern firm, and Gina was by now married and ready to start a family. Jack Garrett was one year old, and Audrey was born in September 26 of 2000, three months before Garrett and Von Oehsen closed shop. The partners had loved working together, but both were ready for new challenges. They stayed in close touch over the years.

Gina is now Gina Cleary, mother of four, practicing law as Gina Von Oehsen, Esq., and living in New Canaan, Ct., not far from their old Stamford offices.

It is best for her to tell her own story of her partnership and warm friendship with Scott.

21. Partnership As It Should Be.

By Gina Von Oehsen Cleary Esq.

Friend and former law partner.

I met Scott while working at Cerussi & Spring, a law firm in White Plains, New York. We were associates who worked for the Managing Partner, Mike Cerussi, an infamous trial attorney at an insurance defense firm who hit it big when a blue chip computer company was sued for claims that its keyboards caused repetitive stress injuries. Scott and I travelled across the country conducting depositions, attending court hearings, and assisting trial counsel. Before long, the litigation mushroomed and suddenly we were very young lawyers tasked with doing things usually reserved for very experienced lawyers. We worked hard and rose up through the ranks.

Scott with partner Gina in their law library in Stamford

After a few years, this particular litigation began to wind down when the plaintiffs' attorney stopped filing new actions to concentrate on more lucrative mass torts including asbestos actions. It was then that Scott and I were ready to start something new and begin a new chapter in our professional lives. We conspired to leave Cerussi & Spring and start our own law firm. We would meet after work at a local dive bar to plan and plot our next move. Over beer and the best chicken wings in town, we dreamed our dream, never realizing how much we would learn and how different our lives would become. Garrett & Von Oehsen, LLC was born.

Scott was so good at everything, making lists – phones, insurance, letterhead – of everything we needed to do. We had the support of Terry, who was Scott's right hand woman. She helped us set up the firm - a one-room office with desks facing each other on the second floor in a dilapidated bank located in Stamford, Connecticut just across from the police station and the courthouse. Thanks to her, we had the perfect font on our letterhead, as well as the finest business cards and formal announcements. We went to the bank, took out a loan and the rest is history.

How much fun it was to work so hard alongside Scott to make this dream become a reality. I remember setting up the office with Terry, while Scott and my future husband painted the walls. Reflecting on my career, those were the best of times for me. I was fortunate to be in a partnership with a brilliant, fair, honest, family oriented, and fun person. I had the privilege of working with one of my best friends everyday. His love for life was contagious.

When we hung up the shingle of Garrett & Von Oehsen LLC, Joe Garrett delivered to Scott a copy of Teddy Roosevelt's famous speech, "Man in the Arena":

"It is not the critic who counts, not the man who points out how the strong man stumbles, or where the doer of deeds could have done better. The credit belongs to the man who is actually in the arena, whose face is marred by dust and sweat and blood, who strives valiantly; who errs and comes short again and again; because there is not effort without error and shortcomings; but who does actually strive to do the deed; who knows the great enthusiasm, the great devotion, who spends himself in a worthy cause, who at best, knows in the end the triumph of his achievement and who at worst, if he fails, at least he fails while daring greatly. So that his place shall never be with those cold and timid souls who know neither victory nor defeat."

It is something that I pull out often in my own life to re-inspire me and to reflect on how Scott felt when Joe first gave it to him.

Scott and I took Stamford by storm, flooding the mailboxes of everyone we knew with Garrett & Von Oehsen LLC announcements, coffee mugs, pens, golf shirts, and picture frames. Scott was a marketing machine, even calling the mayor of Stamford, Dan Malloy (current governor of CT) to alert him of our arrival. Scott figured that maybe the mayor would want to meet us, since we were new in town. Well, Scott did indeed meet the mayor, and what an impression he left! In ways only he can pull off, Scott – in just a short time – was appointed the Grand Marshall at the annual Stamford UBS Parade! Can you imagine…Scott came to Stamford not having many contacts, and in a few short years, he was leading the biggest parade in the state with government dignitaries and the local business leaders following behind him. Who does this… other than Ferris Bueller?? Scott Garrett, that's who.

Our practice grew over the next several months. We went from that little one-room office, to a palatial place - class "A" office space, with copiers, scanners, luncheonette/file room, a conference room that had a stocked library of the Connecticut and New York law, and a reception area with staff cherry-picked from employees we met at Starbucks who saw us come in every day and believed in the vision we had. Joan Garrett designed our office, which was custom built and beautiful. Being an artist, Joan surrounded us with a look that was right out of an office design magazine. It was Feng Shui with regal paint colors…an office that made Cummings & Lockwood and many of our adversaries green with envy.

And did I mention the coffee mugs? Every step of the way, Scott included his family in this journey of ours.

Scott excelled at his work, rising to chair the litigation committee within the local bar association. We tried cases in Connecticut and New York, where we opened a second office. Smart, energetic and always prepared, Scott made even the mundane fun. One day while dragging and complaining that I didn't have time to do the G&V's Christmas cards, Scott insisted that we sign each card individually. I balked and told him to just sign my name to his cards. He asserted that it was the little things that would set us apart from other firms. He was right. It was that bit of personalization that did set us apart. Often life isn't fun or exciting, but Scott always had a way to make it fun. That particular day, he told me we had a meeting. He grabbed the cards (unbeknownst to me), bought me a Bloody Mary at a local establishment and said - "Sign the cards!". Who does that?? Scott did.

Scott made me laugh even when I sometimes wanted to cry. He hated to see anyone down. It was distracting to him. One day, the woman we hired from Starbucks to be our receptionist was missing in action. I assumed that she finally felt it time to move on, as she had been pretty unhappy at work lately. Sometimes the filing, typing, bate stamping and taking calls for us may not have been her 'cup of joe'. I told him not to worry - she was probably too scared to quit, and that we should just forget about it. Scott didn't let it rest. He noticed that she didn't have much family and was worried that she was depressed. He paced the office, swirled his tooth in his concerned way and called the Stamford police department. He asked for an officer to check on her... just to make sure she was all right. He needed to know that she was ok and that she knew he cared. She ended up calling to thank Scott for his concern. Scott cared about everyone, whether it was the Mayor of Stamford or a receptionist… every person was worth caring for.

Scott loved expressions. "Nothing ever happens unless you go outside"; "Can't never did anything"…the list goes on and on. I, on the other hand, was terrible at expressions. Scott kept a running list called "Gina-isms" of all the expressions that I butchered. How lucky I was to have someone who could laugh at me in such a way that showed endearment. Who has a list about me??? Scott did.

For Scott, it was all about family. He loved Terry, Jack & Audrey, Joan, Joe and Jon. He loved his friends. Even when super busy, Scott was great about keeping in touch with family and friends. He would often take a few minutes during the day to call a friend on speakerphone, and if he got their voicemail, would break out in song when leaving his messages. Scott would break out in song often. . .Sometimes in the least likely places.

Oh how his life became so much more fun when his beautiful kids were born. I remember how excited Scott and Terry were to show me the mural that Joan painted on the ceiling of Jack's nursery. He was so in love with Terry and the kids. He loved Jack and Audrey and was in awe of his new world. He brought Audrey to work one day in the bucket car seat when she was very young. As he fed her while we discussed business, he at one point just stopped talking. He just wanted to concentrate on looking into her eyes and feeding her. He knew what was important in life. He loved his family and was so proud of his wife and kids. Scott had very strong women in his life. He was so proud of Terry, his mother and even me. He was a very strong proponent of equality and fairness for everyone and anyone.

While at G&V, we learned very quickly that there is no one right way to do things, and often we just had to put ourselves out there and try. Once, Scott and I tried a big case in New York. We struggled the night before the trial began with a complicated statute relating to New York's Dead Man statute. We left the office that night not knowing every fine detail of the statute, and were not confident that we knew the in and outs of that particular statute.

The next day while our adversary was examining the witness during the trial, I wondered whether we should object, and Scott and I started scratching notes to each other. Scott scratched 'no' while I scratched 'yes' – this back-and-forth continued for a while – until I finally took my high heeled shoe, raised it under the table in the court room and buried it deep into Scott's shoe. He howled, stood up and proclaimed: "Objection - Dead Man Statute!". The Judge asked for argument, and it was clear that our adversary didn't get the statute either. Scott was brilliant on his feet under pressure, and was able to speak clearly, concisely and coherently. The court sustained Scott's objection, and the witness was prevented from testifying about what the dead guy had told him. Well, we laughed about that day many many times afterwards. For the record, I still don't get that statute.

Scott loved speakerphone and any mode of communication. We had cell phones, intercom systems, and many other tech gadgets in the office. I think our office was one of the first firms with software that turned talk into text, which in the beginning came in handy when we didn't have a secretary. He loved to talk. His friends were my friends, and his family was my family. He would leave messages - often in song - that were so long. He was such a bright light.

Scott also loved recreation. He loved to play golf and tennis and had G&V embossed on his golf and tennis shirts. One time he played tennis with a group in White Plains when a man suddenly collapsed on the court next to him. Scott rushed over to him and performed CPR. The paramedics finally arrived and took over. When the man was released from the hospital, he tracked Scott down to thank him. He relayed to Scott that the doctor had told him that it was Scott who saved his life. Scott had revived a complete stranger, giving him a chance to continue in life.

Scott made some decisions quickly, and others he took his time to make. The hard decisions he made after careful consideration. He told me that he would escape to his basement filled with jade and beautiful art to make some of those decisions. He wanted the best for his family. He loved Terry and the kids, and wanted the next move to be the very best.

You see, very fast and very quickly we were doing it all - being lawyers, counselors, bill collectors, business persons, employers, administrators, billing clerks, mass marketers, payroll and investors.

After much consideration and deliberation, Scott, Terry and the kids planned to move to the mid-west, and I was pregnant with my first child. Scott wanted me to continue on alone. I just couldn't and didn't want to do it alone -- not without Scott. Scott made going to work fun. It was a sad day for me when my friends moved out of the little grey house

in White Plains. I always admired Scott for being so good at transitions.
He was able to move several times, make special friends all around the
country, while still keeping in touch with old friends. I often called him
often for advice. He helped me through major transitions in my life. He
was the person I trusted for sound advice.

Scott enriched so many lives. While we are physically able to
continue in life, life would be just so much more fun if Scott were still
here. He showed us how to live. So what do we do now? How do we

Scott and Gina Doing Feld Research

carry on and continue on without him? I don't know how. But, what I do
know is that we should all be more like Scott. I know he would like it if
we reached out to friends more, were proud of our spouse and kids more,
communicated more, were more fun loving and hard working, were more

focused on the little things to set us apart, enjoyed recreation more, cared for others more, were brave enough to stand up and go outside when we don't have all the answers.   For sometimes we just have to be the Man in the Arena. Scott sure was.

22. October Sunsets

"There is no season when such pleasant and sunny spots may be lighted on, and produce so pleasant an effect on the feelings, as now in October.

--*Nathaniel Hawthorne*

October, he knew, would be his last month of relative freedom before the long slog through bone marrow transplant and the incredible boredom of very restricted movement during a year of recovery.

He was free at last of the worrisome and irritating Picc line embedded in his arm. It had hounded him and limited his movements since June. For the first time since his illness began, he had enough freedom of movement to resume playing golf. He could hug his children, go to their games, have regular meals with them, eat at restaurants, see friends without worrying about infections, spend time doing things with

Terry. He felt liberated, and his mood brightened. Still, he and Terry had a lot to think about.

Always near the surface, leukemia owns our family. The disease commands constant attention. IT insists on being the center of every thought and activity. Everyone defers to iT. Leukemia is all consuming, altering normal life patterns and distracting from quality time together. The disease is the hidden invader working tirelessly, like a mythical new God imposing new rules, always threatening. Leukemia is the thought leader sucking all other emotions from the room, like a child demanding attention. Leukemia is what everybody thinks about. All other concerns take a back seat to IT. IT obliterates. IT commands! IT dominates! Above all, we pay attention to IT.

Scott comments some on his illness, aware that things could go wrong, marveling at the current therapies of poisoning the body with chemo. He and I talk about chemo as being primitive, akin to blood letting of old, with real solutions just around the corner through treated stem cells with the power to chase mutant cancerous cells from the blood. Almost every week, new research indicates that these research stage therapies have the promise to be revolutionary cures, but human trials require a long time, too much time to be helpful to Scott. Sick patients want treatments and drugs now, not human trials with control groups receiving placebos. Those are a waste of time to those already inflicted.

On October 1, Scott played a full round of golf with me at Blue Mound, finishing at 3 PM. After a four-month layoff, battling a slice, he shot 84 from the blue tees, on a difficult course.

The next day, he played another 18 with fellow club members, and rested in the afternoon while watching the Packers and the Brewers both win, then had s'mores with Jack and Aud on the back patio.

On the 3rd, he stayed in bed most of the day, rebuilding energy after two very active days. The next afternoon, he was up for nine holes with his boss, Jim Stern. Scott and Jim, as noted, have a strong, mutually supportive relationship. He sees Jim as direct, smart, and with a big heart. Jim has been extremely supportive during Scott's illness. His own older brother, Bill, had died from cancer seven years earlier.

Back at golf on October 5, shooting a 79 today, very strong after extended inactivity. Shish-kabob dinner at home, listening to Audrey's practice recital on the piano. She is a talented young woman musically, and with a strong personality and acting presence, her ability could take her far in the arts.

Milwaukee weather now cool and crisp, with Fall colors everywhere. *So pleasant an effect on the feelings is October.*

October 6. Scott went to the office early, with intention or staying until starting a nine-hole tournament at Blue Mound. He came by our rental house after dinner to bring ice cream and candy. Stayed for half an hour. He looks better now, regaining weight, but knows he is not well. He and Terry are planning a driving trip to St. Louis Thursday, the 13th, for several days, while the kids have some time off from school. He talks about the house on Lake Waupaca, two hours away, which he would like to own with Dr. Jim Bowers, his Father-in-law, but Terry is understandably reluctant until health issues are resolved.

Audrey came by to show her new Dutch Bob, after donating her hair to a charity for constructing wigs and hairpieces for kids with cancer who have lost theirs. She is very happy, and exceptionally poised.

October 7. Scott and Jack golfed several holes with Jim Stern and Jim's son John, then they all ate dinner at Blue Mound. Jim said that if Scott's score were extrapolated to eighteen holes, he would hold the course record with a 62. Scott had birdied three of six holes.

October 7 also happened to be the birthday of his aunt Norma Phinny, who passed away in June, a fact which we acknowledged as a family.

The next night, Scott and Terry hosted several couples of good friends for a back yard barbecue, a very successful payback to generous pals at Christ King Church and school who had been so thoughtful and generous to them during these past months. It would be their last opportunity to host such an event before Scott re-entered the hospital.

Sunday, the 9th, family dinner of pizza and salad. Scott continues his critique of inconsequential details of any and everything, side-effects, we are certain, of the steroids and other caustic meds he has been getting. He knows this and we laugh together.

Lawns covered with leaves now, trees turning rapidly, storm windows going up, preparations for winter in progress.

October 12. Every day to be relished. Golf again today, followed by sushi dinner. The next four days are in St. Louis, for six flags with the kids and golf with his brother Jon and brother-in-law Dan Bowers, Terry's youngest brother. Scott and Jon enjoy each other's company, valuing their time together. Scott and his family are back in Milwaukee Sunday night for dinner of tacos with Joan and me. *October a pleasing effect on the feelings.*

October 19. Back on the testing treadmill at Froedtert. 17 vials of blood drawn through a temporarily reinstalled Picc line. Radioactive blood was injected for cat scan tracing, a pelvic bone marrow biopsy, and a two-hour psychological test with psychiatrists to determine his mental fitness for bone marrow transplant. Some questions, per Scott, centered on what his reaction might be to severe depression, typical with intensive chemo, the transplant, and the long recovery period.

Another tried to determine his likely reaction if the procedure failed, and the prognosis became terminal. It was surmised that the hospital was protecting itself and the patient in the event of any violent or unpredictable behaviors resulting from the stress of transplant, immune system suppression, and recovery.

He ate nothing at all until dinner, when the family had roasted chicken, rice, salad, and skinny cow ice cream bars. Tonight was the opening night of the world series between the St. Louis Cardinals and the Texas Rangers.

Next day, Scott was back in the office, trying to contribute. A new female attorney has been added to Jim Stern's staff, presumably to pick up some of the work load from Scott, but that was not mentioned.

Scott and Terry are preparing Jack and Audrey for his month long hospital stay, in isolation, but likening it to "extra homework for extra credit", saying Dad' transplant is just going the extra step to insure the cancer does not return. The analogy seemed to be effective.

October 21. Today is brother Jonathan's 44th birthday. Scott called him to wish him a great day. Ashley Fairchild, Jon's girlfriend, is with him, in Peidmont, Mo.. We are glad he is not alone.

On the 22nd, Scott and Terry co-host a party with their friends Kevin and Kate Moss. Scott wants Joan and me to drive his Dodge Durango SUV back to California when we go, since he can't use it, and has no place to store it. His Porsche would have to go into paid storage unless the Dodge goes to California. We like the idea.

This pattern of living in beautiful October continued much the same, with kids volleyball games, some golf, some tests, but basically free of the treatment collar until end of the month. On October 25, a meeting with Dr. Jeanne Palmer, transplant team head, required that both Scott and Terry sign informed consent forms acknowledging risks of the procedure. Dr. Palmer points out that 15-18 % of patients die from the procedure, that he must expect nausea, vomiting, seizures, extreme weight loss, a long term compromised immune system, even when blood counts read normal, and full loss of hair. In other words, pure torture, but with it the possibility of life at the end of the tunnel.

Liver failure could occur even a year after leaving the hospital. During the hospital stay, he will have to be fed intravenously for a week or longer due to mouth sores preventing chewing or swallowing food. He will often be wearing masks, mainly to protect his mouth from his hands. Travel by plane is forbidden.

Scott obviously is aware of the risks of going ahead, but is committed to achieving full cure, knowing that remission through chemo alone usually does not last. Relapse is then even tougher to deal with.

He and Terry have had their wills and financial documents updated and witnessed in his hospital room at the end of October, forming the appropriate trusts as part of their estate plan. Papers are all in order in the event they are needed

Before reentering, he continues to do conference calls from home with his staff, discussing particulars of cases and strategies. How long this pattern can continue is unknown, but not long, given that he is entering a blackout period of perhaps two months, during which he will be unable to give direction, and his staff will have to carry on.

October 27, Scott and Terry host Joan and me for lunch at Eddie Martinis, an excellent nearby eatery, one of Scott's favorites. We make plans to be with the kids Halloween night, since Scott and Terry will both be in the hospital. Audrey will go dressed as FLO, the Progressive Insurance girl, and Jack is uncertain what he will be. Both are concerned that their Dad will miss Thanksgiving dinner, a favorite of theirs. They are aware that neighbors have already held an early full Thanksgiving "type" dinner for Scott, knowing he will miss the real one.

October 29. We had an unbelievably great Father/Son 18 holes at Blue Mound, our last together before his treatment resumes. A memorable day in full fall color. At one point, on the back nine, Scott stopped the cart in the middle of the fairway and just sat there taking in the scenery. Finally, he spoke and said he was just absorbing the moment and reflecting on it. Then he said,

"I want to thank you and Mom for all you have done to help keep me alive."

I choked up, not having expected those words, and mumbled to him that he was going to be fine, and that all of us were very proud of him and his family.

The following night was our last family dinner together, consisting of homemade pasta with sausage and octopus. We again held hands and Scott gave thanks and asked for kindness and respect and cooperation. His children listened carefully.

In happier times, practicing his golf swing, PGA West, La Quinta, CA

After dinner, in front of a roaring fire, we watched "The Ocean", by Disney. Everyone knew it was out last night together for four or five weeks. Jack wore Scott's jade Buddha necklace, which Scott had been given by T.Y. Hung, a friend and Monsanto agent, during a trip with me to the Far East.

OCTOBER 31: DAY OF DAYS: Reenters the hospital, in the BMT wing, and a PICC line installed. A new set of nurses, new routine. Tests get underway in preparation for intensive Busulfan chemo to begin tomorrow morning, around the clock for five days. He brought with him his laptop, his I Pad, his Blackberry, and various personal items including pictures of his family and his special comforter. He made and received lots of phone calls from well-wishers. Then he went with Terry to the hospital cafeteria for dinner, his last outside his hospital room for an indefinite period. His new room phone number is 805 7223.

An especially beautiful October with its pleasant effect on the feelings, is over.

November will be the pivotal and decisive month for Scott. The transplant is scheduled for November 8, assuming the donor's marrow is collected as planned, tested as healthy, transported by courier from somewhere in Europe, probably Germany, and arrives on schedule in Froedtert. There are so many things that might go wrong, and these weigh heavily on both Scott and Terry. Terry prays for the donors health, wonders about his family, hopes that he continues willing. She wonders if he has children, and about his circumstances.

From this point on, everything must go just right. If so, he may be home by mid December in time for a more or less normal Christmas in front of the fire, stockings hung, and a dinner of fondue, with Terry and Jack and Audrey, and Madison, the puppy he loves.

23. A Time In Springfield

Springfield, Missouri proved surprisingly urbane. With a metro area population of near 450 thousand, goods and services were readily available. Missouri State University, with a student population exceeding 20 thousand, give the city a youthful spirit and attracted a wide swath of academia and aesthetic sophistication.

Springfield, at the population center of the country and the third largest city in the state, is known as the queen city of the Ozarks. Tourists from all over the world visit the attractions of the rolling Ozark forests, with many roads leading to nearby Branson, the country music stage of he Midwest.

The city has an important and vivid history. One of the first battles of the civil war was fought here, won by the confederates, but quickly recaptured by the Union. On a different scale, Wild Bill Hickok had one of his pistol duels in downtown Springfield, in 1861. Springfield was the historic origination point for U.S. route 66, the first fully paved road stretching from Chicago to the Pacific. Remnants of the old road can still be traced in downtown.

In 1906, a mob overran the local jail and hanged three black men, allegedly for raping a white woman. Thereafter, most blacks moved away from the area. Even today, the black population of the county is under 5 percent.

The famed mobster, John Gotti, lived out his days incarcerated in a large mental institution in Springfield, part of the Federal prison system.

The city is the hometown of many celebrities, including Brad Pitt, Stan Musial, the golfer Payne Stewart, Kathleen Turner and John Goodman, actors, and John Ashcroft, the former attorney general of the United states.

It was to this city that Scott and Terry moved their family to a lovely two story colonial house with wrap around porch and a three -car garage, on a large corner lot. Chris and Carla Weber, a doctor and his wife and young daughters lived next door. Across the street was a Walmart heiress, granddaughter of Sam Walton, and her husband and twin sons. Audrey was three month old, and Jack was 16 months. Within a short time, the kids were known throughout the neighborhood.

Springfield was a good, safe, family oriented town, with lots of activities for kids and a lot of good restaurants, one of which, Haruno's. Scott soon staked out as having perhaps the best sushi he had ever tasted.

Scott and Terry ate there often, and introduced Joan and me to it when we bought a small condo at the other end of town from Scott's home.

In Springfield, Scott was to discover the underside of law. His preference was to steer clear of criminal cases, but civil cases were sometimes heated, especially intra-family ones. One such case in which Scott was asked to testify for his client, a family in dispute with a renegade and suspected mob member, resulted in Scott and his family being threatened by the defendant. This same man was also a murder suspect in another case, and clearly was capable of violence. The hint of threat went nowhere, but precautions were taken.

The Ozarks held lots of " bubbas,", many of whom were backwoods methamphetamine makers. Their stills were hidden in deep forests, and, while raids were frequent, the ease of production and great mobility of the offenders made stopping meth production impossible. Criminals intent on capturing the large amounts of easy money found ways to stay ahead of law enforcement. Like growing marijuana plants in secluded places, meth labs can be just as hard to find, and harder to capture. The utter futility of the so-called war on drugs was once again on full display.

In three years at Husch and Eppenberger, Scott handled a wide variety of civil cases and issues, appearing often in court. Having been a member of the New York and Connecticut Bars, he was grandfathered into the Missouri Bar, with full practice rights in the state. Husch practiced almost all areas of business and litigation law, with hundreds of lawyers in 15 locations, including Washington. D.C. In 2008, through merger, it became Husch Blackwell, one of the largest law firms in the world.

On the side, Scott invested with some fellow lawyers in real estate ventures in Springfield, which turned out very well. St. Louis was just three hours away by car, easy access to Terry's family there. And our condo in Chesterfield Square, with its big association pool, was a ready summer attraction for the kids. Springfield was also day's drive from his Texas grandparents home, about which he still had good memories. He took the family to Plainview for reunions on a couple of occasions.

He cut his litigation teeth and courtroom manner here, gained experience, gained the respect of his clients, and was made partner in the firm in 2003. He stayed very busy, even as Terry became seriously ill and had two major surgeries, during which Joan came from California to stay with the family until Terry got her strength back.

Still, practicing with a law firm and keeping time sheets in fifteen minute segments began losing its appeal. The pressure is always on all lawyers for more billable hours, seemingly disconnected from overall purpose and goals. He began keeping his eyes open for an opportunity to see law from the other side, as a corporate lawyer with a larger scope, where the opportunity might exist to grow with the company and perhaps move up in its hierarchy.

He flirted with joining Anheuser Busch, and interviewed with them during one of their weekend trips to St. Louis. A recruiter contacted him about an opportunity in litigation with Caterpillar Corporation, headquartered in Peoria, Illinois. He drove up to Peoria to investigate, and fell in love with the people he met there and the story they presented to him. *Time to take another shot!*

He and Terry had enjoyed their time in Springfield, really the first home of their children, and their lovely home there, which they hated to leave. And, they had settled in with a membership in a local country club with kid friendly pool. But the offer came from CAT and it was too good to turn down, so they opted for still another venture, this time three hours North of St. Louis. In the summer of 2004, off they moved to Peoria, locating themselves in another attractive two-story colonial with a walk-out basement on the edge of a Boy Scout protected forest preserve. It was a perfect exploration ground for the kids, much as Atlanta's protected preserve had been for Scott more than thirty years earlier.

CAT's corporate offices were in a high rise in the middle of downtown, on the banks of the Illinois river. The heavy earth moving business had evolved from what had been production of various kinds of farm equipment. As automation reduced demand for farm equipment, facilities were converted to heavy machinery, and the rest is history.

A city of 115 thousand, Peoria was long considered a cultural bellwether. Comedians used to say, "Will it fly in Peoria?" If so, the joke was, it would be acceptable. Founded in 1691 by French explorers, it is the largest city on the river, and is named for the Peoria Indian tribe.

Much of the city's economy depended on the large, navigable river, barging manufactured goods from the city and large crops of soybeans and corn from the surrounding area farms. Before prohibition, Peoria was home to more than twenty distillers, and, after prohibition was in force, became one of the bootlegging centers of the country.

The local university is Bradley, a respected institution. The local technical college graduates technicians who are in high demand.

Teddy Roosevelt thought Peoria's Grandview Drive, on cliffs along the busy Illinois river route, was the most scenic such drive in the country.

Scott liked the working atmosphere of the corporate environment. He had high praise for his fellow lawyers, and especially liked and respected Jim Buda, Caterpillar's general counsel. A good friend and fellow litigation attorney to whom Scott initially reported was Lance High, who, it turned out, was a Dartmouth grad and friend of Howard Roughan when both were undergrads there. Scott took over Lance's litigation job when Lance went to Mergers and Acquisitions and a new career opportunity. (Lance remains with CAT, and is now based in Singapore. He writes his own chapter about Scott, to follow.)

Lance lived with his family in a golf course development known as Weaver Ridge, and he and Scott became regular golfing companions there. Other CAT attorneys were also avid golfers, and the group very often met at other clubs and public courses to compete as foursomes. Golf had always been Scott's sport, and this group in this setting felt very right to him.

Later, he joined Mt. Hawley club, near his home, where the kids could also swim, but continued to play some golf at Weaver Ridge. But the work was satisfying, within a huge and well organized and well managed legal department. CAT always had plenty of litigation issues to defend against, a natural consequence of the production of a wide array of heavy equipment with computer directed moving parts. Unforeseen accidents sometimes happened to operators, some resulting in suits against the company. Others might be illness related, with claims that some aspect of material used in manufacturing might be to blame. And there were many other issues that intrigued him, including the chance to look in on corporate management as it developed new strategies and set corporate priorities.

He became a black belt in Six Sigma, the quality improvement system pioneered by General Electric, and adopted by CAT. He had a chance to work with CAT's Washington office as they formulated plans on various subjects. And he went along with Jim Buda on one of the CAT corporate jets for some meetings. He became part of the CAT pro-bono effort to offer legal assistance to those in the community who could not afford lawyers. The charitable arm of CAT enlisted him. He and Terry attended a number of charity dinners as part of the team representing the company.

CAT was a fertile learning ground for Scott. He found he could thrive in a big corporate setting. It was his first close-up look at the inner-workings of big business, its relationships with Washington, the interaction with state and national representatives. He felt new doors were opening for him far beyond what he might have experienced if he had stayed with Husch. The choice to leave his partnership at Husch to become a litigation attorney at CAT was another reflection of his flexibility, his embrace of change, his desire to move ahead with a new and different dimension of legal work. This adaptability was totally consistent with his personality and his willingness to take risks.

This trait surely came built into his genome, given to him by ancestral grandfathers who took similar risks as the country was founded and expanded. Henry Garrett served with George Washington then moved on to farms in North Carolina, Kentucky, and Tennessee. William

Dickson Garrett, Scott's great grandfather continued the migration to Oklahoma and Texas. Alexander Shakespeare Morris, Scott's maternal great-grandfather, rode horseback from Charlotte to West Texas after the civil war, and later homesteaded land in the territory of New Mexico. Ben and Sophie Johnson emigrated from Sweden to find opportunity in the new world, first in Minnesota, then California. All were pioneers who sought change and improvement in their lives, and risked their own and their family's personal safety in doing so.

24. My Friend Scott

By: Lance High, Fellow Attorney at CAT

I have never been to Pebble Beach to play golf, but my friend Scott played there. Scott loved the stories that came from the California golfing region—how he spent mornings wandering around the pines, wetting his feet with grassy dew, preparing to puncture the Pacific fog with his drive off the first tee. Scott played Spyglass, Spanish Bay, and, of course, he played the links course. He loved it….really, really loved it. The whole spectacle of it gave him a charge of energy.

Anyone who has the faintest inkling about golf knows that Pebble Beach is hallowed ground. All of the world's greatest golf champions have played there. And, Scott played there, too. He played as well as any.

I choose to believe that Scott is still there—walking, talking, playing. For me, Pebble was the sight of Scott's greatest victory, and a moment in time is etched into my memory. Scott Garrett, a champion at Pebble Beach.

I played golf with Scott several times over the years, in almost all conditions. Once, we took the first tee time at a little course in central Illinois in early March, and it was so cold that our hands were numb by the time we putted the first green. It was painful. We shouldn't have been out there. But Scott wanted to play, so we drove back to the car where Scott produced some hand warmers, and off we went to the #2 tee box.

I've see Scott hit some weird golf shots, too. Scott wasn't particularly strong, and he wasn't particularly long, but, as with all great athletes in virtually any sport, he was consistent. And when it came time to close the game out, to hit the shot that would beat his opponent, he had the mind to do it.

The shot that I remember most was not particularly elegant, the course not particularly memorable or challenging. Scott had a way about him when he was going to hit a shot out of a very difficult lie. He would pick his club, size up the shot, address the ball, backswing and......a big bellyful of "Unhhh" would come out of his mouth as he swung at the ball. It was as if Scott was weightlifting, or maybe playing tennis. His "Unhhh" was saved for the hardest lies, which was usually followed by a little smirk as the ball went right where he wanted it to land. Not always, but usually.

Anyhow, we were playing a scramble at a charity event, and our lie was in the middle of the fairway of a long par 5. We had a long way to go to get to the hole—300+ to get home. Scott approached the ball with his driver. I said, "what are you doing?"

"Driver off the deck."

"You're going to hit a driver off the deck?"

"Yep, driver off the deck." Approach, Address. Backswing. "Unhhhh."

He laced it. Straight, rising trajectory, right up the middle, to put us a short iron away.

The point of this little anecdote is not that Scott put the ball in the hole, or even that Scott's shot got us onto the green. The shot was fairly ordinary, but it set us up for a birdie if we could get it down in 2, which we did. The shot is memorable because it displays the focus that Scott was able to muster in that instant.

Anyone who knows golf knows that a 1-iron is almost impossible to hit. But, a driver off the deck is unheard of. You never see the pros do it. Never. But, Scott did it, and I witnessed it.

Acute focus on getting the job done. Driver off the deck.

I met Scott and Terry sometime in 2004, when I interviewed Scott about joining CAT as a litigator. I managed a small group of lawyers and we needed an experienced litigator. We hired Scott for the job.

At the office, Scott was particularly driven when compared to his peers. I think it came from the fact that Scott was a few years more senior —he felt like time was running short for him to achieve his career goals. I assured him that his "trajectory" was good, but I don't know how comforting that was to him.

Not having enough time can make people decisive, and, to be fair, I don't know if it was pressure from Father Time that made Scott decisive, or he was just naturally that way. We did have a lot of discussions about our careers over the years and one characteristic our careers shared is that we were a little older than many of the attorneys we worked with. Scott would often raise his age, (around 40 at the time) and so I am confident that the notion of "time" affected how he approached his work. Time created an urgency for Scott.

Scott was a good leader because he was decisive. His decision making was quick, and he rarely felt uncomfortable with a decision he had made.

In one instance where we were reevaluating and changing roles of our outside lawyers (in other words, we were moving work around which always made on law firm happy and another firm unhappy), Scott had no problem evaluating the status quo and deciding that we wanted to assign work in a new manner for his cases, even though the the lawyers with that firm had performed extremely well over the years. Scott saw a change that he wanted to make, he put together a plan to get those changes done, and then he did it. I asked him how he was going to approach the firm that was losing the work and what was he going to say to them. Scott knew exactly what needed to be said—that we see a better and more efficient means to get the work done, that we've made the decision, and that there's no turning back. Scott was direct and clear.

Scott did not shy away from tough decisions. He understood that leadership involved "decision making," and that leaders don't get to choose between the easy ones and the tough ones. Whether deciding to take a tough case to trial, deciding to settle a tough case, or in dealing with personnel issues, or in working with our lawyers, Scott had no trouble in pulling the trigger.

Maybe, just like hitting the driver off the deck, he knew when he had to go for it. And, in doing so, he mastered an element of leadership that I've always valued---you can't look back!

As part of work, every couple of years, our company would host a conference with a select group of our outside counsel. We were lawyers-litigators specifically-and we needed to hire many outside lawyers to litigate our cases throughout the United States. We worked for a big company, and in the United States, big companies get sued with some regularity. There was no way that Scott or me or our colleagues could litigate the cases ourselves, so our role was to manage teams of outside lawyers, working together to come up with strategy and tactics to represent our company in litigation. We did that, and we continue to do that, with unparalleled effectiveness.

Our combined team—all the in-house litigators and all the outside counsel litigators—was pretty close one—many people look at hired outside counsel as suppliers of services. We looked at them as our trusted counselors, our business partners, and our friends. That closeness is what set our litigation program apart from all the rest of corporate America.

Anyhow, Scott and I, along with another attorney named Brendan, planned this conference for about eighteen months, and it was going to be a memorable one for everyone. It was to be held at Pebble Beach, and, after all, it's not every day that one gets invited to business meetings that will be hosted by arguably the best and most famous golfing area in the United States and perhaps the world.

About four weeks before these meetings were to occur, I was offered a career broadening experience that would involve global responsibility for high-profile mergers and acquisition projects. In my mind, this was a "must do," there was no question about the quality of the job or the doors that it could open for me. So, I took it. I transitioned my leadership role to Scott, and Scott would be responsible for making sure that the conference delivered all that it promised to be.

Over the course of the next month, Scott and I stayed in touch, and the excitement that Scott felt about heading to Pebble Beach was palpable.

On the other hand, I was melancholy. To this day, I have never even seen Pebble Beach. And, with the time and effort that I had invested in the planning process, I was looking forward to going. But, with my new job, I was no longer part of that group. As with any transition, you need to look to the future—you can't live in the past.

On the internet, you can find the Pebble Beach webcam that broadcasts from the 18th green. I did not know that it even existed, but Scott had told me about it. It's for people like me—people who can't go to Pebble Beach, but who have friends or family who play there.

On the last day of the conference, the group was done with meetings, showered up, and there was to be a group photo by the 18th green. Scott was one of the first ones out to the green area, and he called me. I was sitting at home after a day at work, in my kitchen, and the sky was dark, because I was two time zones ahead of California.

"What are you doing?"

" Nothing. Sitting in my kitchen," I replied. I knew full well what Scott was doing, but I asked anyway.

"Hey, you should get on the internet," he said. While I fumbled with my laptop, I continued to talk to Scott, and more of my friends and colleagues were joining Scott by the second. Scott passed his phone to several of them so I could chat, as my computer booted up and I logged on.

I found the webcam, and when Scott got back to the phone, I said, "where are you? There's no one there." The green was empty.

And then Scott came walking into the frame—dressed in blue blazer and tie and slacks, with his slicked-back hair. Strutting in with his bow-legged gait toward the center of the green. "Do you see me," he asked, waving one hand toward the webcam, holding his cellphone to his ear with the other.

"Yeah, I see you Scott. Looks awesome there."

And then, he said something that just floored me. "I wish you were here," he said. I hear the echo today, almost five years since. I can't even tell you about the rest of the conversation.

As I write this now and reflect, those words are what made Scott a champion to me at Pebble Beach. Forever linked in my mind, Pebble Beach and Scott Garrett. Scott had displayed to me an act of friendship and kindness—very simple, straight from the heart. It was totally unexpected, and it was a moment that I will never forget.

And so the final lesson Scott taught me is that friendship takes effort. It doesn't take a lot, but it takes some. Scott was the type of person who always reserved a little energy for his friends, no matter the circumstances. He always had something to say or do to let his friends know that he cared about them. It could be a call or an email; It could be a joke or a gag, or it could be, "I wish you were here," straightforward sincerity.

I live in Asia now, and as I write this, I can look out the window of my airplane and see the glassy South China Sea. I cannot help but think that Scott Garrett has helped me get to where I am today. At work, I have achieved many goals, and have many more to pursue. But the lessons I have written about are all related to my experience in knowing Scott, working side by side with him, and being his friend for those few short years. He was a champion at life, and led his in a manner that I admire.

25. Fateful November

"The afternoon knows what the morning never suspected."

--Robert Frost

Faced with roller-coaster emotions and anxieties from the beginning, Terry stayed strong throughout Scott's long illness, determined to be his watchful advocate and his solace.

Her devotion kept her by his side night and day, holding his hand, encouraging him, caressing him, monitoring every aspect of his care. She soothed him in his pain, walked with him nights when he couldn't sleep, called for help when he needed help, and talked with him about their future together with Jack and Audrey. They had celebrated their 17th anniversary two days after his diagnosis of leukemia.

As she always had with her children, she listened carefully to Scott as he wondered about the effects of his illness on their children, his career, his worries, his hopes and dreams and whether they would be realized.

She slept next to his bed, in a chair or rollaway, awake when he called, making certain he never felt alone or in need. She brought him special foods, fed him when he couldn't feed himself, made certain that his sleep was not interrupted without good cause.

As she did all these things, Terry earned the admiration, friendship and respect of the very professional nursing staff, and the respect of Scott's team of doctors and specialists.

In her role of mother, she was equally devoted to her children, aware of their need to be informed, loved, and cared for. She was determined to be honest with them about Scott's illness, explaining the details in terms they could grasp, answering their many questions fully, and never, ever ignoring their interest or concerns. They were always kept in the loop, going confidently to school each day, with continued excellent grades a testament to their sense of well-being.

Terry was with her children every moment she was not with Scott. Joan and I were her surrogates when she was away with Scott, but she almost always tucked them in at night before returning back to the hospital.

Her sense of purpose and pure love and devotion to Scott and their children will forever be looked upon as acts of the purest altruism. She gave all she had, every single day, with the sole desire of keeping her dear family intact, together in pursuit of their dreams.

In this most critical of her life's trials, she remained courteous, helpful, and appreciative, to both friends and family, and hospital staff, true to her character and benevolent nature. In other words, she was and is the Terry we have always known.

NOVEMBER was transplant month, the most logistically difficult, the riskiest medical procedures, with consequences very good or incredibly bad. All the opinions had been gathered, the decisions firmly made, the required hospital papers signed, the personal documents witnessed and notarized. All the preliminaries were over, and the time had come for the showdown. Last night, Halloween, Jack and Audrey trick or treated the safe Wauwatosa neighborhood with a group of friends. They each came home with big hauls, and were showered and in bed when Terry got home from the hospital at 9:30.

The bone marrow donor has been identified as a white male European with 0 blood type, which matches Scott's. New marrow, it is understood, may change certain body characteristics in time, such as the rate of growth of body and facial hair. This marrow constitutes a new engine producing blood cells at a new rate, with the DNA of the donor expressing through the recipient. Because of privacy agreements, the identity of the donor may never be known, certainly not for one -year minimum after the transplant.

NOVEMBER 1: CHEMO BEGINS NOW.

The drip through his PICC line started at 6:15 this morning, finishing at 8:15 AM. He is to receive a new bag of BUSULFAN chemo every six hours around the clock for four days, with two hours on, four hours off. A new bag, each containing 68 milligrams of the toxin mixed with 60 milligrams of diluting fluid, starts the cycle over again. The contents work to destroy his immune system to prevent rejection of the new marrow when it is introduced into his body.

I called at 10 AM, and found him already nauseous, much sooner than expected, but he knew this chemo would be more toxic than earlier versions. This evening, in his room, he was groggy from lack of sleep and drifted in and out while Terry and I talked.

November 2. Joan and I visited early with scones and coffee. He was not sick at that moment, but bored with the slow pace. He had made his own pot of coffee at the nurses station. Scott has always been particular about coffee, insisting on it being strong and hot.

He took a call from Bob Neimeier, a good friend at Caterpillar. CAT's General Counsel, Jim Buda, is in town today, Bob reports, and may drop by, but not certain of his schedule. Buda has a reputation as a foodie, and Scott suggested several good restaurants to Bob. Buda and his wife have been very friendly and cordial to Scott and Terry since they first met, and Scott would welcome him as a visitor.

With 30 to 40 more days in this hospital room facing him, Scott needs projects to fill the time. He is a prisoner here, confined to this small place with limited distances he can pace, very tough for a high energy, hyper person, which Scott is. The latest science on the genomes of high energy, super-alert people is that they have inherited ancestral hunter/ gatherer genes making them more conscious of their surroundings minute to minute, more sensitive to possible danger, therefore more easily diverted from one task to another. The advent of widespread agriculture replaced dangerous, nomadic hunting, evolving genes less dependent on security and hyper vigilance.

This description fit Scott perfectly. Today's psychologists and sociologists no longer label this energy a disorder, but a simple gene driven difference found in many people who go on to become high achievers.

NOVEMBER 3.

An emotional day for Scott's family, void of his ordinary boundless energy. He lies there, taking instructions from doctors and nurses, showing little to no appetite, unable to see his son or daughter. He seems helpless.

Starting Saturday, a still stronger chemo, CYTOXIN, is to be infused for two days, ending late Sunday, but the most damaging effects of chemo are just kicking in. There will be sores in his mouth and nausea and headaches.

Tuesday is transplant day, when the new marrow, the one-chance life saving marrow from an unknown on another continent, the marrow on which his new life platform will be built, is to be infused, just like chemo, from a simple transparent hanging bag, within a period of just 45 minutes. There will be no pain, nothing strange or out of the ordinary, just a life or death bag of fluid hanging from an ordinary "Estavez" metal pole. There will be no ceremony, no blessing, no recognition of any kind of the precious contents of the bag.

Afterward, the fight begins to see if his system will accept or reject the new engine. A critical, anxiety filled two-weeks must pass before blood counts will give a full indication of success or failure. The medical assumption is that, with a very good match, which this one is, there will be very little of the host/graft disease, i.e., rejection.

Joan is emotional about the risks connected with what is about to happen, and clings to Scott as her baby. She remembers every day of his life. Terry is much the same. Scott, meanwhile, is on the phone receiving good wishes from friends and family, including his brother Jonathan.

NOVEMBER 4.

This is the last day for BUSULFAN, then CYTOXIN begins for just two hours, followed by 22 hours of flushing the drug out of his system quickly before it does irreparable harm to his kidneys and bladder. BUSULFAN is thought to be routine, but events will prove it to be anything but.

A Dr. Silber comes to say everything appears to be on schedule, even though his blood pressure is very high from the chemo and volumes of fluids in his system. He prescribed no meds, saying it may self-correct by tomorrow.

Silber said the new marrow is not here yet, a surprise, but says there are "contingency" plans in the event donor collection or transportation foul-ups delay it. Clearly, there was no alternate donor, and Silber seemed not to want to go into detail on the subject.

At noon, his first food of the day while doing humorous parodies on Restoration Hardware, the furniture retailer, insisting that they must soon go out of business because he has never known anyone to buy anything there, and because their products are so oversized and wrongly styled.

He also has discovered an "app" for his iPad allowing him to record emails of any length, which the app then sets to music. The addressee hears Scott singing his message.

This afternoon, Joan will cut his hair and shave his head, thus avoiding clumps of falling hair sure to come within the next few days.

NOVEMBER 5, SATURDAY:

Today is chemo-bottoming day, and Scott was sick all day, vomiting, unable to keep anything down. CYTOXIN is now in his system, causing havoc. He is completely uncomfortable in his skin, tossing and turning all day, sleepless. Terry had the morning shift, and Joan relieved her in the afternoon. He was awake but clearly not able to converse. At 6:30 PM, he was dry heaving repeatedly into a pan, still retaining no nourishment. He is dangerously weak and vulnerable, humiliated by what is happening. For us, his family, this was perhaps the most difficult and draining day so far.

The stark reality before them and him was that only he could fight this potentially deadly condition, that family can do little to comfort him, that his being singled out is arbitrary, unfair, and unjust. Families think this way in crisis.

Why this man, full of life and potential and having accomplished so much? Why this young needed father? Why this honest, moral, and ethical son and husband, eager to advance his career for the benefit of his family? Why has this young man, in the prime of his life, holding so much promise, been struck with this primitive, mysterious, stupid disease, the only standard treatment for which, at this point in medical science, is horse and buggy vintage?

We watch him struggle bravely with it, alone. We cannot help. We can only watch and hope, and thank all those who are hoping with us. All parental defensive instincts kick in when their child, no matter what age, is threatened or hurt. The middle-aged son becomes a young boy again to his parents, who want to lessen his pain. Parents are never, ever free from the emotional instinct to shield their offspring from hurt and suffering. The physical and psychic toll on parents/spouses/children is gut wrenching, paralyzing, breath taking, a reaction to arbitrary unfairness of life and the world.

NOVEMBER 6.

Terry called from his room to report he is still vomiting, but is less restless, possibly a result of two doses of morphine, is quiet but uncertain whether he slept. His eyes are closed, in apparent rest. The last bag of CYTOXIN is being dripped into his system, after which he hopes there will be no more chemo, ever.

Terry posted a new Caring Bridge, and comments, good wishes, prayers are being posted from all over the country. Terry is tearful, worried. He asks Terry, "How am I going to get through this?" She answers, "One day at a time, just like last time."

A week ago, he was playing golf. Today, a helpless contrast to a week ago, struggling to tolerate the poisons erupting his system. Today, this week, his life is at risk.

His son Jack finishes his volleyball season tonight. Jack is agile, smart, and a good team player, much improved over last year. Both sets of grandparents will be on hand tonight, as well as his sister Audrey.

NOVEMBER 7, MONDAY:

Groggy but able to hold down noodle soup and crackers, his first food in three days. The burn out, tear down effects of the two chemo drugs are beginning to lessen. Now he is receiving an infusion of TACROLIMUS (PROGRAFT) to further suppress his immune system.

He will receive it twice today, two hours each time, and will be finished with it. Along with it, a bag of sodium chloride to help flush his system of CYTOXIN. He had ATAVAN last night, to help him sleep.

Dr. Silber visited this morning and encouraged Scott to take the anti-nausea drug to calm his stomach, so that he could eat for needed nourishment. He also encouraged walking, which Scott has done earlier in the morning.

The doctor and duty nurse claimed they did not know whether the donor marrow is on hand or what time the infusion would take place, a response questioned. By noon in Milwaukee, the day in Europe had already ended, so the donor marrow would have had to be collected, packaged, couriered to an airport in Europe, and on its way to the U.S. by commercial airlines. With transfer in New York, Boston, or Chicago, and transshipment on to Milwaukee, there would simply be no way to schedule events so closely and definitively without this knowledge. Conclusion was that hospital staff was following policy of not revealing any such details in the event anything might still go wrong.

Tomorrow morning, roughly 12 hours from now, he will be propped up and ready for the transplant, with no announced fall back plan in the event the donor material is not on hand or does not test out as being healthy,

NOVEMBER 8, TRANSPLANT DAY:

A new engine goes under the hood tonight, about 9 PM, analogous in many ways to becoming pregnant. Another person's genes are implanted into Scott and a new internal factory is born, with the potential of producing a human being with slightly altered characteristics.

The donor marrow arrives at the Milwaukee airport at 6 PM tonight. If all goes well, the courier should arrive at Froedtert around 7, the material checked out in the lab, brought to the BMT floor to be made ready for infusion.

Silber said that fourteen days from now, ENGRAFTING should occur when the new marrow starts producing new healthy white blood cells, and, a week later, starts producing the normal mix of white, red, and platelet cells. And if all goes well, discussion could begin about discharging him. Scott points out that he will then be incarcerated at home, also in a confined space, but that he will take it.

In the period before engraftment, he will be receiving blood transfusions and other fluids to allow the new factory to gradually come on line. Scott's chief concern is what to do with himself during his long and restricted movement recovery at home, not being allowed to go to work, and avoiding most social contact, while going back to the clinic almost daily.

SCOTT WANTED ONLY TERRY WITH HIM FOR THE TRANSPLANT TONIGHT, SAYING , "IT WAS NO BIG DEAL."

The donated marrow began entering his body at 9:45 PM, and by 10:30, was all done.

There were no ill effects. The bag was strawberry red in color, about a pint in volume. His defenses had been stripped naked by chemo and PROGRAFT, and he now has a new magic refinery in his body, and fourteen days to wait to find out its productive capability.

It's a donation of life, a new beginning for Scott, and an act of complete selflessness by the generous and kind human in Europe.

NOVEMBER 9.

The first day of the rest of Scott's life, made possible by medicine which didn't exist a few years ago. And the current technology, one size fits all, will certainly be considered quaint and even obsolete a few years from now as genome sequencing customizes leukemia treatment, and killer cells are infused to take out mutant cancer cells in the blood. New research results all point in this direction.

Terry stayed with Scott until midnight last night and called this morning to say their stress levels were lightened. She is back with him this morning, bringing food.

At 6 tonight, he is feisty and argumentative, a very good sign. He wrote a dozen or so emails while talking about vacations next summer, college for Jack and Audrey, and about parenting. When the kids go away to college, he said, he plans weekends with Terry often in Chicago, outlining detailed plans for these weekends. He spoke to Terry's parents, Jim and Joan Bowers, on the phone, and said they should consider joint ownership of a vacation home in Florida. He searches for real estate online.

He talks of winning the Blue Mound Club Championship next August, and that maybe a new driver with a slight draw face should be in his bag. He thinks he will stick with the belly putter Jim Stern gave him recently. He reviews a lesson about the perfect golf swing on his iPad, which he seems to consult every five minutes or so.

His round the clock nurses are Christina, Ashley, and Luci, with Julie as the PM tech. They are kind and diligent and truly seem to like both Scott and Terry. They tell him he will be on intravenous feeding for several days because of mouth sores, and that he will have a self-administered morphine pump for pain. Late tonight, he called Joan and me to talk about vacationing next June in Las Vegas and the Grand Canyon, then the Hyatt Tamaya near Santa Fe, then Plainview and St. Louis, as we drive his truck back to Milwaukee from the West Coast. This plan could actually have legs, we think as we listen to him.

NOVEMBER 10, TRANSPLANT PLUS TWO:

Some nausea and light foods only today. Rested and went to sleep early. First light snowfall in Milwaukee, leaves down everywhere, temperature expected to warm during the day.

NOVEMBER 11. THIS IS 11/11/11

Terry called to say Scott is sneezing some, and the new protocol for visiting would be hospital gowns, masks, and gloves, until it is determined he does not have an infection. The all clear came later this morning.

At 10 tonight, Scott called his parents and said, "I just called to say I love you, and I want to thank you for all you are doing to keep me alive." He had said this to me once before, on the golf course, so he obviously felt the need to express this sentiment. We told him we loved him dearly and tried to reassure him that he would win this battle.

He went on to describe, in detail, his plans for a new portico on the front of his house, new lighting, a new circular driveway, shelving in his garage, new furniture arrangements in his basement, all for $25K He has been going through magazines and collecting pictures depicting his ideas.

When told he seems to be having a decent day, he bristled, and says his days are "shit", with nausea, headaches, and forced meds. There are no good days in a hospital bed, he claims, with some authority. There are constant interruptions by multiple teams of doctors and nurses taking blood counts, blood pressure, temperature, and other measurements, all fed into a computer stored in his room. Staff follow explicit directions and timetables specified by doctors.   Patient comfort, as noted earlier, is somewhere down the list of priorities.

NOVEMBER 12, SATURDAY:

Stomach discomfort, with headaches, he suspects from PROGRAFT. Some moaning and sighing with esophagus burning down to his stomach.   Dr. Silber said counts are good but that he needs to keep eating and exercising, regardless. He asked for a small filet with rice, carrots, and cucumbers with a side of A1, which Joan prepared. He ate only small bits at a time. He remains feisty, argumentative, bored by the hospital routine, trapped, and discontent. He is officially neutropenic now, and extra precautions must be taken to avoid infections. He is no longer allowed to walk outside the BMT unit.

NOVEMBER 13. IGNITION EIGHT DAYS FROM NOW:

He is talking more to his kids on the phone now. He talked twice with Jack today, and seems very sensitive to their needs.   Jack went shopping for a new winter coat today, and found a North Face with hood that he really liked. Scott wanted details. Scott is very pleased that Jack wears his jade pendant at all times.

Jack researched the Garrett family crest today as part of a homework assignment. He found one online saying that Garrett origins were English/Irish, and Germanic before that. Scott is pleased to hear this. Going into the final week of waiting for marrow ignition, his blood pressure is down to normal, and he continues to receive PROGRAF, the anti-rejection med. Some walking and exercise, but almost no appetite.

NOVEMBER 14, ONE WEEK TO ENGRAFTMENT.

With hardly a complaint or whimper, Scott suffered desperately through the long days and nights of this last week before the life giving marrow was scheduled to take hold and begin producing good blood.

Mouth sores extending to his intestines made solids impossible to take, and intravenous liquid nourishment was begun. Morphine and hydromorphone worked only partially to lessen unbearable headaches and stomach pains, with side effects inducing hallucinations and memory loss. His speech was slurred, often incoherent, his voice barely audible. Sores covered his outer lips and gums, to the point he has trouble opening his mouth wide enough to be inspected by doctors and nurses. His mouth may require vacuuming. Some nose bleeding and low-grade fever. His mental state muddled, grim, in and out of full consciousness. He wants no visitors and is not allowed any because of his lack of immunity.

His body is void of hair, and will remain so for seven months, he is told, while he continues to take PROGRAF in pill form to fight rejection. He is cranky and angry. *Another hell and going through it.*

The week was the bottom, the worst of times, the tunnel of darkness, endurable only by the promise of new marrow giving new hope for life. In lucid moments, he wants to talk, and does with great difficulty. Park City, Utah and San Francisco are mentioned as good vacation destinations for the kids.

He forces conversation with the office, trying to brief Jim Stern on a big case in Washington, D.C. coming up next week. He talks to his cousin, Stan Cribbs, about their ownership of Porsches.

I   personalize his pain and suffering, angry that this fine and deserving young man is struck with this life threatening scourge. The situation is surreal, as if it is happening to someone else, but the mind numbing reality keeps coming back. Like every parent in this situation, I wished over and over again that I could take his place. Terry and the children are also sharing his pain every minute, and devoting most of their waking thoughts to him. There can be no doubt that those closest to cancer sufferers also suffer greatly and with anger at the disease and its cruelties.

Joan and I cannot visit now. On the 18th, he called us from his room and talked for 40 minutes, funny, sometimes making sense, sometimes not. He expressed opinions about Leno and Letterman, his incessant headaches. We hang on every word. He hung up reluctantly when a nurse came in.

He is now on oxygen most of the time, with five bags of fluid and nourishment pumped by Estavez into his two PICC lines, one in each arm. He has to be demoralized and a little delirious from the narcotics, but seems to be optimistic and hopeful, hanging on to the trends and what the doctors keep telling him is the normal trough for transplant patients.

He pushes the morphine pump as often as the timer allows, twitches with every breath, says nonsensical things, wonders if this happens to alzheimers patients. He falls asleep in mid-sentence. He experiences the most excruciating pains, unlike anything he has ever imagined. He gargles liquids then spits them out, saying they hurt his throat.

Nurse Christina announces that he is being switched off morphine to higher doses of hydromorphone.. She also tells him he will get a final dose of chemo, a metatraxate push into his PICC line, tonight, to suppress his counts again, but good blood counts should be rising after that. At 3:06 AM on the 19th he emails that his white counts are up to 700 from 200 yesterday. He will be neutropenic until white counts reach 1000 and holding. In the evening, his pain is greatest and he thinks the new medication is not working, and that his condition is worsening. He tries to drink Power Aid, but suffers nausea.

On the 20th, he says he is afraid of the narcotics he is getting. Pain has not subsided. He is vomiting and has no voice, and has severe headaches. Terry becomes adamant with the medical staff that they find a way to modify the pain. Terry spent the night with him, and he was awake and calling for her, sleeping only two hours. Terry says we have to manage our expectations, not expect straight-line improvements. He can't talk, and can't eat. Her firmness with the docs paid off. They decided that his PROGRAFT levels were much too high, most likely causing the pain. Why did it take a confrontation to get this decision? He is taken off

PROGRAFT, took a new pain pill, and got relief in 45 minutes. He slept during the day, and showered when he woke up.

Terry says that his eyes are the clearest in ten days, and he feels like walking. White blood counts are holding at 800, reds are 25, and low platelets require another transfusion tonight.

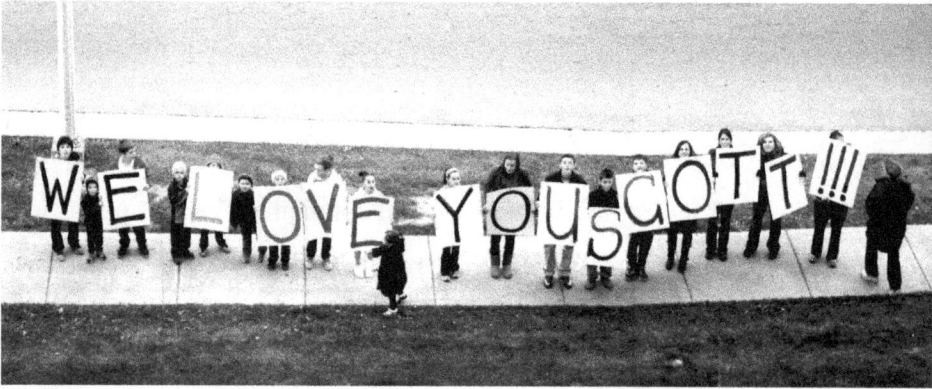

Friends of Scott and Terry paraded posters outside his hospital room.

During the day, several families who are friends of Scott's and Terry's line up on the street below his hospital room, carrying a large banner sign saying, "We love you Scott." Twenty people participated in the effort. Scott and Terry saw them. The effect was very emotional. Terry's Dad took pictures from the lounge near Scott's room.

Tomorrow is D-day... ignition day, the day for first production from the new factory. If the numbers are good, he may get to come home in another ten days.

NOVEMBER 22ND: LIFT OFF DAY.

White counts are up to 1800, platelets are good, but reds lagging and requiring a transfusion. The larger concern is the new stomach pain which kept him awake all night, for which the nurse would not give him pain medication. He was angry at the nurse and her attitude. He is taken down for a cat scan of his stomach to make sure there is no serious blockage before any laxative can be given. Strange, since he has had no solids for days, how can he be constipated now?

Head pain is down to a 4 or 5 from 9 yesterday. Parents visit deferred until the scan is done and some solution is found for the hard, distended stomach, and his feelings of blockage.

They visited at 3 PM and were told no blockage but large amounts of trapped gas, constipation resulting from narcotics. Some blood in his urine. All urine and feces now being held for lab examination.

Nurse Julie said numbers are trending right, and each day hereafter should be better. A junior tech thinks he may get to come home on the 29th, if all goes well. Seems a long way to go.

He walked twelve laps around the small BMT unit. Nurses want him to keep walking as much as he can in order to encourage bowel movement. He is getting plenty of nutrients, but no solids, so constipation is strange under this diet. He puts on his nose fed oxygen, which nurses want him to wear constantly when he sleeps.

NOVEMBER 23. IGNITION PLUS ONE.

All counts are up today, the first time all have risen in unison. This is the liftoff expected.   If these counts hold up and his pain can be managed, tomorrow will be a real Thanksgiving Day.

He appears to have come through this trial, this dark tunnel of doubt and pain and despair.   The three weeks since getting the new bone marrow have taken a huge toll on his body, his organs, and his psyche. Much has happened he and his family did not fully understand, even though there had been attempted explanations.

The clearest lay observation is that this standard paradigm for bone marrow transplant patients brings the patient to near death, choking off his natural ability to fight simple infections and diseases.   This therapy is the only one known.   Every patient is assumed to be like every other patient, requiring the same chemo, the same suppressants, the same narcotics, the same fluids, the same invasive tests.   Torture and grief before gain is thought to be a fundamental requirement, much like therapies of old used in treating blood infections.

But the treatments for leukemia are on the verge of changing radically, away from standard to individual gene therapies, away from standardized chemo drugs, toward targeting the trouble causing mutant cells.   How long this transition will take depends heavily on intensive research and trials to perfect the new frontier. For now, we only know that the gene therapy is not available to Scott.

Thanksgiving suggests a theme of gratitude, of generosity, appreciation, praise, and honor....a day to count blessings. Thanksgiving should not ideally be the day to express our actual sentiments. Words like resentful, critical, thankless, scornful, angry, and cynical would more accurately describe our attitudes leading into this holiday. Scott has just willingly spent the most unbearably painful, demeaning month of his life, in fair exchange for the chance for new life. There are still miles to go.

26. Milwaukee: Home At Last

"Nothing can stop the man with the right mental attitude from achieving his goal."

--Thomas Jefferson

CAT was a great workplace for Scott. Introduction to law from the corporate perspective contrasted sharply with law firm practices of maximizing billable hours and jumping from complex to simple legal issues, made even more challenging by client

Terry's 41st birthday, Milwaukee

requirements and attitudes. Corporate law was more consistent, more goal oriented, always with a single, predictable client.   Scott liked this consistency and stability.

He also liked his fellow lawyers and legal assistants. He greatly respected Jim Buda, CAT's general counsel. He admired CAT's approach to problem solving and issue identification through the Six Sigma discipline. CAT's products intrigued, and the breadth of the company's manufacturing and marketing operations provided the platform for individual growth and diversity in assignments.

At the same time, the depth and quality of the legal staff there brought the need for tight organization and hierarchy. With some 180 in house lawyers and growing, formal performance reviews and seniority dictated orderly advancement in the ranks. Cross training in a variety of domestic and international assignments was the standard route to promotion. Jumping the organization in any significant way was highly unlikely and would have upset the natural order of expected progression.

Forty years old when he joined CAT, he developed a personal goal of becoming General Counsel of a significant public company by age 50. While he did extremely well at CAT and earned promotions, he saw clearly, at age 43, that his chance to become a GC would be in a more nimble, less structured, smaller legal department, which meant a senior management with the latitude to go outside the organization for fresh leadership talent.

He and Terry liked Peoria and made many good friends there, but, as in Springfield, came to believe that a larger city would be a better fit for their lifestyles, and their children's long-term educations.

Always alert to new opportunity, Scott interviewed for a position as Head of Litigation for A.O. Smith Corporation of Milwaukee, and immediately liked what he saw and heard there. Jim Stern, just a couple of years older than Scott, was Smith's General Counsel. The two liked each other immediately, and, after meeting and talking with the CEO, Paul Jones, and other key members of management, Scott was offered and accepted the job, effective April 1, 2008.

Uncle Cal with Scott, about 2004

Smith is a 100-year old industrial company specializing in producing and selling residential and commercial hot water systems and water purification products. One of their earliest products, no longer produced, was steel-frames for Henry Ford's Model T assembly lines. They also made glass lined industrial containers, and, in the past, large cylindrical metal silos for grain storage on farms, many still visible in the wheat, corn and soybean belt of the middle West. The company was founded by the Smith family, and some members of the family remained active on the Board of Directors and in governmental affairs and the A.O. Smith charitable foundation.

Sales were about two billion dollars, with a good growth rate, with international production and sales a large component. China, India, Europe, Mexico, Canada, and the U.S. were manufacturing sites.

Scott saw in Smith and Jim Stern the chance for managing a wide variety of litigation issues, and, as a member of key management, to have a closer, hands-on experience with the decisions of top executives. His relationship with Jim would allow seeing the full scope of the General Counsel role, in preparation for becoming qualified to take the job if Jim left Smith, or, if opportunity presented itself with another company. He had six years to realize his goal.

Both Scott and Terry saw Milwaukee as the ideal size, with all the amenities and services they needed. A metro area of about two million with great cultural and educational facilities, its location on the southwestern shore of beautiful lake Michigan, its air travel and shipping hubs, and lots of reasonably priced housing options, were highly appealing, as was major league baseball. And just 90 miles north of Chicago, with its big city attractions.

Founded by the French as a trading and fur trapping center, German Catholic immigrants soon turned Milwaukee into "beer town", the center of beer making in America. Industry flourished in Milwaukee as a key port city for the shipment of raw materials and finished goods to America and the world.

Most important for the Garrett's was choosing a home in the small suburban city of Wauwatosa, and the Christ King Catholic parish and

Christ King School, where Jack and Audrey formed immediate friendships and did well academically. The Christ King neighborhood became Scott and Terry' social hub, and remains so. Like-minded young Catholic families were attracted to Wauwatosa for the same reasons. A tight familial bond was soon formed with many of them, who pitched in and supported each other in times of need. Jim and Maureen Stern were members of Christ King church and had two children in Christ King School. They encouraged Scott and Terry to join there and enroll Jack and Audrey in the parish school.

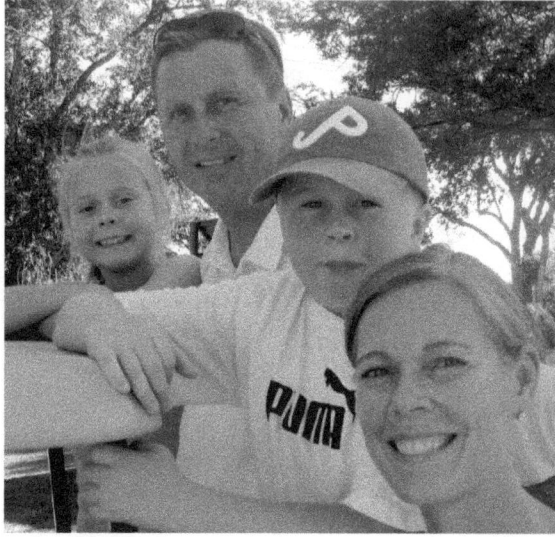

The happy Garrett family at a Hereford, Texas memorial golf tournament for his Uncle, Cal Garrett

Scott with Audrey, sailing with the family on Lake Michigan.

Downtown, its beaches, parks, yacht clubs, world famous art museum, and Discovery Center, were just 15 minutes away. Miller Park, home of the Milwaukee Brewers, just 7 minutes away. Very nearby were the Milwaukee State fairgrounds, and the excellent Milwaukee Zoo, and leading shopping malls. Mitchell field, the airport, only 20 minutes away. To the west, the University of Wisconsin at Madison, the state capitol, was 60 miles. The

Coaching son Jack in Jr. Hilltoppers football, 2009

Aboard the 63 ft. Swedish

mahogany sloop he won for a day.

Wisconsin regional medical center, where Froedtert Hospital and the Medical College of Wisconsin are located, only 5-7 minutes away. Clearly, Milwaukee had critical mass and resources to support world-class arts, sports, healthcare, restaurants, and transportation facilities which smaller cities, attractive as they were, could not match.

The home they chose and

remodeled extensively was a large 80-year old center hall brick and frame colonial on the Menomonee River. It was on three levels, with a large extra lot to its South, which became an open playground for the kids and their friends.

In short order, Jim Stern had introduced Scott to the Blue Mound Golf Club and Scott applied and was accepted into membership. The club was directly adjacent to Scott's home, perhaps a seven iron away. He very soon had found a comfortable golfing home. Between work, Christ King Parish and school, Blue Mound and the close knit Wauwatosa community, Scott and Terry felt they had found a home for the long term.

Scott came to Milwaukee first and rented until the kids finished their school year in Peoria and joined him. There seemed to be no issue in adjusting to the new school, where Jack began third grade and Audrey second grade in September, 2008. Terry, meanwhile, immersed herself into the school picture by volunteering to do various jobs.

Scott was already involved in a variety of cases at Smith. He travelled heavily the first few months, acquainting himself with Smith facilities, personnel, and issues. But other than the interruptions and delays of remodeling, everybody felt comfortable in Milwaukee, and pleased with their choice.

27. Scott: Like a Brother

By: JIM STERN:
Friend, Fellow attorney & General Counsel

In the four short years I knew Scott, he had a profound impact on my life, the life of my colleagues, and the lives of my family. Here are some of the reasons why.

SCOTT WAS THOUGHTFUL.

In 2008 and 2009, I travelled to China quite a bit (I think some fourteen times. Almost every time I would go out of the country, I would call home to hear that my family had just gotten back from the Garrett's for taco night or that Scott had stopped over and dropped something off for Maureen and the kids. The Stern family now has taco night in honor of Scott.

But it wasn't just when I was out of town. He was the kind of friend that if he knew you had an issue or some trouble, he would come to your aid. He was always offering to pick up the kids when I was busy, or planning something with them when he knew I was out of town.

GREGG JENNINGS CELEBRITY GOLF OUTING

Scott had been with A.O. Smith less than a couple of months when we had the opportunity to play in the first annual Gregg Jennings celebrity golf outing. Our mutual friend, Rodney Van Bibber, had invited us along with his colleague, Dan Potter. As luck would have it, our celebrity was Gregg Jennings, of Green Bay Packer fame.

It was a magical day on the golf course. Because of rain, we only played 16 holes of the scramble, which included one par, one eagle, and the rest birdies. We all played great and the camaraderie was like none I have ever experienced in a team golf event. Around our 6th or 7th hole, when we knew things were going well, Scott teed off and hit the ball long down the middle of the fairway. As he is swinging, Scott lets out a very loud, "Yee Haw!, and when he was done, grabs his tee and starts running down the fairway saying, "Come on guys, let's go!" Gregg Jennings turns to me and asks "Is he always like this?, to which I replied, "I don't know. I have only known him for three months."

But as all of us knew or were going to know, that was the essence of Scott: An excited, full-of-life guy who thoroughly enjoyed life and the camaraderie of a good round of golf.

THE COURSE RECORD AT BLUE MOUND

In October before Scott went into the hospital for his procedure, we took our two sons, John and Jack, on a Saturday afternoon to play golf

Blue Mound. Neither of us had played much,, but the prospect of spending the afternoon with our boys playing the most enjoyable hobby, was one of life's simplest pleasures.

This was a beautiful early October afternoon. Scott played the best golf I had ever seen. He birdied one and two, lipped out on three for birdie (but getting the par), and parred # four. As good as he was playing, our boys were not really into the game, as we found them goofing around in the bunker on # five. Five is a beautiful par 5 at Blue Mound, and, on this day, Scott birdied # five to go three under after five holes.

But being the great Dad that he was, he understood that Jack and John were not having as much fun as we were. Scott suggested that we skip holes six through eight, and play # nine to end our day. Scott parred # nine to be three under after six holes. Seeing that three under after six holes would have translated into nine under after eighteen holes, with a 61 for Blue Mound, I believe Scott shares the course record at Blue Mound.

THINKING OF OTHERS EVEN IN HIS TIME OF NEED

Scott went back into the hospital right around November 1. My birthday is November 2nd, and when I visited Scott in the hospital, he gave me a beautiful Hartmann portfolio. He had seen me for the past four years walking around with a beat up seventeen-year-old Hartmann, a gift from my then fiancé, now cherished wife, for Christmas. I was blown away that he was thinking of me even as he was grappling with this life determining procedure. Even in his most challenging days, Scott was thinking of others.

SCOTT KNEW EVERYONE, AND QUICKLY

I distinctly remember a day in June of the year that Scott joined Blue Mound. Scott and I played that day, and we must have come across eight members that I tried to introduce him to, but that he already knew and seemed to be good friends with. That was so Scott. After your initial meeting, it felt like you had known him for years. Same thing happened at Christ King, where everyone thought of Scott as a good friend. He just had that way of making people feel comfortable. We certainly got that feeling as we remembered him during his funeral. He was a friend's friend.

I only had one friend in my life who I think "got me" as well as Scott, and that was my late brother, Bill. It is that kind of chemistry where you can make eye contact during a meeting or at a party when you both know something seems funny or strange or a bit off-kilter. Scott "got me", and I would like to think that I "got him." It helped that we had kids the same age, were members of the same parish and golf club, and were blessed with great parents and sole-mates for wives. We made the working relationship work, and our friendship outside of work is something I will cherish forever. JIM.

28. The Bone Marrow Transplant Unit

About the size of a tennis court, the space reserved exclusively for bone marrow transplant patients is a double rectangle, with 12 patient rooms on the outer perimeter, and the nurses stations and desks forming the inner rectangle. Six nurses and techs man the desks there. Each desk has a computer for record keeping. Each patient call or nurse visit is entered into the patient file.

There is a complete change of air in the BMT unit every 7 minutes, to reduce the chance of infection from airborne bacteria. Through the double doors at the North end of the unit is a patient lounge with several game tables holding jigsaw puzzles, seating, two exercycles, a TV, and large picture windows with expansive views North and East. He can see treetops in his own neighborhood through these windows.

At the far west end of the unit is a small half kitchen with microwave where patients can keep refrigerated foods, labeled. Coffee is brewing all day.

The south end double doors open onto a main hospital corridor leading to guest elevators and the larger hospital. While the BMT unit is semi-isolated, there is no barrier preventing anyone from entering or leaving the unit, no visible security, and no check on whether visitors may be disease carrying. A receptionist is on duty to answer questions. Nurses in the unit work here exclusively, seven days on and seven days off, 10 hours each day. Dr. Jeanne Palmer and her team devote themselves to BMT patients only.

The corridors are busy with activity day and night. Nurses and techs monitor patients almost constantly. Maintenance crews come and go. Specialists see patients and check the patient data entered by nurses.

Scott's room is about 10 X 12 feet with large picture windows looking north. On one wall is a 3 by 4 ft. white bulletin board laid out in a grid showing each day of the month. In hand written black marker, the board indicates blood counts each day, particular drugs being infused, and nurses and doctors on duty and making rounds. Visitors can check the grid to see what is going on and planned. Left of the grid is a cork strip for pinning up personal messages or routine medical advisories.

Across from the foot of his bed is his private bathroom which only he can use. The wall behind his bed holds devices for measuring his temperature, blood pressure, and pulse rate. On a chest high stand along the South wall is a laptop computer where each nurse and doctor visit is logged in, along with their tests and findings. Any hospital staff entering the room can readily see where he is in his treatment and be brought up to date.

A small tube TV is mounted high on the East wall, bordered by bookcases. Two chairs, one a recliner, are in the room. Scott uses them when he feels well enough to sit up.

His bed is a typical hospital single, adjustable to suit him. His cover is a down comforter he has brought from home. A cable with a large control panel extends to his bed. With it, he controls the TV, calls the nurses, adjusts his bed, brightens or dims his room lights. A telephone on a stand next to his bed allows him access to the outside world, and to order food from the cafeteria. He uses his I-Pad and Blackberry extensively.

The room is decorated in neutrals, peaceful, nothing garish. A drop down plenum carries pipes for the sprinkler system. There is recessed lighting, a ceiling mounted camera, and smoke and fire detectors.

At home, this room might be considered a well-equipped smallish bedroom. Here in the BMT unit at Froedtert, it is his prison cell, from which he would like nothing more than to escape. He would spend 42 long days and longer nights in this cramped space, much of it in writhing pain.

His room is one of twelve, all devoted to bone marrow transplant patients. Since his admittance, most other patients have come and been treated and been released to home. One of these, Donna, was a waitress at Blue Mound Golf Club receiving her second transplant after 17 years. Ironically, she served Scott and me lunch just one day before falling ill for the second time. During that luncheon, knowing that Scott was scheduled to receive a transplant, she had volunteered information about her own transplant all those years ago, with no indication of relapse. One day later, she was diagnosed as needing another course of treatment, and was in the BMT wing at the same time as Scott. Her second transplant, with marrow donated by her sister, was thankfully a success, and she was restored to health a second time.

29. Thanksgiving 2011

Yesterday, all counts were up in unison for the first time. This was the liftoff that had been expected. He still has head and stomach pain and a sleepless night, but the strong blood count numbers have been the story. The counts are a clear indication that the transplant has been successful and has begun to produce new blood cells in the appropriate ratio.

The data supported hope and optimism that Scott would shortly be back on his feet and recovering at home, away from the noisy freeway that his hospital room had become. He would soon be home with Terry and the kids, in familiar and loving surroundings.

THE EUPHORIA WAS SHORT LIVED!

As events of the week unfolded, a new and totally different phenomenon came to override all other concerns and bring down hopes and spirits. This new intruder was a damaged liver, unrelated to the bone marrow production but to the chemo required to suppress rejection. In retrospect, the symptoms were there.

In the past week, he has suddenly gained thirty pounds, while taking in few solids, and has severe edema in his legs and ankles. He is back on the morphine pain pump, and having difficulty emptying his bladder. A catheter may be needed if urine flow does not improve. The rounds resident doctor says to expect three or four more days of head pain and stomach discomfort before it clears up, apparently unaware of what has developed.

Pain worsened during the day, to the point that Terry insisted more be done. A direct injection of hydromorphone was given, and nurses were instructed to give him more injections as needed for pain. He could have no visitors today, and wanted none. Injection brought relief and he slept.

Urine is bloody. His liver is being monitored and tested. He is groggy and has difficulty talking. A brain scan shows no issue. An ultrasound is scheduled for Thanksgiving morning..

Thanksgiving morning brought news of the devastating new complication, making sense of the awful, unbearable pain of the last few days. Through scans and blood tests, the doctors have discovered that Scott has an obstructive liver disease, resulting from intensive Busulfan chemo he received four days starting November 1. The terrible effects of the drug have taken this long to be understood and diagnosed. The disease must still be confirmed through biopsy of the liver.

Terry and Joan and I are stunned and heart broken by the news, dreading what is ahead, paralyzed by the implications of this development on the heels of such heartening news yesterday.

The disease has a name. Hepatic Sinusoidal obstruction syndrome, (SOS), formerly known as **VENO OCCULSIVE DISEASE** (VOD). It is one of the rarest and most feared complications of bone marrow transplant. It results in a basic loss of liver function caused by a thickening of the walls of major veins carrying blood away from the liver. This constricted flow causes a back-up, or clogging, of blood entering the liver for filtering before passing out to the intestine as used or wasted blood cells.

The liver ceases to function. At this point, a liver transplant, assuming a donor liver, would be too invasive a surgical procedure for a weakened patient to endure.

A key indicator in liver disease is the level of something known as serum Bilirubin. This strange new word is descriptive of an orange, yellowish substance, according to the medical literature, which goes into the liver in indirect uncoagulated form and is there transformed into direct or coagulated form, made water soluble, and is excreted into the intestines. Bilirubin gives the stool its brown color. The normal count of Bilirubin is expressed as "1". Today, Scott's is at a level of "2", not good at all if it continues to rise. Doctors say that if the level rises to 10-15 range, the prognosis for the patient becomes poor, unless the level comes back down quickly.

Literature states that the survival rate from mild VOD is 70% overall, but much poorer in moderate to severe cases. Time and a liver biopsy will tell the severity of Scott's case.

According to Dr. Saad, the diagnosis means that Scott must remain in the hospital another month, meaning the earliest he might come home would be December 25, Christmas Day. Another month in confinement will be extremely hard on both Scott and Terry, who are already exhausted by the emotional extremes of the past month, and are frayed and tender from worry and anxiety. And Jack and Audrey will have fears and questions which eleven and twelve year olds should not have.

Choosing the language to explain to them this new illness will not be easy. They know about life and death and they are smart. Nothing can be kept from them. This dreadful thing happening to their father will be expressed by them in some manner, perhaps in anger or resentment.

Terry is distraught, and we all see the situation as surreal, as if it is not really happening, or happening to someone else. Surely, this life threatening prognosis must be wrong, must be brighter than the cases heard, must have a positive outcome restoring him to his energy-filled self. And how can he be the one in one thousand with this affliction, how can anyone be that unlucky and unfortunate? It must not be true!

Scott is drugged, but insists on explaining the situation to us himself, aided by Terry. He talks without hesitation about the rarity of the disease, the chances for survival, dry eyed, while we and Terry wept.

The discussion in his room was a moment of truth, a reckoning, a spoken realization of the worst that could happen, and awareness of how totally and helplessly dependent we all are on fate and the hoped for magic of modern medicine. Positive outlooks one hour become highly negative in minutes. The turnabout is too sharp to readily comprehend. Denial is the first instinct....the natural reaction.

Scott is short of breath, taking oxygen, vomiting from time to time to release some of the fluids being given him. His voice is raspy, and he speaks in short phrases due to the shortness of breath. Scott normally elaborates at length on any subject, especially those he sees as absurd or stupid, but he doesn't have the breath to do that now. His shallow breathing is directly related to extreme bloating in his midsection. There are some moans or heaving in between phrases. His head and throat pains are still at high levels.

In his favor is overall good health up to this point, and a history of a healthy heart, liver, kidneys, and lungs. He has really never been seriously ill in his life. This profile gives family and doctors hope.

His family left his room at 4 PM. He hugged them and told them he loved them very much, unusual for Scott, but today it was his impulse. The love was returned. This long illness has given family a complete new understanding of each other as human beings, not just father/son or mother/son. Every moment of his life from birth has been reviewed, and old memories refreshed vividly, which might not have otherwise come to the surface. He is treasured, appreciated, and loved more consciously and deeply than ever before.

Terry will go home briefly and bring the kids up to date, then come back to spend the night with Scott.

FRIDAY, NOVEMBER 25

He sent an email this morning at 2:53 AM saying his white counts are now up to 7000, double yesterday's count. Platelets are in the 70's, and the red count is also rising, all good signs of functioning bone marrow.

These counts are back up to his blood levels when he entered the hospital the last day of October. These data seem to settle the bone marrow issue. The new factory is working as advertised.

At the same time, his Bilirubin count is rising. Too high, and it clogs the main vessels carrying blood away from the liver. Sustained high levels mean big trouble. The liver stagnates and enlarges, unable to process anything. High white counts indicate that he is not neutropenic. Nurse Jolie says the liver can be biopsied by going through the jugular vein, avoiding external puncture wounds which could become infected. Decision is made to biopsy his liver this way.

About a dozen samples of the liver were taken this way by a specialist in performing this procedure. Later today, there will either be confirmation of VOD or simply temporary effects of all the drugs he has been getting. There is a thread of hope remaining that the blockage could be self-correcting.

Scott's appearance and demeanor have been transformed in the past few days. He now appears older, more dependent, bald, exhausted, gasping for enough oxygen, helpless to help himself. The ravages of major illness express themselves quickly. This personality is separate from the vital, lively, animated, opinionated Scott we expect.

The last twenty years of his life have unfolded hundreds or thousands of miles away from his parents, yet they have tracked him closely through phone calls, emails, and visits. Scott and his brother Jon have been the sustaining center of our lives, always with the natural assumption that each would progress through careers and relationships, never allowing the thought of life threatening illness to intrude on this traditional order.   They and their families have gradually become the carriers of not only their own hopes and dreams, but our emotions and aspirations as well. The older generation had their run at life, and are now investing in and betting on the young.

This is likely true of every parent/child relationship. Their happiness is the parent's happiness, their hurts and suffering deeply felt and shared, their disappointments cried over, their lives fused into one, their successes celebrated together.

Scott's life is cradled in a blanket of thousands of prayers from his and other churches, his children's school, fellow lawyers the world over, from Caring Bridge posts, from old friends. For the family, questions of faith and the power of prayer creep in.   Now is the time to hope for synergy between the power of prayer and the science of modern medicine. Perhaps they can both work together to pull Scott through this trial. He is a worthy man, a good and needed husband and father.

This afternoon, with us and Terry in the room, doctors came in to confirm the biopsy results of VOD.   The small remaining hope for a different outcome was not to be.   The spoken words were dreaded, shocking.   The family notes that 19 days have passed since infusion of bone marrow to the day his liver biopsy happened.   This raises questions about the wisdom of waiting to do definitive liver tests until the disease had clearly developed, versus a possible different course of treatment had the biopsy examination been done before the BMT. Doctors are human! Human beings make mistakes!

ENTER DEFIBROTIDE:

A short time later, a new doctor, David Margolis, enters the picture, and, together with Dr. Saad, recommend an experimental new drug, named DEFIBROTIDE, be started immediately to treat the disease in it early stage. Dr. Margolis is head of Froedtert's Children's hospital, where the drug has been used to clear the livers of jaundiced newborns.

DEFIB is not yet approved by the FDA, but has had some success in Europe, and is in limited trials in this country. Without FDA sanction, its use must be approved by a medical Board, and Margolis has already secured Board approval. Small quantities of it can be borrowed from Children's hospital while additional amounts are ordered rushed from Italy, where it is produced, or borrowed from other U.S. hospitals. The drug is intended to reduce the levels of liver clogging Bilirubin and restore the flow of blood.

The technical name is polydeoxyribonucleic acid. It is an anticoagulant derived from cow lung or pig intestines. It is intended to work in dissolving blood clots by preventing the clotting function of platelets in the blood. The manufacturer in Italy is Gentium.

Dr. Margolis, experienced in using the drug in children, leads this effort. Defibrotide will start being infused this afternoon, for two hours each six hours, for two weeks. The doctor thinks the disease should be brought under control after the two-week cycle, and his stomach swelling and severe pain should subside. He describes the drug's function as "unclogging the toilet", saying the volume of blood entering the liver should be matched by the volume of blood exiting the liver. Side effects can include internal bleeding in 5 % of cases.

This new terror is one Scott never thought he would face just a few days ago when all looked right for him to get to come home by the end of November. His appearance today is sallow, withdrawn, worried. He can hardly speak. The frustration is that neither we nor Terry can make things better, that what is happening to him is wrong and unfair, that he has done nothing to deserve this pain and suffering. The great hope is that tomorrow and each day thereafter will be better. DEFIBROTIDE is the name of hope.

NOVEMBER 26, IGNITION PLUS 4.

He had received two bags of DEFIBROTIDE as of 10 AM, preceded by five bags of plasma last night and one bag of plasma this morning. He peed five times during the night and had his first significant bowel movement in several days. Bilibubin count has risen to 2.9, but all blood counts look good.

A stomach scan during the night showed no obstruction. Doctor had been particularly interested in his spleen, but learned nothing from the scan. The fact that pain is concentrated on his left side rather than the right side location of the liver is a lingering question not fully understood.

He slept on and off in a chair, administering the morphine pump himself. The automated pain medication has been stopped because it could possibly interfere with the action of DEFIBROTIDE. He is put on LASIX (FUROSEMIDE), basically a water pill, to help reduce excess fluids in his body.

Terrible images now creep into consciousness in spite of attempts to lock them out. Scott's life hinges on the effectiveness DEFIB, which must work for him to survive. There are no other options. We all understand clearly that his life is precariously on the edge. Everything MUST work now. There are no backup drugs or strategies, no surgeries, no remaining therapies.

The mental picture is terrifying and absurdly unreal. Extended family and close friends have been notified of Scott's condition. Supportive messages are pouring in from them, all comforting and prayerful.

Jack and Audrey are informed by Terry in carefully chosen words. Their big question is, "Will Dad be home for Christmas?"

This afternoon, the medical team tap his stomach and take off 2.2 liters of fluid, relieving some extreme pressure buildup. If fluid begins to collect in his lungs, they are prepared to tap the lungs in the same manner to drain it off. The latest scan shows no cause for concern yet.

At noon today, his appearance frightens. He moans in constant pain in both head and stomach. He has five bags of meds being infused through his Picc line, including the critical bag of DEFIB.

Terry will spend the night with him again tonight. Nobody wants him to be left alone at night, even though he may be only vaguely aware that someone is there. He needs an advocate and his family needs the emotional security of being by his side to make sure he gets an answer anytime he calls. Tubes running into him, swollen stomach, legs, scrotum, and ankles, life at risk, helpless, presents an image which will not go away, and which comes back in sleepless nights.

Dr. Saad reports that the coming Tuesday should give a good indication as to whether the new medication is working. Sunday and

Monday will be the longest, most worrisome 48 hours ever stumbled through.

Tonight, Jack looks and acts so much like Scott did at the age of 12, but Jack is calmer. I watch Tosh.0 on TV, and remembers that Scott loved the guy's weird humor, and I wish we could watch the program together. And I fantasize that we might play golf tomorrow at Blue Mound, as we did in late October, and then have lunch outdoors, even if it is raining. There are so many things to do over with him, routine things that are now remembered as very rare and very precious.

SUNDAY, NOVEMBER 27, IGNITION PLUS FIVE:

During the night, his white counts went to 14,000, reds held at 26, and platelets went to the low 80's. Fluid retained is still huge, and his pain causes him to moan with every breath. Bilirubin count is 4.5 from 2.9 yesterday, still not dangerously high according to doctors. His scrotum is huge from fluid buildup, and walking or going to the bathroom requires him to call a nurse.

He is receiving antibiotics again, getting minimal pain medication because it goes directly to the liver and interferes with the DEFIB VOD drug. He is confined to bed only, no more chair. A possible tube in his throat is being considered to relieve trapped gas in his intestines, and another stomach tap to drain fluids is a possibility. It's a messy picture, with an expected turnaround possible in the next day or two. He remains in agony with pain, and by 2 PM, the medical team agreed to increase his self-administered pain medication from 0.2 to 0.8 per hour.

Dr. Saad reports that the supply of DEFIB be depleted at midnight tonight, and attempts are underway to get more from other hospitals here or in Texas. This may delay critically needed infusions of the drug for 24 hours, which seemed not to concern Saad. By midnight, Scott will have been given nine doses of the drug. Terry may call Dr. Margolis to get further explanation.

His LASIX dosage is being increased to try to fight fluid retention, which continues to build in his stomach, scrotum, legs, and ankles. His testicles are swollen to softball size, quadruple normal, and are difficult for him to manage in any position. An ice pack is kept under them to help reduce swelling. Saad has no real concern about his spleen or his elevated Bilirubin count, saying he is still on a good track. Scott reported a pain level of 8, the best he has been today. He got a shower with the help of nurse Jolie. He is not allowed to leave his bed by himself. Nurses intend to make certain he does not fall, and to manage his many tubes and his oxygen bottle. His dependence on them has grown hourly, and he knows he needs the nurses to steady him.

Finally, a liver specialist, Dr. Rezat, is called in at 12:50 PM, and shows us a computer image of Scott's enlarged liver, which is causing pain on both sides of his stomach and pressing against his lungs, but he says the blood flow to his heart is adequate. The heart rate is high because of having to work harder, but Rezat says it "should come back down" once the DEFIB kicks in. Rezat says he would like to get Scott out of the hospital before Christmas. His words are soothing, but given the direction we see things going, we wonder why this optimism.

A new breathing device, named an Incentives Barometer, was brought in and Scott is encouraged to use it to expand his lung capacity. It is a 10-inch high plastic tube with a blue ball inside, and a mouthpiece.

He sucks in air ten times, as hard as he can, thereby expanding the base of his lungs and increasing oxygenation. As he sucks on the mouthpiece, the ball inside rises in measurable degrees. He tries it with great difficulty.

At 8 PM, a catheter was attempted to be inserted through his penis into his bladder to drain urine, but the nurses could not get the catheter past his grotesquely enlarged testicle sack. Urology experts will come and insert the catheter tomorrow, we are told.

His parents said goodnight to him at 10:30 as he thanked them for being with him today. He is thoughtful and courteous in spite of terrible pain and the frightening appearance of his swollen body. He knows he is in trouble, but has remained hopeful always based on what he is being told.

NOVEMBER 28, IGNITION PLUS SIX:

All counts and vitals signs are within acceptable range this morning, with edema causing great discomfort. His scrotum continues to require frequent salving and ice bags, which the nurses attend to on schedule.

The last bag of DEFIB is going in now. More has been located in Chicago, but the red tape protocol to get it released and couriered to Milwaukee may cause a delay of up to 36 hours between doses. Terry is unclear about the impact of this delay. His kidneys are stressed by the increased LASIX, but still more is being given. Pain meds may be increased again this morning, with doctor approval.

He struggled through a short walk this morning, sat in the lounge for a few minutes, and asked for a cup of ENSURE, is peeing some, but almost no bowel movement. The big issue remains getting the liver function right, which would unwind all the problems.

There is a complete and total loss of privacy and dignity now. He has no control over sleep interruptions, how naked he is, or which substances go into his body or come out via his PICC lines. Nurses have to be in the shower with him, wipe him, wrap his scrotum, and dress him. He is completely worn out from lack of sleep and pain, but has no ability to stop any of it. How long can this pain and exhaustion be carried on without itself becoming lethal?

Terry called to say that some amount of DEFIB will be back on stream within 24-36 hours, but, once begun, will continue for a period of three weeks, not two as previously said. This means that the earliest he could be home would be December 20. If, after three weeks, the drug is working only partially, it will be continued on some schedule to build to full effectiveness. *At this interval, after nine infusions, there is no evidence that the drug has begun to work.*

An impression is confirmed that none of the doctors have had meaningful experience with treating patients with VOD, because of its rarity, even though some case histories do exist. Only two cases have been treated at Froedtert in the past five years. DEFIB, we also understand, is being administered by a medical team with limited knowledge about the drug, therefore small ability to predict what might happen at various stages.

A chest x ray this morning showed some light shadows in the lungs. There has been some coughing, but no fever or symptoms of pneumonia, but Saad thinks it best to begin antibiotics against the pneumonia possibility.   Nurse Elizabeth says that LASIX injections sometimes cause coughing.

Saad orders maximum rest this afternoon with few interruptions. Fatigue alone is cause for alarm. Terry spoke to the nurses about coordinating their room visits to insure fewer interruptions.   He needs much more rest.

The old adage, "never enter the hospital with a serious condition on a holiday weekend" seems to hold true here.   Over Thanksgiving weekend, the corridors were deserted, the pharmacy closed, doctors were off, staff on short schedules.   Medical personnel also want holidays off if possible, but their absence can mean life or death.

At 3 PM today, Doctors Palmer, Margolis, and Saad conferred in Scott's room and revealed that a full quantity of DEFIB would be here and in use within 36 hours, saying they had little concern about the down time when he was not receiving the drug.   This was Dr. Palmer's first visit to Scott's room in more than two weeks.

Jim Stern, Scott's General Counsel, had offered the Smith company plane to get the drug sooner, but Scott and Terry seemed satisfied with the troika and their plan, and turned down his kind offer. The doctors urged patience in allowing the drug to work, but the slow attack of the drug, the delay in its infusion, combined with the myriad of antibiotics and other drugs and LASIX going into his body, with pain killers, produced considerable anxiety.

Scott walked two turns around the BMT unity, but showed weakness and dependence on Terry for physical and emotional support.

Late tonight, Scott was asleep, catheter and oxygen and bags of med going into his body from the incessantly beeping pumps. He awoke at 10 PM with a deep, harsh, rumbling cough originating deep in his lungs, with no sputum and no clearance, a sure symptom of possible pneumonia to complicate his other agonies.

QUANDARIES OF AGE:

At 76 and 78, Joan and I were not prepared for changes in life's natural order. Our lives had been those of traditional parenting, mentoring, hoping, as all parents hope, that as our sons grew to be adults and became educated, they would take their places in society in pursuit of careers, and ultimately become parents themselves.

With the usual teenage stutter-starts, this model seemed close to becoming reality. Scott married, practiced law, set career goals, and had beautiful and smart children. Jon chose a different, less conventional path, striving in different parts of the country in various entrepreneurial efforts.

Our generation watched this natural sequence unfold, content to share their successes and temporary set backs, accepting the few disappointments as essential elements of achieving understanding and maturity.

We were never conditioned for a sudden reversal of this comfortable order. We fully expected to live out already long lives in the shadows of our son's progress. With the stunning news of Scott's confrontation with mortality, we realized we had no roadmap, no contingency to deal with a life and death battle we knew nothing about fighting. We had no failsafe path through the pain and crippling sadness.

We became walking wounded, with few outward signs of disability. There was no bravado, no stoicism strong enough to bring order to this sudden chaos. Literally, we became damaged souls.

BMT: A FATEFUL CHOICE:

Arguably, had Scott chosen not to go for bone marrow transplant when he was already in remission, he would not have VOD liver disease today. His choice was a brave one to go for the long-term cure.

Speculation is pointless, but the decision is yet another example of the consequence of choosing one path from other options. It highlights the risks in all life's choices, of spouse, career, lifestyle, and moral and ethical elections. Once committed to a path, retraction and reversal of course if often impossible.

Were his decision possible to make again, would he have chosen to stay in remission and take his chances, or would he have made the same choice to do BMT, unaware that he would be in the tiny minority unlucky enough to be struck with a rare and potentially fatal liver disease? Would Scott and Terry, as a team, make the same choice, thinking the transplant direction best for family and career, escaping the fear of lapsing back into leukemia?

Almost certainly, Scott's personality and optimism would have led to the very same decision. It was the only one consistent with his character and his view of how his life was to be lived.

THE NEED TO CONTROL

When the chips are down, the family impulse is to contribute ideas for making everything better, partly out of frustration, but mostly from the need to be proactive rather than passively allowing diseases and their treatments to take their own good time in arriving at cures.

I felt the need to question the doctors and nurses more closely when there is little or no improvement in his condition. Lay people become impatient, incapable of standing by. Antibiotics, we think, should work immediately to alleviate the terrible, rattling cough. The fluid buildup in his abdomen and lungs should be drained away now. His obvious great pain requires extra measures to give him relief.

In some instances, desperate measures may be the right ones, but the medical team and their drugs must be allowed to do their work, on their timetable, in spite of the work seeming to be too little. The overriding instinct is to take charge, to cut through red tape and standard protocols, and get the job done. Fathers always think they can make any hurt better, help solve any problem. The instinct is correct, but the protocol of the team in charge still follows slow but sure steps, while loved ones become anxious onlookers.

In times of deterioration, aware of the gravity of the disease and its course if not reversed, words of finality or failure cannot be used. Death and dying cannot be uttered. Doctors speak only of "possible" outcomes. Emotions welling up in human minds do not allow the articulation of the unacceptable. There is hidden guilt that speaking these terms makes one complicit, contributing to negativity.

The left brain comprehends reality so damaging as to threaten his survival, but the right brain intercedes and insists on life, a return to robust health, to the image of his watching his children grow through their educations and to families of their own. The right brain overpowers reason, preferring to see him resuming his career as strong as ever, back from the brink, marching onward to a long and happy life, fulfilling the natural order.

NOVEMBER 28-30, TRANSPLANT PLUS 20-23:

These last harrowing days of the month were cause for hope and terror. A new supply of DEFIBROTIDE has arrived from New York, and is being infused, yet his Bilirubin counts are trending too high. The trend needs to be sloping downward, toward allowing the blood to circulate through the liver, and that is not happening. The catheter is in, so he no longer has to wrestle himself out of bed to pee. He can sleep better.

Another stomach tap is being considered to remove fluid, while he continues to be infused with still more liquids than he can eliminate. He drank three insures this morning, and did breathing exercises.

Patients and their advocates must monitor and take charge of their own treatment management to some extent to block excessive intrusions and interruptions. Terry is growing increasingly impatient with routine inspections which could easily be done at other times, clustered to avoid separate, deferrable actions. Two unknown nurses barged in between 6 and 8 AM and announced that they were to do routine skin inspections of all patients. Scott immediately told them no, that theirs was not a high priority, and to go through his nurse before coming back.

Priest and volunteer ministers offering communion are also troublesome, and Scott has told them no in certain terms, asking his nurse to bar them. Without guidelines and some direction from the patient, hospital staff and do-good volunteers will overrun him and make life miserable with needless questions. Routine activities such as pill taking can be synchronized with other nurses who have to take blood or give shots, or hang bags of meds, or change beds and take out the trash. Nurses now know to bar all non-essential personnel while he is sleeping. He and Terry are taking ownership of this space.

Drugs have him in a partial stupor. He calls the nurse for a special cough medicine, but cannot remember why he called when she arrives. He briefly has trouble remembering which grades his children are in, but finally gets it right without prompting.

His condition is critical, and he must begin to show improvement in the next two or three days.   He is a wounded warrior. This cannot be happening!   He can't keep going without improvement.   His voice is weak, and breath shallow.

Terry is brave in facing reality. She is now on top of every little test and every change in his treatment and his meds. She said Scott slept well through the night, without interruptions. Some signs of perking up, with more energy. He is walking, drinking Insure.   A liver specialist announced that he is "encouraged", and asked for everyone to be patient. More LASIX has been decided upon.

The right brain continues to dominate. Words of encouragement are the ones heard, discouragement fails to register.

One of us needs to be with him at all times, in case of crisis, in case he calls, in case he feels the need to tell us something, in case we want to hug him. We feel isolated and alone when we are not with him. Perhaps he wants to talk about his children or remember a pleasant moment in his life.   We cannot afford to be absent if he chooses to speak of any of these things through his pain.

We relive every precious moment of our lives with Scott, thinking anew of every detail of some event or other, from his earliest days in New York, to Connecticut, to Atlanta, the trips we took together, the conversations we had, the sports we saw him play, the fun we had.   We think of his teen years, his college and law school life, his marriage, his fatherhood, his striving to succeed, his formula for living.   We see him competing in golf as a junior, and as a mature adult.   We see him coaching his own son in football, baseball, and volleyball.   We see him in Springfield, Peoria, St. Louis, Milwaukee, Pebble Beach, Asia, Acapulco, Texas, White Plains, Stamford, and the British Virgin Islands.   We see him eating spicy foods, but avoiding butter, milk, mustard, and eggs. We see him at his wedding to Terry.

He experimented with life and learned important lessons. He grew to accept the counsel of peers and experienced people he respected, and his mentors.

These are the kinds of thoughts which pervade the minds of family and friends while they watch and worry through long vigils.   These thoughts come to us, along with tears, as we watch him sleep, stirring in pain from time.

30. The Support Network

Humans in history have congregated and assembled in tribes with secure perimeters. Common appearance, language, beliefs, blood, and interests define these social groupings. Churches, synagogues, and social clubs are examples of affinity platforms which offer protection and comfort to members. Participants in these communities have extended family status.

Scott and Terry moved to just such a community, Wauwatosa, in the Spring of 08. They and Jack and Audrey were accepted immediately into the tight knit Catholic family. Christ King church and Christ King school were within walking distance, and the kids started the new school year in the highly rated school connected with the church. In four short years, they made many new and valued friends.

In Scott's time of crisis, these loving neighbors stepped forward with an amazing and well organized care network, providing dinner meals to the family for more than six month, holding prayer vigils, calling and emailing to offer help in every way possible, and often hosting Jack and Audrey for special events. Notes and cards came daily expressing prayers for Scott's recovery, and most posted thoughtful, prayerful messages on the special CARING BRIDGE web site set up for Scott.

The close church/school community enveloped them and became their protective tribe, their perimeter, volunteering to help in any way, decorating their home for Christmas, giving breaks for Terry by taking the kids for meals, movies or sleepovers. Their common interests, Catholicism and children, bound them together tightly in a positive expression of the value of religion. Common interest bonding might have come from the members of an athletic club, a sailing club, a book or political club. But the Christ King community revealed itself as committed to live its religious and human values. As it did so, the Garrett family became forever grateful.

30. Cold December

On war within

Journaling his condition daily, recording micro data, seeing marginal improvements in vitals and blood counts, reminds all that Scott's body has become a mortal battleground between two opposing forces. The warring force for cure and survival is the new bone marrow which keeps making tactical advances.   The army opposed is his non-functioning liver which fills his tissues with fluid and threatens to drown his organs. In the course of their epic battle, both armies produce terrible pain as they inflict wounds and suffer casualties, and his neural system staggers with each blow.

From the viewpoint of the civilian…the non-medical professional, the advantage in this battle seems to swing back and forth on the daily data, with hope coming down on the side of cure and survival. Tactics show almost daily advances.

Experienced leukemia, liver, and kidney specialists, seeing the larger macro view, would likely have seen this very battle before, and know from the outset which side had the stronger strategic advantage. They would be inclined to ignore the potentially misleading indications of temporary results. Yet they are unwilling to express the negative view too strongly. They also do not want to abandon hope and raise premature alarms. The family's emotional state must be considered. Turnaround is still theoretically possible.

As Von Clausewitz viewed war, the outcome was probably always clear to professional commanders seeing the big picture with all the elements and resources of both sides in focus, while the daily noise of the micro picture distorted day-to-day conclusions. Short-term data suggests one side may be winning, even as the overall strategic advantage accrues to the other side. Viewing Scott's internal struggle as a battle of unequals seems to fit the Clausewitz assessment at this point.

DECEMBER 1:

Joan and I are deep into a form of mourning for the living. It is a form of unavoidable self-pity. I have trouble going to the Blue Mound pro shop where the Christmas sale promised great bargains. I left quickly, buying nothing. I want to avoid driving Scott's car, sitting in the driver's seat of his beloved Porsche, where he sat such a short time ago.

Joan wants to be alone with him in his room, partly to keep it quiet and allow him to rest, but also to have moments of remembrance with him, to caress him, to cry. These are moments of hidden mourning, not yet articulated or fully understood.

The morning of December 1, his vital signs are good, his cough is getting worse and sapping his energy, he is disoriented to some degree, making hand signals to indicate he wants his bed up or down. His appearance is not better, but blood counts are good except whites at 20K are too high. Intern said most likely stress caused by meds and excess fluids. She said they don't want to tap lungs to removed fluids because of infection risk, nor is kidney dialysis indicated "at this time."

Scrotum pain is at a level of 8 of 10, hugely enlarged and distended, wrapped in a sling. A new batch of DEFIB starts at noon today, and future supply is good. He is uncomfortable in bed with sheets bunched under him, which he constantly tries to straighten. He uses his arms to try to pull himself up higher in bed.

He is fighting courageously, with outward signs discouraging at this point. Doctors say this could be the trough before breakthrough improvement, signaled first by improved breathing when his fluid levels do down. He drinks blue Power-aide to soothe his throat.

This afternoon, Dr. Palmer imposes a new regimen, limiting all visitors in his room to a total of just 4 hours each 24 hours, saying his condition is "guarded." He must get more rest, and is given ATAVAN for sleep, following which he slept 4 and ½ hours. Her first priority is weight loss by getting more fluids out of his system. Since entering the hospital on October 31, he has gained 50 lbs. in spite of having no solids for the past two weeks. His liver can't process all the fluids he is taking in, about five liters per day, two required to accompany DEFIB, and three more through water, Power-aide, and Insure. He must be liquid restricted.

The current excess liquid overloads the blood vessels then seeps through the vessel walls into surrounding tissue, stored there in his swollen stomach, legs three times their normal size, enlarged knees, ankles, and feet. He can walk only with his feet far apart, and has great difficulty sitting on a regular toilet.

More LASIX is ordered to take pressure off his kidney and lungs. Fluids must come down, his blood count and Bilirubin numbers must improve, he must be able to take food orally and do physical therapy, before he can possibly be released from the hospital. Palmer says he "is not out of the woods yet, but will get there if numbers continue good."

She said DEFIB will be infused until December 21, creating obvious doubt whether he can be home for Christmas. She notes that the new bone marrow is performing well, and she has little concern about his deep cough, thinking of it as a way to get rid of excess in throat and lungs.

Kidney creatinine levels, a key measure of kidney function, is a new concern. Normal is .6 to 1.2 milligrams per deciliter. Scott's spiked at 1.7 before dropping back. Pressure must be taken off the kidneys before permanent damage is done.

The new rule for visitors is not going down well. Terry has been a loving companion for Scott throughout this ordeal, and she is having trouble imagining Scott being alone at night, when he asks for her. Being cut off from him the very moment he needs her most , when he is so severely afflicted, saddens and wounds her.

My reaction to everything going on is a form of guilt. Guilt that I am healthy, functioning, exercising, eating, shopping, hugging Scott's children, when Scott cannot even leave his bed without assistance, can walk only a few yards with help and tubes and oxygen bottles, cannot see his children nor they him. Guilt that I am not the sick one, not suffering pain, not confused or disoriented from an overload of pain medications. Guilt that I cannot soothe him or bear his pain for him. This is supposed to be happening to my generation, not Scott's.

Tonight Scott will be alone and perhaps lonely, and frightened when he wakes up and calls for Terry and she is not there. Dr. Palmer's visitor restriction will not last.

DECEMBER 2, FRIDAY, DAY 33 IN THE HOSPITAL, 10 DAYS SINCE NEW BONE MARROW TOOK HOLD.

A good night's sleep according to Don, the night nurse, with 300cc more liquid expelled overnight than was infused. This is about 11 ounces, two thirds of a pound, one positive measurement with at least 50 more such reductions needed before fluid equilibrium is restored.

He weighs 252 lbs now, up 65 lbs since entering the hospital, yet fluids essential to dilute otherwise toxic meds continue to pour into him. The meds are his lifeline, yet the fluids have the potential to drown him. A very fine line is being walked by the doctors and nurses, betting that the fluids can be induced to come out of his system. His legs are as hard as stone, his skin stretched to the breaking point. He is a tragic site, uncomplaining, not seeing himself as a victim, which he never did, but seeing all this pain as the necessary precursor to cure.

Prayer is the default mode in situations like Scott's. Every civilization has one or multiple deities they tribally invoke when there is nothing else known to do, when other options have been used up. Beyond science, beyond immediate medical protocols, an unconscious belief system with religious incantations kicks in, embedded in our primary language and tilted to the right brain. This "faith" is thought to bring help above and beyond mortal intelligence and scientific effort. Pure emotion, pure hope override negative evidence. There is no denying that this is where the mind goes seeking answers, during the darkest times of inevitable human inadequacy.

At the gym this morning, I am greeted by Arnold Sims, my champion body-building friend. Arnold grabbed my hands and held a spontaneous prayer session for Scott, bringing tears. Arnold is a man of great faith, who prays that "God's will be done with Scott". His words were much appreciated, but I noticed that God's will presupposes a master plan for each of us, and God himself is off the hook whichever way Scott's illness goes. Would a just God do such a thing as some sort of pointless test, the kind repeated over and over again in the old and new testaments? I am no closer to understanding religion or its grip on much of humanity.

This line of thinking leads to wonder about where Scott and Terry and their children go from here with their lives, and how? Assuming his full recovery and resumption of a near normal routine, will he be the same man, with the same intellect, the same energy, the same emotions?

Will Terry and Jack and Audrey be the same, or is this mortal battle so indelibly imprinted as to always shadow their every thought and action for the rest of their lives? Will Scott have the same career, or even desire it? Will his relationship with Terry, Jack, and Audrey be wiser, more caring, more sensitive, thoughtful, and forgiving?

This entire family has been taken to the edge, and every life-changing event surely forces changed outlooks, values, goals, and changed needs. Nothing can be as it was before.

Jim Stern thinks Scott will return to work at 110% of his old self. But new bone marrow has literally reshaped him, producing a slightly modified human being with its own genetic longings and quirks.

Perhaps he will be content to have a local law practice, not one which takes him far and wide. His goal of becoming a General Counsel will almost certainly have to be adjusted to a role less stressful and demanding. His value system may now make him a man of faith. Maybe he will become a teacher of law, a mentor for young hopefuls, a volunteer in a charitable organization providing low cost legal aid.

Terry is already a strong and well-educated Catholic, and deeply affected by Scott's illness and its effect on their children. She has proven herself strong, capable of managing difficulty, up to the big emotional challenge. She and Scott, together, may now assess their lives and branch out to entirely new interests consistent with newly formed values. Corporate striving is unlikely to be the brass ring anymore, replaced by personal family happiness and deeper convictions now dominant in both their lives.

And Jack and Audrey will carry this vivid worry all their lives. It may color their choices of education, spouses, careers and emotional responses to many issues in their lives. Even if Scott survives this ordeal, an incredible canvass has been painted for them which will become a new reference point. They will tell their children and grandchildren about their father's battle with leukemia and transplant, and how it made them feel.

They will probably ask GOD to spare them and theirs such a terrible trial. There are no ages exempt from impact.

Joan and I know can never feel secure or complacent again where our family is concerned. We see how tenuous health and happiness are, how superficial some of our usual concerns, how completely unimportant material things are in the scheme of life, how fortunate we have been to have our sons in our lives. We now see the path to becoming more appreciative, less cynical, less critical of small things, more loving and generous to our immediate and extended families.

At noon today, he eats watermelon, and is cleared by Palmer to eat pineapple, melon, and grapes, so long as the fluids are counted into his daily allowance. These are the first actual food textures he has tasted in over two weeks, and should activate a near dormant intestinal track. His voice is better, and his personality is coming through in his requests for certain fresh fruits.

Still, Joan comes back sobbing from the hospital, unable to fathom that Scott is so devastated by this illness. She is somewhat soothed by the good vital signs and continued good numbers, but not much. She is terrified.

Sleepless, restless at night, new doubts creep in. Are these the very best doctors? Is this course of treatment the best one? Was proper monitoring done in the early stage of prepping for the transplant, when Busulfan intensive chemo was infused, damaging his liver? Would this liver disease have happened at some other cancer hospital like M.D.Anderson, Mayo, or Johns Hopkins? Are the medical teams here consulting with the best doctors in the world on the treatment for VOD?

Are his kidneys being adequately monitored? We don't understand kidney functioning well enough day-to-day. Should DEFIB have been given in advance of the bone marrow transplant as part of conditioning his system properly? We don't want to look back and think that we were too timid and non-assertive, if being so would have made the slightest difference.

This is desperate thinking, leap-frogging the science in hopes of finding what went wrong and fixing it quickly. But looking at Scott, seeing the gravity of his predicament, these thoughts are constantly present. Yet there is no family advocate, no independent counselor we can turn to who will spell out our concerns in medical terms the doctors will listen to. The family has no independent medical team to represent them, nobody to argue for them, nobody to effectively challenge what is going on and make sure that it is the very best that is possible. Trust is the operative word for everything that goes on here.

Most families face this same dilemma. In the future, independent medical advocates who represent the patient and his family may become commonplace, but are almost unheard of today, except for second opinions, themselves often postured in politically correct watered down language. Doctors don't like to contradict fellow doctors, which is fine and civil, except when such contradiction could make life and death difference. Medical mistakes of judgment are common, yet few doctors intervene openly or insist on changing course when they doubt the judgments of other doctors, according to medical experts.

THE MATH ON FLUIDS:

A pint of water weighs about a pound. With the excess water Scott has in his tissues, about 65 pounds, or over 30 quarts. Assuming he can be made to eliminate one quart per day more than he takes in, more than 30 days would be needed to work off the excess and relieve pressure on his kidneys and lungs. Yet this rate of depletion has not yet been spoken of, much less begun to happen. There is talk that the rate of elimination increases once the outflow begins. Even if that is true, and as little as 20 days would do the job, that kind of added stay in his hospital bed, on top of the 34 days already logged this stay would weaken him physically and mentally to the point of danger. Thus, new emphasis is placed on physical therapy.

His edema can only increase in the bed, so he must be made to get up and move. He is game to try, but is already weak and off balance. He gives it all he has, and follows nurses directions without complaint. Two quarts of liquid have to leave his body each 24 hours, continuously. He and the physical therapy team know they have a big job ahead.

SATURDAY, DECEMBER 3, DAY 34 IN HOSPITAL, 26 DAYS AFTER TRANSPLANT, 12 DAYS AFTER NEW BONE MARROW STARTED PRODUCING, AND 24 DAYS TILL CHRISTMAS.

Numbers continue good today. Ate fruit during the night and again this morning. Babbling about leaving the hospital and going home as an outpatient. Slept too much yesterday during the day, so little last night. Staff wants more visitors today to keep him awake. Dr. Palmer's edict of strict visitation is modified by reality. Ducolax laxative said to work well. No reduction in body and leg swelling. Net elimination of fluids did not keep up with inflow.

Staff wants him to order and eat soft solids, but he wants fruit or sponges for moisture in his mouth and throat. Weight is 253 today, same as yesterday. Anyone who knew the slender, willowy Scott would not recognize him today. He did request a peanut butter and jelly sandwich, which Joan brought him and he ate rapidly, his first such food since around mid November. He then ate more fresh fruit and two popsicles. At 6:25 PM, he said he was going to sleep, and did so.

Today, he is like a young child, totally dependent on others. He can't roll over, talks haltingly, can't get out of bed on his own. Every movement must be assisted. Yet move he must.

SUNDAY, DECEMBER 4.

Another day of monitoring and hope. Confused and babbling some unrelated thoughts, drug induced. Kidney creatinine count within acceptable range, say two kidney specialists, who visit. They say he needs more protein, and that getting water off his system will be a long process, which we knew. Liver enzymes are trending down, which is good.

A breathing treatment at 10 AM consisted of strapping on a plastic mask over his nose and mouth and feeding in enriched oxygen for 7 minutes. He has been wheezing a lot lately, and this treatment seems to help a little. Legs and feet are so distended as to be unrecognizable, as is his midsection, but not his arms, shoulders, or upper body. He moans with pain, and pushes the pain button every 15 minutes as it allows.

Good trend lines today but until larger quantities of water start to leave his system, there can be no turnaround. His family continues sleepless and intensely worried, trying to force only positive thoughts, but deep breathing, attempts at self-hypnosis, repetitive mantras, and sleep aids all help for only short periods. Scary negative thoughts slip in, and efforts at mind control fail.

Jack and Audrey are perceptive and also worried. They have not seen their Dad in 35 days. He had 40 days of hospitalization earlier, during which they could see him occasionally. Now they cannot, and get reports only from Terry about his condition, who is truthful with them.

Grades have slipped a little this past week. Jack bombed a literature test, which he never does. Audrey also did poorly on a test and her attention wanders, a contrast to her regular A+ performance. They see their grandparents worried, and their mother sometimes distraught. The weight of their father's illness may now be taking its toll on them.

The best news of the day came from Dr. Palmer, who told Terry, "getting him home for Christmas is not off the table." When the DEFIB is done, most of the other meds going through his PICC line might still be given to him as an outpatient. Scott hears this and will do everything in his power to persuade the doctor to release him.

But looking at him in bed tonight, watching the Green Bay/New York game on TV, listening to him breathe, I wonder how he can possibly be well enough to be released in time to meet the Christmas target. The date seems so distant and totally unreal.

At A.O. Smith's legal staff Christmas party at the Stern house this afternoon, Scott's associates and subordinates expressed love and prayers. They are quality, sincere people, and we are heartened by their feelings of true love and admiration for Scott.

MONDAY, DECEMBER 5, 36TH DAY IN HOSPITAL, 28 DAYS SINCE TRANSPLANT, 21 DAYS TILL CHRISTMAS.

Condition is still precarious, with his body swollen and grotesque in spite of good numbers. But his weight is up to 257, four pounds over yesterday. Kidney specialists want more restricted liquid intake, but how to achieve this while infusing meds is the issue. Still more LASIX diuretic is ordered. Palmer not concerned about his disorientation, saying there are no stroke-like symptoms.

THE WELL-WORN PATH:

Froedtert Hospital is five minutes from Scott's house. A mile down Menomonee River parkway, right on Swan, two miles to a left turn onto Watertown Plank road, right on hospital drive, one quarter mile to left turn into hospital entrance, right into five floor parking garage, pick up ticket from automated machine, drive straight ahead to the last bay, turn left up the ramp to any open space.

Enter the hospital through two sets of sliding doors, walk 150 paces forward on the 10 ft. wide brick patterned corridor to the D elevator, passing, in sequence, the gift shop on the left, the pharmacy on the right, the main reception desk on the left. Pass the chapel on the right, always empty, the family center on the left, always empty, various administrative offices.

Take elevator to 4th floor, wash hands carefully in small bathroom on the right, then walk 90 paces straight ahead down multi-colored corridor to the BMT unit, left through the double wooden doors. Have parking ticket stamped at reception desk, greet nurses, proceed a dozen steps to the right and room # 3, marked S. Garrett and Dr. Palmer (the rounding physician that week), sanitize hands and enter Scott's room.

Since June 11,we walked this path, round-trip, over 200 times, not once encountering any form of uniformed security. There is no screening for infectious diseases or colds or fevers, no metal detectors for weapons or explosives, no challenge to anyone, no matter how ragged and suspect. Thousands of visitors and staff of all ages and backgrounds enter and leave these busy corridors each day, with no overt concern about where they are going, or what they are taking with them in their bags or on their persons.

Like airports, large concentrations of people and valuable equipment in hospitals could become potential targets for the disgruntled seeking revenge, for those with evil intentions to carry out any mission they choose with explosives, bacterial or viral contamination, random shootings, disabling vital equipment, or interruption of medical procedures. Drugs could be taken by force from various wings of the hospital. No one seems to be watching, there are no apparent barriers to entry.

AK 47's and explosive vests could be walking the halls at any given moment. The tiered parking garage could be brought crashing down by one explosive packed vehicle, detonated remotely. There seems to be no concern. Security is clearly not a priority. Froedtert seems to have confidence that nothing bad will happen, because it never has. Maybe Froedtert is right...maybe not.

Tonight, Scott is awake, chewing on wet sponges, asking for chicken noodle soup. Stephanie, the night nurse, agreed to prepare it for him. He ate two cups of it from Styrofoam cups, mostly noodles with the liquid drained away. One moment, he is talking gibberish with no context. The next, he is making complete sense, asking for this or that. At 7:20, he asks the nurse what he is allowed to drink. He is not ready for the peanut butter/jelly sandwich by his bed.

His forehead is flush red, perhaps from medications. He watches TV on and off, mainly listening with his eyes closed, making unrelated comments.

A new bag of DEFIB was started at 7 PM. I told him goodnight at 7:30, saying that he was better and was going to be alright. He said, "we will see."

DECEMBER 6, 37TH DAY IN HOSPITAL, 29 DAYS SINCE TRANSPLANT, 19 DAYS TILL CHRISTMAS.

More micro data this morning extends hope. Bilirubin, enzyme, blood, and kidney numbers all trending correctly. Kidney doctors say they are not worried.

Weight at 256, even though he offloaded about 10 ounces more of fluid than he took in overnight. Still groggy and mumbling. At 1 PM, a rigorous physical therapy, but he began coughing and the session had to be stopped. He is under blankets, asked that the room temperature be upped to 77 degrees. His forehead is warm to the touch.

He talks some on the phone with friends. He wants to see his children, but can't. He insisted Dr. Palmer and her team focus on him in a coordinated way and set a goal of getting him out of the hospital by Christmas. This is the goal oriented Scott, and a good sign.

Not on oxygen, and less congested. He wiggled his toes when they were touched, and exchanged greetings. Dr. Palmer said that December 17 would be the last day of DEFIB, which should lessen his overall fluid intake. He is about to start a small bag of antibiotics.

Between 5 and 7 PM, Terry said he walked a full lap within the BMT unit, went out to the lounge and sat for awhile, went to the bathroom. He is down to one pump that he has to take with him when he gets out of bed. No LASIX tonight to avoid stressing his kidney with too much diuretic infusion. The nurses note that during his walk he is off oxygen…a good thing.

DECEMBER 7, 38TH DAY IN HOSPITAL, 70TH ANNIVERSARY OF PEARL HARBOR, 18 DAYS TILL CHRISTMAS.

His stomach seems to him bigger this morning, a consequence, it is thought, of his catheter not working properly. Urology is called and they fiddled with it and got it working again. They will check back later this morning for a more thorough look. An inefficient catheter pressures the kidneys more, testing at a 22 level at 9 AM, versus a 25 level that would be cause for alarm. Nurse Jolie thinks a stomach tap might be necessary today to drain away excess fluids, but Dr. Palmer has vetoed the idea so far.

In spite of stability in his numbers, his appearance is still not showing improvement. Legs and scrotum are especially angry and painful. Last night, 600 milliliters more fluids went in than came out through the catheter, about 18 to 20 ounces. He does not have room in his tissues for this added fluid.

Christmas décor is going up at home, anticipating the possibility that Scott may be home on the couch when the gifts are opened Christmas morning. Jack and Audrey came home from school in 28 degrees, and insisted on walking the 6-8 blocks. They have not seen their Dad in 38 days, getting only second hand information about his condition. They know about the liver disease, and understand the delay in getting him home. Still, there is no doubt in their minds that he will be coming home in time for their usual Christmas Eve dinner of fondue in front of the fire. Terry has vetoed Skyping between them because she doesn't want them to see him in his present condition.

Terry reports that a stomach tap is now likely this afternoon, done with a local anesthetic and a needle drawing off fluids. Too much fluid off-take means a loss of essential electrolytes, which kidney doctors don't want. Later in the day, Terry thinks two liters were actually drawn.

Physical therapy is working his legs now, saying he is strong. His legs are so swollen that bending at the knees is almost impossible. Dr. Margolis comes and says DEFIB may have to continue longer than December 17. He wants his Bilirubin number to be 2 or less, which it is not, and wants him off oxygen before stopping DEFIB. Palmer wants him walking around, shedding fluids, and eating solids. Tactical signs continue good overall, but strategic signals may be working the other way.

At the end of the first week in December, the battlefield is littered with debris. Each detail is captured and logged, but no one is yet ready to call victory or defeat in this struggle. More resources will be brought to the front this coming week, and the battle will continue.

31. Week Two In December.

"Joy and sorrow are inseparable...together they come and when one sits alone with you, remember the other is asleep upon your bed."

--Kahlil Gibran

The Christmas spirit normally fills this week. Last minute shopping and wrapping of gifts, decorations on the tree, anticipation and excitement building. But this Christmas season, even Scott's children are muted. They have perfunctory lists, with little joy or expectation, realizing that Christmas this year is overshadowed by the larger and much more personal event of their father's grave illness. They see great concern on the faces of all adults surrounding them. They see tears flowing.

In this context, the commercialization of Christmas is reason for great cynicism. How can anyone embrace this tradition in the ways expected? Unhappy, resentful families go through the motions of buying pointless gifts to avoid disappointing children, yet there is no connection whatever to the meaning, if any, which should be at the center of the observation. Incessant Christmas songs blare in every mall, while parents endure the stress of fighting crowds simply to comply and conform to societal demands. Respect for the whole season is lost, leading to the conviction that such religious observations such be confined to the church rather than foisted on the public at large. Everything about the current system seems phony and cheapened.

CHANGES BROUGHT BY HIS ILLNESS:

Part of the reason for our rebellion against Christmas is the insidious change in our family brought by Scott's illness. Our thoughts and actions are so focused on him that current events, politics, personal concerns, all take back seats and have faded from priority. Normal interests have disappeared. Each shortened December day is lived hour-to-hour, slogging through the minutes, dreading the nights and the beginning of another day and what it might bring.

This syndrome of gloom is clearly recognizable in families when one member is seriously ill without a clear prognosis. Everyone changes his orientation, making room for the intruding, aggressive stalker who has forced his way into their lives. Suddenly there is a new mountain to climb that was not there before. This becomes the thing which has to be conquered, crowding out all the daily routines, the social correctness, and sensitivity in relationships. This is no time for laughter, fun, joy, playfulness.

When we are healthy, we take wellness for granted. Well-being should bring love and appreciation for the positive happenings in our lives, but we think of good health as our right, our entitlement, as our steady state of being. Self-awareness and conscious celebration of good health could lead to open expressions of thanks, of less cynicism, and more in the moment enjoyment of our families, every day. And this perspective, the celebration of good health offsetting the depression of bad health, is the way it ought to be, not the way it actually is.

Terry is stressed between spending hours each day with Scott in the hospital, seeing his condition worsen, and then helping the kids with their homework and keeping up their spirits and talking to them about their concerns. Conflicting priorities demand her time and attention while tearing at her emotions and elevating her anxiety and stress. Her life...her family's future, is on the line now. She is strong and seems to have the resolve to deal with whatever happens, but the situation is taking its toll.

Jack and Audrey have full school days and nightly studies, but maintaining their attention and desire is difficult. Teachers have written notes about their absent mindedness or sudden lapses with otherwise easy test material. Who would expect otherwise? Their father is deathly ill and they are reacting normally, yet unable to express their emotions fully. Terry does her best to keep them on an even keel, and their overall school performance continues to be excellent, a tribute to her.

ABOUT FAITH

The faithful offer prayers. Friends and family of Scott and Terry have half the country praying for him. He is on the prayer lists of dozens of churches and at least one convent. Dedicated prayer meetings and rosaries have been held for him. Prayers for him have come from all over the world, from East to West, from North to South, consistently, over the past six months, and we await a sign yet that this multitude has been heard by anybody.

Are all prayers selfish, asking for exceptions? How can one prayer be answered and another not? Do all prayers challenge or refute God's will? How can one supplicant be rewarded and another denied? This inconsistency is not often addressed from the pulpit, and, if it is, the unsatisfying answer often expressed is "it's God's will." "Have faith, don't question" is the bedrock message of all religions, yet these very words admit powerlessness over the randomness of illness. They confess that outcomes are predetermined, and, thereby, admit the futility of all prayer asking for change.

Doctors should be the best scientists, the most knowledgeable and up to date on therapies, and recognized leaders in their fields. After that, if they happen to be men and women of faith, that is fine so long as their faith or dogma does not interfere with or trump science. Hope might augment but must not replace good science. Wishes for good health must not replace state of the art medical delivery. No doctor should believe that his patient, if lost, is "in a better place."

This afternoon, when Joan was with Scott, urgent, sudden pains in his abdomen brought nurses and doctors to his room. A stomach X ray showed only trapped gas as the cause. Finally the pain passed and he was able to rest. At 5 PM he was awake and asked to go to the bathroom for the first time in two days, not surprising, given the absence of solid foods.

His nutritionist gave him a list of foods she wants him to eat, which should get his bowel going again, but first, he has to eat them.

DECEMBER 9, 40TH DAY IN HOSPITAL, 31 SINCE TRANSPLANT, 17 SINCE ENGRAFTMENT, 7 REMAINING OF DEFIBROTIDE, 14 DAYS SINCE DIAGNOSIS OF VOD, 16 DAYS TO CHRISTMAS.

The forces of good and evil continue their battle inside his body. Yesterday's severe pain is a reminder of his very fragile condition. His legs are "weeping" fluid through his pores, the fluid forcing its way out of his body through the only remaining way it can escape. He has lung congestion today and bouts of coughing produce bloody phlegm. Fluid pressure on his lungs brings shortness of breath and double the normal heart rate. Getting in and out of bed is exhausting. He must roll on his side and have his huge legs lifted in and out of bed by a nurse.

He seems vulnerable to infection. He shakes while lying in bed. His arms are bruised from needles drawing blood or injecting drugs. Almost every moment of the day, his rest is intruded upon by teams of doctors who want readings of his lungs, liver, and kidney functions, and want to inspect his mouth sores, his pain levels, all with a series of redundant questions already asked by a series of PA's and nurses.

He is not eating and has no appetite, yet desperately needs protein. He no longer gets nutrients from infusions because they add to the fluid bulk. His liver is not adequately processing and passing drugs and their accompanying fluids. His sodium level is suspect. Almost every part of him is in pain at some point during each day, yet all pain meds given have to be metabolized by his liver, which is busy itself trying to heal with the action of DEFIB, the only drug for clearing the liver.

How can he recover from all this mess? Doctors say be patient, one day, one hour at a time, not to expect rapid fluid or weight reduction. But the package of total treatment he is undergoing must work very soon, or the stress on his body will surely overwhelm the best efforts of the medical team.

Scott still believes that his pain and suffering he is experiencing will end with him going home and regaining health, so he complains little. He continues to follow all directions explicitly. The staff regards him as a model patient.

Terry called at 9 AM, sounding discouraged and frustrated. His weight is above 260, up 4 pounds from yesterday. Bilirubin count is above 3 and creatinine kidney numbers also up slightly. There are some tears in the skin of his scrotum where bandages had been removed. Last night's sleep drug did not work, so this morning he is given Ambien again after having been off it for several days. Terry is now convinced that Scott will not be home by Christmas. Today's session with Dr.'s Palmer and Margolis will be important.

If kidney dialysis is needed, according to nurse Jolie, he will go into ICU and stay there for some time, since the dialysis will be through his carotid artery to his kidneys to try to avoid infection and stress on his system.

The assessment is slightly degraded from yesterday, the loss of another crucial day when the battle should have been turning the other way. Better news tomorrow is the fervent hope. Anything but a favorable outcome is still inconceivable. Success is still fully expected. There has been no real emotional preparation for anything else.

Dr.'s Palmer and Margolis gave their report at 2 PM. A setback with his weight gain, which must start going the other direction as fast as possible without stressing the kidneys with too much LASEX, yet continuous infusions of LASEX are prescribed, oxygen, ATAVAN for sleep, and pain meds on demand. Both ATAVAN and the pain meds make him goofy/spacey.

Tomorrow, a likely feeding tube through his nose to deliver nutrients and medications and help relieve abdominal pressure. The docs think the next two or three days will be crucial in turning him around. They want his liver and kidney numbers down, with more fluid outflow. They see evidence that the DEFIB is working, otherwise his numbers would be worse, possibly requiring a ventilator.

Our boy is in big trouble, and his appearance and helplessness tears at Terry and Joan and me. We are not up to seeing him in more pain and suffering. It is now clear that the doctors don't know how this will turn out. We all need to prepare ourselves for the worst, but cannot even think of that, much less prepare for it. We leave his room reluctantly, wounded deeply by what we see. We don't want him to be alone, ever, and Terry has insisted on spending the night with him. Palmer has agreed.

DECEMBER 10, DAY 41 IN THE HOSPITAL, 15 DAYS TO CHRISTMAS.

From the first day, it was clear that VOD was life threatening, and very rare. At other major hospitals around the country specializing in bone marrow transplant, VOD is equally rare. There is no VOD dedicated specialist simply because the rarity of the disease does not warrant specialization. Nobody, therefore, can be called an expert in the diagnosis and treatment of VOD liver disease. We grilled Dr. Palmer about consulting relationships with experienced VOD doctors worldwide, only to find that no such experience is on the record, that there is no great body of literature on treatment procedures beyond those being implemented here. VOD is a fluke, striking one in one thousand. It is random bad luck without explanation, without a significant body of medical research, and without a pharmacy of drugs designed to treat and cure it. Scott is a victim of chance, the one in a thousand bet that went wrong.

Today, the forces for good are losing. All blood, kidney, and liver indicators are discouraging. The most fearful day yet. Doctors also seem baffled. Dr. Palmer talks of walking a tightrope between too much LASIX, which would anger his kidneys, and too little, which would aggrevate liver and lungs by allowing more fluid retention. The drug cocktail of ATAVAN, HYDROMORPHONE, PROGRAFT, and antibiotics being infused with LASIX, keeps Scott out of full consciousness most of the time. Still, he was sitting up in bed, partly because his bed was broken and a replacement was on its way. His weight is up slightly from yesterday in spite of fluid in, fluid out equilibrium of 2500 MG overnight.

Scott asked about Jack's basketball game last night, and was told that Jack's team won 29-27. He was told about calls and good wishes from Ken Hurley and Jim Stern, and his response was, "I love those guys." His mid-body is quad -sized, holding an extra 70 pounds of fluid which have squeezed his lung into a narrow cavity, making deep breathing impossible. Respiratory people came in with their deep breathing mask treatment to force more oxygen into the lungs. They come four times a day. He does not tolerate the treatments well, sometimes gagging.

Finally, he walks with me to the lounge, with oxygen bottle, and sat while frozen plasma was pumped into him. He is mostly coherent sitting there, with only occasional phrases making no sense. His sentences are very short and interrupted by shallow breaths. He negotiated with nurse Jolie to get him back in bed, but she said no, that he had to sit up until the bag of plasma was finished, and his new bed in place.

Walking the halls of the BMT unit, they pass the open doors of other BMT patients who seem to be recovering nicely, and who do not have the dreaded VOD. How we envy them, on their way to release to home for Christmas, while Scott's stay will be much longer.

How did he suffer this stroke of life threatening bad luck, and they did not? No one can ever know. During daytime visits with him, he stands and walks with great effort, but optimism rises.

At night, reviewing the day's meeting with doctors and nurses and their comments, gloom takes hold, and dismay forms bad dreams. Nothing can keep the demons away. Jack and Audrey come to their grandparent's house for a visit tonight, but both want to sleep in their own beds, reflecting worry and insecurity they see in the faces of their mother and their grandparents. It is clear that questions and concerns are just beneath the surface of their young but knowing minds. They have not been told yet of their Dad's turn for the worse. Terry is waiting for the right time.

32. An Ominous Turn

**DECEMBER 11, DAY 42 IN HOSPITAL, 19 SINCE
ENGRAFTMENT, 32 SINCE TRANSPLANT, 16 SINCE VOD
DIAGNOSIS, 5 DAYS REMAINING OF DEFIBROTIDE....AND
THE FIRST DAY OF A CLEARLY POOR PROGNOSIS.**

Numbers severely worse this morning, weight above 264, highest ever, everything is going the wrong way. Added LASIX has not done its job. Palmer decided to go to BUMEX, an advanced generation diuretic to fight fluid buildup. Hope is waning and panic is clearly setting in. His body is surely about to crash.

He cannot sleep, regardless of drugs. Helpless to do anything for himself. We are very, very discouraged and distraught by what we see, and want a conference with doctors and specialists to figure out a way forward. While on the scene and doing what they think is best, it is clearly not enough to prevent Scott from slipping away.

Emergency options now? Dialysis? A lung tap to remove fluids? Another stomach tap? Ventilator and a coma to allow easier breathing while DEFIB has one last chance to work at turning things around? Isn't it time for emergency measures to save his life?

Joan and I and Terry are now on the verge of breakdown every minute, fighting back tears as some degree of reality is faced. Thousands of parents have faced the death of one of their children, and wondered how they can possibly carry on. All this has happened before, but not to us, and we have never before understood the depth of despair this situation can bring. A son dying in combat in a senseless war, a daughter dying in a car crash or from a drug overdose, are sudden, cataclysmic events. But the slow eating away of life from an insidious and rare disease, with day-to-day deterioration, brings a sadness and loneliness that is suffocating and paralyzing and indescribable.

We are consumed with fear by what Dr. Palmer told us this morning. For the first time, the words death and dying were used. "Imminent danger" was also spoken. Decision will be made later today whether to remove him to the Intensive Care Unit and put him on a ventilator, as supportive care to let the liver try to heal. If on a ventilator, he will be sedated and in a coma. And once on the vent, his respiratory system may become dependent so that he can't be taken off.

We are at a critical crossroads, and Scott could die within the next day or two unless there is a miraculous turnaround. We tell him we love him every minute and pat him gently so that he knows we are there. He is agitated, wants to sit up, wants ice and water, green tea, wants to go to the bathroom even though there is nothing there to move. He is eating nothing.

Terry is engulfed in fear. She has been so full of hope, so prayerful, so believing in recovery, so in denial that this could go so terribly wrong. She simply is not ready to accept, as we are not, that this could be the end. Her emotions are so exposed and fragile that she nears collapse at times when talking about her feelings. She fears for her children mostly, seeing their reactions once they know their Dad's true condition.

She is planning to bring Jack and Audrey to see Scott this afternoon, before the ventilator decision, knowing that this may be their last best chance to see him and hug him and kiss him and tell him they love him, and for him to say important words of love to them, before he is placed in a coma from which he might not recover.

As damaging as this could possibly be to Jack and Audrey, Terry will not deny them this chance to see their father. She knows that they both will carry memories of his swollen, distended, breathing assisted condition, barely conscious of their presence, and able to talk to them only in short utterances. But that is a downside she has wisely decided to risk. Not seeing him again, for them and for all of us, would be the worst of all possibilities. Not knowing the truth, not being allowed to touch him, to cry over him, to hear his voice, would always be unbearable. The opportunity to say goodbye, however painful, must always be taken.

Joan is also near emotional collapse. Scott is her baby, to whom she gave life, who she remembers holding and rocking to sleep as an infant, in whom her own body and genes are invested, and who she expected to live out a fruitful and productive life as husband and father of two wonderful children. Now, that dream is threatened. In her life, knowing that all human lives are finite, she has never been confronted with any situation so harrowing, so emotionally damaging as witnessing her dear son lose an epic battle she thought he would win.

She sees him continuing to be the fighter, never giving up, never giving in, always willing to work harder and go the extra mile to do anything and everything the doctors and nurses ask him to do, even though he is exhausted and very weak. And the apparent futility of this effort heightens her fear and her sorrow.

Today marks six months that Joan and I have been in Milwaukee, seeing him two or three times each day, in or out of the hospital. It is now clear that whatever happens, we will remain here as long as Terry and the kids need us. Our lives are so invested in Scott and Terry and the kids that life without them is unimaginable. Have we been too invested? Have we failed to cut an essential parental knot that might have been loosened long ago? Have we been thoughtless and immature in our complete attachment to Scott and his family and their day- to day lives and hopes, successes, and dreams? Have we wanted to see and be with Scott and Terry too much? Is too much possible? Are we different from most parents? Are our lives too intertwined?

Our lives are completely bonded together, and especially so at times like these, when, beyond our experience or dreams, we are filled with love and appreciation that we have been permitted to build and hold this bond. It means everything to the continuation of our lives.

LATER THIS AFTERNOON, the saddest moment of our lives when Scott was removed from the BMT unit to the Intensive Care Unit on the sixth floor, and put on a ventilator. Before he went up, his kids and Terry's parents had the chance to visit him and talk with him and touch him. It is an image which will be with them always.

Joan and I said a tearful goodbye to him and patted his shoulder and kissed him and told him how much he is loved, and he expressed his love for us. He was wheeled away, in his bed, waving his hand as he disappeared down the hallway. We sat in his empty room, collected his personal items to take home, and both broke down and cried for half an hour before we could move, trying to comfort each other. We are lost in what to do next, and tried to think about what Scott would want us to do. This went nowhere, and we left the room unable to keep emotions in check or heads clear. We did not dare to think that this would be the last time we would see him conscious, see his eyes, hear his voice, or that he would feel our touch.

In the much larger ICU unit, he is "intubated" and completely sedated, unaware of what is being done to him, although the male nurse thinks he may be able to hear when people talk to him. Terry reported that he is resting comfortably, breathing rhythmically at 20 breaths per minute, with his heart rate down to 108 from 125-135 when he entered. The same bags of meds are still hanging and being infused, including DEFIB and LASEX. Kidney dialysis is not being considered for now because it removes fluid from the blood stream only and not from body tissues, where most of the fluid is stored.

A roller coaster, emotionally damaging day, with big decisions made, all risky. His PICC line is changed from his arm to his neck because of suspected infection. Infection from the inserted ventilator tube is a major risk in ICU. This must be watched closely, and he is being given an all-purpose antibiotic to guard against it. He is also being given PROPOFOL, to help sleep, the same drug which killed Michael Jackson in overdose.

His arms are black and blue from needles, over and above his Picc line bruising. Some sores have erupted on the surface of his legs as fluid forces its way out of his body.

ICU staff are general purpose emergency trained, with no specific expertise in leukemia or VOD complications, therefore, they follow what Dr. Palmer directs. ICU people handle any emergency that comes through the door. The need for quick and frequent patient access means no doors, only curtains, and lights are left on at all times since patients are sleeping.

This day will be with us always, no matter what the outcome of Scott's illness. We are different people tonight from the humans we were this morning. We have grieved every minute, have seen our dear son's precious life seriously threatened, have cried and held each other through a pain we never expected, have been a part of monumental, life changing decisions, have been humbled by the intricacy and fragility of the human body and a valued human life....our own son's life.

33. Three Days In December

DECEMBER 12-14:

We were traumatized with shock, loneliness, and total helplessness during these awful, heartbreaking last days. We felt paralyzed and suffocated, completely unable to process the reality in front of us. How could this be happening? How has it come to this point? This can't be happening to someone so alive and vital, to our Scott. Events unfolding are otherworldly, happening to someone else. Every minute we are caught in disbelief, our brains rejecting what we are seeing. Surely his is not about to die! It can't be!

There is a four-day remaining supply of the so-called "miracle" drug, DEFIBROTIDE, to try to save his life, and infusions are ongoing. There are nightly stomach taps to draw off five to seven liters, about 14 pounds of fluid to lessen pressure on kidneys, lungs, and heart. Yet his weight is not going down, defying the laws of physics. Tubes in his throat and nose are now doing his breathing for him.

The ICU staff is all business, with little time for visiting or answering questions because of the volume of patients.   Chris is the morning nurse, and Terry is impressed with his 12 years of experience. Greg, the PM nurse, seems a capable young man with a year and a half experience on the ICU floor.

At 6 tonight, there were more tubes in his throat, as well as in both nostrils, three ports in his neck Picc line, and the older Picc line still in his left arm. LASEX was being infused in the neck line at 10 ML per hour, as was PROPOFOL for keeping him asleep, ACETYLCYSTEINE, and an antibiotic, VANCOMYCIN. In the left arm line, a bag of nutrients was being pumped, alternating with DEFIB..   Both sets of pumps were dripping bags of sodium chloride, necessary but adding to his body fluids. Potassium is scheduled to go in at 6:45 PM.

Two doctors have said that the bowel produces liquid on its own and releases it into the tissues, adding to his net weight. Net addition to weight from this source is not logical. The added weight must be coming from liquid infusions, in the absence of food intake.

His $50 thousand dollar hospital bed is designed to rotate him once every hour, left or right, to shift his body weight and fluids. He looked peaceful and pitiful lying there, breathing mechanically. He is completely entrapped and dependent on these machines.   Even assuming a liver turnaround at this point, how can he ever unhook from all these devices and medications, rid his tissues of massive unwanted fluids, get off of the myriad of meds and antibiotics, and have his kidneys, heart, and lungs work in unison to restore normal functioning? What is best practice and medical theory at this point? We don't think anyone here knows. To the lay-person, recovery does not seem feasible.

He tolerated a bronchoscopy this afternoon to test for infection or fungal growth in his lungs. A small camera was lowered into his right lung and cultures taken. Test results will take two or three days, and the logical question is "what's the point?" Afterward, his system wanted more oxygen, and more was given at a level of 9.5. Just four days ago, he did not require any external oxygen. His own breathing supplied all he needed.

I talked to him and rubbed his head and arm and told him I loved him, hoping he could hear. I will never know.

He is in total lockdown, unable to move, to speak, to open his eyes, arms at his sides, his beautiful, graceful, capable hands quiet with his long fingers extended and thumbs against his forefingers. His stomach, hard as wood, does not give to the touch. His mouth is open, forced so by multiple tubes. His breathing is shallow, with oxygen processing efficiency very low. PROPOFOL keeps him in deep sleep, unable to fight the tubes and other invasions of his body, which would be human instinct if he were conscious.

Looking at facts, DEFIB has been a complete failure. The drug was the only therapy to possibly reverse VOD and unstop the liver, but the evidence is that it had no effect. With only two days remaining of the drug, the liver is functioning no better, and all other indicators are negative. None of us is prepared for the unimaginable, but, rationally, we know that all being done for him is not enough to save him. His condition is so far gone, his body so damaged and distended, that we must face conclusions we never expected to have to confront.

Today, December 13, is deeply troubling, and we do not have a clue how to deal with what we know. The tide of battle has turned to favor the dreaded enemy. Scott's features have sharpened and darkened in ICU. His nose is more angular, his eyelids appear bruised, his face so covered with patches and tubes that seeing him clearly is hard.

Kidney specialists have decided on a modified dialysis method involving inserting a tube through his left lower neck into his heart to begin filtering fluids from the blood. They emphasize this is not a cure, but a holding action while desperate efforts are made to get liver function. Two additional bags of red plasma are given him to prepare him for the dialysis procedure.

A new acronym, PEEP, is introduced, meaning POSITIVE AND EXPIRATORY PRESSURE. This is a measurement of pressure remaining in the lungs after exhaling. A PEEP of 3 is needed and normal to keep the lungs from collapsing after each breath is expelled. A higher number means more pressure is needed to keep lung function. Tiny sacs fill the lung linings, known as ALVEOLI, and these are the workhorses which actually capture and diffuse oxygen through the lungs to the bloodstream. Scott's PEEP number is 10, translating to a need for much more pressure to keep the lungs from collapse. This is still another in a long line of concerns.

For the first time, Terry broke down emotionally, wondering why and how this happened to her dear husband. She is very scared, unable to think ahead, not allowing herself to think forward, but dark images creep in. She has begun to talk to Jack and Audrey about the details of Scott's illness, and they get it. Audrey says, "It's like Dad has a big grocery list of things he has to do to get better." She is older than her eleven years. Jack's questions clearly reflect that he grasps the gravity of his Dad's situation. No longer expecting him home for Christmas, they both ask whether they should fill Dad's Christmas stocking, and answer their own question by immediately deciding to do it.

Terry relives every moment she and Scott have had together over the past 17 years since their beautiful St. Louis wedding. She sees the handsome, happy Scott then, never dreaming that this illness would potentially destroy their lives together. She worries every minute about the kids and their lives without their Dad, and her own life without the man she loves so dearly. She cannot accept, as none of us can, that such a life force could be struck down this way, and with him, his family's future. At this time, her hopes and dreams and theirs together are a complete shambles. Life as she has known it and expected it to be has evaporated. She cannot imagine her life without Scott.

She is shaking with fear, not eating, with barely enough energy to talk to her children or anyone. We are concerned about her health in this mind-numbed state of grief. She is also angry with the situation, with her God, and with the failure of tens of thousands of prayers for his recovery.

And she has not stopped fearing for Scott, for his pain and suffering with this disease over all these months, and the unfairness and callousness of how his life appears to be ending.

AT 3 PM TODAY, WE WERE OFFICIALLY GIVEN THE NEWS THAT SCOTT WOULD NOT LIKELY SURVIVE.

The 13th day of December will be forever imprinted on our memories. This became the darkest, most disheartening, most sorrowful day of our lives. We now understand that any parent would give his own life to save the life of his child. And how it is entirely possible that grief can be so great as to die of a broken heart. Normal processes stop. The neuro system goes into reverse, unable to comprehend. Emotions freeze, paralysis sets in, the heart races, emptiness of mind and spirit takes over, incredulity rules. This simply cannot be true.

Mother's memories flood Joan's mind, her grimace and posture reflecting all she is feeling. She holds Scott's limp hand and his face, talks to him as she did when he was two or three years old, calling him her baby, telling him that all will be alright, that the hurt will go away.

All this grand technology and science have not been able to pull off saving this man's life, starting with a relatively healthy, cancer free body and a clean slate filled with optimism on October 31, the day this dance with eternity began. Nothing has been able to stop this from becoming our day of deepest, suffocating sorrow, our greatest pain, our worst memory…the day we were told our son would die very soon. Our souls were crushed, our spirits broken.

The short winter days in Milwaukee are now ominous, more threatening, more symbolic of our misery. Our lingering hugs and goodbyes to him tonight were filled with tears and heart-stopping grief. We hope he heard us telling him of our great love.

34. December 14, SCOTT-FREE

*"To laugh often and much, to win the respect of intelligent
people and the affection of children, to leave the world a better
place, and to know even one life has breathed easier because
you have lived. This is to have succeeded."*

--Ralph Waldo Emerson

**DECEMBER 14, 2011, DAY 45 IN THE HOSPITAL, 11 DAYS TO
CHRISTMAS, 19 DAYS SINCE VOD WAS DIAGNOSED, DAY 3 ON A
VENTILATOR IN ICU, DAY 2 ON CONTINUOUS DIALYSIS, FIRST
FULL DAY OF TERMINAL PROGNOSIS, END OF LIFE IMMINENT.**

This day began like the others, with hope. A sleepless night was
filled with images of Scott as a child, as a young, adventurous boy

exploring and discovering life and his own beliefs, as a law student, as a young husband and Father, as a sportsman who loved the outdoors.

Every day of his life, remembered, now has special and precious meaning. Golf, his Porsche, spicy foods, his love affairs with Caterpillar and A.O. Smith and his litigation teams, his ambitions for himself and his family, his ideas for home design and additions, his desire for a lake house in Waupaca, his optimistic philosophy, his belief in doing, his goal to become a Catholic once out of the hospital, for the sake of Terry and his children. His every moment was filled with new ideas for his children and their futures, his special love for Terry and Jack and Audrey.

Father John from Christ King came to his room to offer last prayers for Scott. Terry had requested him to do this, and these prayers were of great importance to her.

AND NOW, SURRENDER.   Defeat.   Total, humiliating, inglorious defeat. Anger, disgust, remorse, resentment, regret that the best minds of science and their tools could not conquer a simple clogged liver and release the jam of depleted red blood cells that caused it to stop functioning. How primitive medicine is! How humbling and inadequate its efforts to perform such basic tasks.

The grand strategies have failed. The generals, the planners, the thinkers, the alchemists, now move on to the next battle, vanquished. But the fighter in the arena, the man who risked all with great bravery and daring, is dead, killed by a stealthy and unseen enemy which outflanked and outfought the teams of specialists with their high powered weapons.

And those who supported the fighter, his family, must now also die inside, their spirits diminished by his loss, never to be the same.

And so Scott Edwin Garrett died.

Months later, those words still cannot be comprehended and processed. The words "Scott died" echo daily, hourly, when we think of him. Yet the words simply cannot penetrate. They are blocked by protective barriers which will not allow entry of that kind of finality, that cruelty, that foreverness, to enter the brain. "Scott died" still cannot be what really happened that day or any day since. The words will not be admitted. The shocking, surreal phenomenon is repeated endlessly, day after day after day. "Scott died" could not have actually happened. It had to be something else.

> *His last breath came at 5:25 PM on Wednesday, December 14, 2011, in his bed in room 13 on the sixth floor of the ICU unit at Froedtert hospital.*

He was held and and loved by his Wife, his Mother, his Father, and his wife's parents. They held him close and shed tears on his face, his hands, his feet, begging him to stay close to them always. Terry would not leave his side and cradled against him, in his bed, and told him of her love for him, and that Jack and Audrey loved him so much, and that he must always be with them.

This was the last place on earth that his family wanted to be, but the one place on earth they were most privileged to be and had to be. We were with our dear son when he drew his last breath, showering him with love and kisses and tears. He was 47 years, three months, 14 days and four hours old.

An hour earlier, he had been removed from life support with family agreement, after his team of doctors met us and advised that they could do nothing more. That extending his life a few more hours would require "epic" intervention, be totally artificial, and prolong suffering. The doctors assured that he would be kept comfortable, not in pain, and would die with dignity. After anguished and tearful questions and discussion, Terry nodded her assent.

So the drugs and the oxygen were stopped. The tubes were taken away. He breathed his last hour on his own, never regaining consciousness. His freedom from medical pumps and devices restored his appearance to near normal, and his children came to see him one last time, but were traumatized in doing so. His shallow breaths became less and less frequent, farther and farther apart, and, finally, ...just stopped. His heart beat one last time, and he entered eternity....

The appointed doctor came, examined him, and made his death official.

We could not leave the room. We just sat there and cried and held each other, continuing to hold him. We had trouble imagining where he would be taken next, and did not want to let him go. But we finally had to.

The special commemorative quilts covering him were removed, folded and given to the family. His hand impressions in clay had been taken earlier, to preserve the memory of his touch, and these were given to Terry for the kids.

Nurses from the BMT unit had visited throughout the day, expressing their sorrow and love for Scott and Terry. They presumably were hardened by illness surrounding them every day, yet cried and held us as if they were part of the family. Jolie, Christina, Azure, Amber, Donna and others came multiple times and held us and said goodbye to Scott.

Scott's brother Jonathan was called, having been alerted earlier, and now he was inconsolable, unable to speak through his grief, unable to believe what had just happened. He had last seen his older brother over Labor day, had always loved him, and now felt more sorrow than he knew he could feel, more wonder that this had happened so quickly, disappointed that he had missed Scott's call a few days earlier although it was not his fault. We had not estimated the depth of emotion Scott's death would evoke in Jon. He will be always be in pain as he remembers this moment. We agreed to talk later in the evening.

We finally gathered Scott's personal belongings and pictures which had been brought from the BMT unit, and left him there in the care of nurses, leaving the building for perhaps the last time, barely able to see where our next steps would be. We drove to Scott's beautiful home and sat in front of a warm fire with Terry and the kids and Terry's parents, wrestling with the notion that he would not see this room again, nor see his kids lying in front of the fire, nor be with Terry on their favorite couch, nor hold their dog Madison, who he called "the best dog ever." His name for her was Pork Chop.

We composed the final Caring Bridge post announcing events of the day, and the end of the saga. Our hearts were searching for the right words, the correct words, to convey what Scott had meant to us, and how he was surrounded with love at the end. It was posted around 7:30 PM, and tributes and prayers immediately began pouring in from all over the country, all expressing grief.

Later, we called Jon again and tried to console and calm him, unsuccessfully. The call lasted more than an hour. He desperately needs something of Scott's to hold on to. He will drive to Milwaukee tomorrow to be with us.

Phone calls to other family members and friends followed, some of whom had read the Caring Bridge post, others who were shocked by the news. Like the family, they had assumed Scott would survive and soon be back at home with his family. There were many tears, long silences, and great disappointment, as we tried to console each other.

35. Separation

"Ever has it been that love knows not its own depth until the hour of separation."

--Kahlil Gabran

In the days that followed, we moved zombie-like through the necessary motions in making funeral arrangements and planning his memorial service. The hours since separation had indeed brought a new depth of understanding of our love for Scott. The stunning reality that he was now gone brought emptiness and anger at whatever Gods may be.

Christopher Hitchins, stricken with terminal esophageal cancer, wrote his last chapters from his hospital bed in the book, "Mortality." He talked about being deported from the land of the well across a stark frontier to the land of malady, and of abruptly becoming a "finalist in the race of life." Scott had now crossed another stark divide, from the land of malady to eternity, having sacrificed himself to the ravages of chemo-poison and the indiscriminate swath of indignity it dispenses in return for offering small amounts of hope. Hitchins points out that cancer has nothing to gain, since it dies when its host dies. Since the battle is a draw, with no winners, what is God's point, assuming some assign God's will to the outcome of the fight?

Hitchins died on December 15, 2011, one day after Scott.

Scott was cremated, as was always his intention. His ashes are with Terry and us today, to remain so unless his children later decide on another resting place.

His service is planned for Christ King church, in Wauwatosa, Wisconsin, at 10:30 AM, Tuesday, December 20.

A group of friends led by Kathy Barczak and Kate Moss took the lead in preparing and printing the programs and pictures to be displayed at the club, following Terry's wishes. They also collected photographs for a memorial book.

The five long days before the service, we clung to each other in search of comfort and relief, but the nights were mostly sleepless, filled with dread and confusion. The same questions came back over and over again. How had this happened so suddenly, without fairness, to someone so needed, at the high point of his life? Why? Because, as Hitchins observed, he was as eligible as the next father, son, husband.

The lyrics of Michael Bolton's song come back hauntingly. "How am I supposed to live without you, how am I supposed to carry on?" Everything is not gone, of course. There is still family and his children. We know in our hearts that our loss is unique, but also know that tragedy occurs in almost every family, and their losses are likewise unique. In context, we are all living out the life and death cycle. Death is the commonest visitor in every family. Our loss is not singularly different, except to us, at this time, during these nights, for the rest of our lives. Others move on, concerned with their own tragedies and mishaps. But objective context does not make a difference when it comes to personal mourning. We must continue our preoccupation… our obsession with loss. We cannot move on.

The lone bright moment of a dark and somber December 15 was the establishment of THE SCOTT GARRETT LEUKEMIA RESEARCH FUND, within the Froedtert Hospital Foundation. We began with $25 K, and it quickly grew to more than $60 thousand. Jim Stern and Roger Smith of A.O. Smith Corporation, Scott's firm, were generous with their contributions, as was the Smith foundation, and many friends and family.

Research grants will be on a merit basis, with proposals reviewed and approved by the Froedtert standard panel for signing off on research projects. Dr. Jeanne Palmer, Scott's lead doctor, will have input to this process, and monitor research progress. Realistically, these funds will be combined with others so that ambitious leukemia research projects can be undertaken on a significant, meaningful scale.

But the goodness of this day could not erase for a moment of the first day without him in our lives. The first day of the endless days during which those of us who mourn him will gradually die away. He will miss his children's graduations, their loves, their marriages, his grandchildren, never be seen by his descendants or his children's spouses. This pattern is part of the reality of living and dying, yet on this day we cannot accept it.

December 16 saw the arrival of our son Jon, our grieving with him until midnight, and the preparation of obituary notices to go out to the Milwaukee Sentinel, the St. Louis Post-Dispatch, The Greenwich Time, and the Plainview Herald.. Scott has roots and friends and relatives and mentors in all these places where his family has lived.

Friends from California, Dennis and Mary Lou Green, came. So did cousins Stan Cribbs from Lubbock and Stan's sister Susan Martinez from Albuquerque; John and Harriet Roughan from Greenwich; Howard, Christine, and Trevor Roughan from Ridgefield, Ct.; George and Nancy Soule and their children from Darien, Ct.; Scott's old friends from his law school days, Steve Ely, Jack Cline, and Greg Wessner from Washington, D.C.; Lance and Anastasia High from Caterpillar in Peoria, and their daughter; Kenneth Schwartz, attorney friend from St. Louis; Gina Cleary, from New Canaan, Scott's former law partner at Garrett/Von Oehsen.

Stacey Connett Spartz, daughter of old friends Gene and Effie Connett, arrived from upstate Connecticut, herself suffering from multiple cancers for the past few years. Stacey baby-sat Scott when we first moved to Connecticut; Ken Hurley and his family from Philadelphia, Scott's oldest friend growing up in St. Louis; Don and Petie McKinley from St. Louis; Dean and Trish Bordeaux and their family, also from St. Louis; Robert English; The Tom Penny family, former next door neighbors in Peoria. And Joan's great friend, Kathy Hetzel from North Carolina. All these, and a host of other lawyer friends from throughout the country, attended his service and participated in the comments afterward.

Of course, Terry's siblings and their families, and her parents, Jim and Joan Bowers, also came from St. Louis, Seattle, and Omaha. Good friend Jim Stern served as master of ceremonies for the celebratory luncheon, relating his own favorite times with Scott at A.O. Smith Company, as Scott's General Counsel and friend.

A Christmas box of fruit is delivered to the nurses and staff in the BMT unit, as thank you to those who helped Scott, so thoughtfully. Jolie, Katie, Jill, Christina, Azure, Don, Ashley, Liz, and Julie. In the ICU, Chris, Ann, Liz, Chad, and Chris Gonzales. Doctors in ICU were Mundey, Borgo, Jednacak, and Kay.

Fruit was delivered to both hospital units, with our thanks to all. Jon was taken to room 13, where Scott died, explained where we all were at the time, and how the end came. This may help him in his grieving.

Joan is at her lowest today, going through papers from Scott's room in BMT before the move to ICU. There were his business cards with smiley faces drawn on them, his hand written notes for the detailed schedule for all of his family to make a planned trip to Las Vegas, the Skywalk at the Grand Canyon, the Hyatt Tamaya resort near Santa Fe, the stop off in Plainview to see relatives, overnight in Springfield, Mo., to see friends, the same in St. Louis, before returning to Milwaukee. Scott saw this trip happening in the Summer of 2012. Joan was devastated reading these notes.

Kathy Barczak came over and went through my photo file to select pictures for his service and memory book, which she then made into a draft program for his service. Scott's handsome, smiling picture was on the cover. We were overcome when we saw him there, in that context, smiling beautifully at us.

And the very saddest, crippling moment in any parent's life is when he reads his own child's obituary. Scott's appeared in the December 18 Milwaukee Sentinel Journal, exactly as I had written it. Seeing his picture and the printed words underneath made it much too real, and made us weak with sudden grief. His brother, Jon, sleeping in the next room, heard us, and came and cried with us. We missed his voice, his touch, his humor, his calling friends "Jimmy" when he spoke to them on the phone, his great energy, the image of him holding and hugging his children. And this morning, Terry and Jack and Audrey were alone in their own home, with the same lost feelings.

Our breaths are short, our stamina gone, our steps halting, our brains muddled. The wound is not with the victim alone, but with all those who love him dearly. In her book, "The Year of Magical Thinking," Joan Didion cites the National Academy of Science Institutes of Medicine 1984 compilation:

Complicated grief, known as pathological bereavement, according to Harvard and Massachusetts General Hospital studies, brings frequent immediate responses including shock, numbness, disbelief, disorientation. Humans, like animals, become lost, stop eating, forget to breathe, grow faint from lowered oxygen, suffer clogged sinuses from unshed tears, experience obscure ear infections, and lose concentration. They forget their own telephone numbers, show up at airports without picture ID. They fail, fall sick, and some die.

"Research has shown, that like many other stressors, grief frequently leads to changes in the endocrine, immune, autonomic nervous, and cardiovascular systems, all influenced by brain function and neurotransmitters."[3]

Mundane financial matters and routine death certificate submissions will have to follow in January, when Terry is left with myriad details requiring official documents to settle. Right now, the task is to go on with the services, take him home, and then struggle to get through the unwelcome Christmas season, with all its expectations.

In all of this, our thoughts go to the caring "motherly strangers" as Hitchins calls them, who nursed Scott lovingly over the months, bathed him, fed him, walked him, injected him, held his head while he vomited the poison chemo, which every day produced new sores or ulcers or swelling or neuropathy, all without complaint, expecting the pain was worth the reward. Illness and death surround these nurses, mixed with some restorations to health, but keeping faith, countenance, and sanity without stressing out and breaking down must take enormous effort. They cried genuine tears for him, holding his head in his pain, seeing him slip

---

[3] Joan Didion, The year of magical thinking, Alfred A Knopf, New York, 2005, p 48, 49, 55.

away. How they keep showing up for these jobs we might never understand...

Remarkable numbers of old friends call to offer condolences, and figuratively hold hands. Dan Hagood from Lubbock; Travis Goree from his ranch in Valera, Texas; Bobby Williams of Dumas, Texas; Weldon Hayes from Childress, Texas; Jerry Jones from Dallas; good friends John and Annette Long from Odessa, Texas, all high school or college buddies. Steve Bethke, a golfing friend from Indian Wells, CA; Paul Chavin from La Quinta; Alex Korn from La Quinta, and Joan's friends Leslie Daniel and Marilyn Johnson, both of whom lost their husbands some years ago.

Terry received dozens of calls from friends and visits from caring neighbors, many bringing food. All these kindnesses will never be forgotten.

36. The Service, December 20

"God's finger touched him, and he slept."

--Alfred Lord Tennyson

"What we have once enjoyed we can never lose. All that we love deeply becomes a part of us."

--Helen Keller

After this long day, most of the mourners for Scott will return to some semblance of normal living. We will envy those intact families resuming their lives and careers, those fathers seeing their kids off to school, dressing for the office, and planning dinner around the table at home tonight. Scott can never be among them. His children can never receive his kisses and his hugs and his praise. His family is altered not just for a little while, but for every day.

Last night, a gathering at a local hotel of out of town and local friends who mingled and got acquainted with each other over food and drinks. The room was filled with people standing and talking and crying and hugging, even laughing. Friends arrived and departed throughout the evening, expressing their thoughts to family.

Earlier, Jon and his I had shopped for CD's of the Grateful Dead and The Rolling Stones to be played during the celebratory luncheon at Blue Mound. This music will say "Scott" to those who knew him well.

This day, I am struck by the irony of dressing for my own dear son's funeral. My suit is the same suit I wore for Halsey Burke's, Bruce English's, Cal's, Gene Connett's, and Elaine Glass's funerals. It is my special purpose suit. I wore it to Scott's and Terry's wedding seventeen years ago.

On this fateful day, I will stain this suit with tears, put it away, then wear it to the funeral of another loved one. Surprises abound at this age. Everybody gets a turn. In early June, I could not have imagined that I would wear this dark brown Ivy-styled suit to my son's funeral today.

I kept the suit because I thought some event would warrant dress up, perhaps a renewal of wedding vows, a christening, a bar Mitzvah. Using it as I am today was beyond the far reaches of my imagination.

And now, it is forever Scott's memorial suit. Joan's suit will also be her Scott's funeral suit. Our clothes will be our December 20, 2011 memorial adornments; the moment we said goodbye to our beloved son, but kept him in deepest hearts.

And Now, 400 people gathered in Christ King church
to remember Scott.

Father George delivered a homily from notes. It perfectly captured Scott's energy, his humor, his enthusiasms, his personality, his essence. Audrey and her cousin Melisa did readings, Jack and his cousin John lit candles. The assembly sang hymns. The student body of Christ King marched in from the school next door. An ensemble of friends provided live music. Scott favorite classical composition, Magnum Mysterium, by Wagner, was played at the close of the service. He had told Audrey that he wanted it played at his funeral.

Memory cards were written and passed to the center isle, collected for a family memory book. Dozens of pictures of Scott and his family were displayed around the perimeter of the church.

At the close of the service, the assembly adjourned to Blue Mound Club, where tables for 300 were set, buffet style. The huge ballroom was decorated with beautiful flowers, and pictures of Scott lined each side of the buffet table. During the meal, Jim Stern led a group of Scott's friends in recalling their individual memories and good times with Scott, going back to high school, college, and law school days. Eight friends spoke eloquently and from the heart, with humor and love. The luncheon truly was a celebration of his life, as Terry had requested.

The group mingled and hugged until 3 PM, gradually falling away as darkness descended on this cold winter's afternoon, with a light covering of snow on the ground. Scott would have liked this cheering section and their stories from all his "Jimmy" friends.

In the evening, dinner together with John and Harriet, Stan and Susan, Howard and Christine and Trevor, Dennis and Mary Lou, Kathy, and Joan and me. We ate Japanese style at one of Scott's favorite restaurants. We dreaded tomorrow's departures.

Tomorrow morning early, they will all leave and his family will be left with emptiness, heartaches, depressing dreams of what might have been. This will be the time of hallowing out, the realization of the permanence of grief. Today, he will have been gone seven days, twenty-two days after he was to have been back at home had things gone right. This is the probable day of his cremation, when decisions must be made about the disposition of his ashes, his urns, the signing of legal papers for the county and state.

By afternoon, they will all be gone, and we will be facing our demons alone, too focused on his end of days, too filled with tears and self-isolation, to move on.

37. Other Paths, Looking Back

IN THE DAYS AND WEEKS THAT FOLLOWED, there were the natural and inevitable second thoughts, second guesses. About what went wrong, what caused this failure, and what might have been done differently.

Every battle is fought over and over to identify what might have been the outcome if different weapons had been deployed, if a different set of generals had been in charge, if new strategies and tactics had been drawn up in the war room in advance of the first shot being fired.

In Scott's battle for survival, the first weapon was the powerful and toxic chemo drug Busulfan, deployed early and intensively for five days to beat back his immune system so his body would not reject the new bone marrow. Later, the doctors said that this drug was the probable cause for the destruction of his liver.

The damaged liver was not detected until two weeks after the bone marrow transplant, and then only by the rapid build-up of body fluids in his tissues, and rapid weight gain.   Seventeen days passed after the BMT before the liver was finally biopsied through his jugular to confirm that "VOD is indicated." At this late date, the doctors conferred and decided to deploy an experimental and non-FDA approved drug from Italy to try to get the liver functioning again. DEFIBROTIDE, described technically as "the sodium salt of a complex mixture of single stranded oligodeoxyribonucleotides derived from porcine mucosal DNA" (pig mucus), was begun twenty-one days after BMT, and, we now know, had not the slightest effect in reducing the clogging of the liver...the clearing it of depleted red blood cells trying to exit the body. The liver blocked all such attempts because of its occluded veins.

The natural issue raised is both strategic and tactical. If DEFIB had been deployed before BMT as a precaution to insure that the liver remained open, might it have then made the critical difference. The doctors call this prophylactic usage, as an upfront preventive, rather than training its guns on the enemy when most of the casualties had already been taken and the damage done, expecting it then to turn the battle around. Strategically, prophylactic use would have put the most powerful weapon to work at the outset to preclude the possibility that the enemy might establish a beachhead. Clinical trials had shown it helpful in preventing occurrence of VOD.   Instead, DEFIBROTIDE was used tactically to try to mop up after most of the real battle was over. The medical literature on the drug suggests that it might have been started days before the transplant, rather than twenty-one days after, when he had already stored thirty pounds of excess fluids in excess of fluid eliminations.

There had been no history of liver disease, and blood and other tests indicated a normal liver in a young, healthy male. Yet, in achieving remission from AML leukemia, extensive chemo had been used through June and July, and booster chemo through August and September. Additionally, there had been dozens of transfusions of blood and platelets, along with antibiotics and cocktails of other infusions including CYTOXIN, METATRAXATE, AND MYCOTRACIN and steroids, all of which had to be processed by the liver, and which, to some degree, most likely assaulted it. Intelligence gathering to know the enemy well before battle might have suggested a liver biopsy at the outset to confirm its good health, or, alternately, determine its likely weaknesses and vulnerabilities...before training new weapons toward the enemy which might misfire and damage our own. A biopsy at this point might possibly have shown a compromised liver requiring separate medical attention or even a possible liver transplant, at a time when he was in remission and in relatively good health. VOD liver blockage is very rare with few documented cases, yet it was known that VOD was a remote possibility, suggesting that all fact-finding and all preventive measures be taken at the outset rather than after the problem develops.

Once the experimental drug showed clear signs of being ineffective, should it have been continued until his death, requiring two liters more of dilute material to accompany each dose? These fluids could not pass the liver, and instead were stored in his vessels and tissues, pressuring his kidneys, lungs, and heart. Each day, without solid foods, his weight increased dangerously. Was continuation of these drugs and fluids good strategy, or should they have been slowed or stopped to allow his body to work down the excess? We will never know. We do know that his death was caused by "liver failure", with no mention of the failure of the drug therapies and what might have been different, more positive outcomes with the same or different drugs administered earlier, later, or not at all.

Patient Advocate:

So far as we know, Scott had state of the art medical care at Froedtert Hospital. "So far as we know" is the operative phrase.

In a hospital, with serious illness, under the care of a cadre of specialists who presumably know best, the patient and his family must rely on the experience and training of the assigned hospital employed doctors and staff. He and his family have no authoritative, independent advocate to represent them, capable of questioning the validity of any procedure, drug, or test, debating the pros and cons of each therapy, challenging daily decisions to infuse this, stop this, add this, double the dosage of this.

In fairness, Scott's doctors are unquestionably among the best in the country in their specialties, with long years of experience. Scott and Terry trusted them. Still the patient effectively has no real control in decisions about his care, except to protest in pain, or simply refuse treatment if he decides he wants to end his life. At the most critical moment of his/her life, he/she has the least voice, the weakest input in guiding the outcome. There is some dialogue, of course, with frustration for the layman who doesn't know which questions to ask.

Of course, this imbalance of power occurs often in daily life, so why would we expect medical care to be different. Yet according to published data, tens of thousands of hospital patients die annually as a result of simple medical mistakes. Wrong drug infusions, in wrong concentrations, resulting from human error, account for the majority. Here, an eagle-eyed advocate might help avert grievous, irreversible, deadly mistakes.

But the power vacuum persists even with a carefully planned hospital stay for treatment of a deadly disease. Rarely can a patient and his family employ their own counselor, as they might in a courtroom setting, to advocate for them and them alone in a medical setting, to translate the arcane medical terminology, to research all possible uses of the drugs or surgical techniques to be employed, to double check that all meds being given have been vetted and are in the proper amounts and in the most sterile atmosphere. There is no one to assure that the medical experts have looked at alternatives, or consulted far and wide for other opinions on the proper course of treatment. The relationship is parent to child, boss to subordinate, master to slave, general to private. The patient does mostly as he is told, committing himself to faith and trust.

In Scott's case, might an objective qualified advocate have made a difference? In choosing to do an early liver biopsy? In exploring the possibility of a liver transplant? Of applying Defib or alternative drugs well before the bone marrow transplant? In cutting short the infusions of fluids when it became clear that he was drowning in fluids which could not be eliminated?   In challenging the medical team in ICU to use alternative means to save his life rather than end life support? Of pushing for a more revealing autopsy which might have identified fault and future course corrections, rather than simply stating cause. So far as is known, the Froedtert team did everything right, and there is no implication that they made mistakes.

An advocate knowledgeable about VOD liver disease, if   one could be found,   might have taken a strong stand against going forward with a bone marrow transplant while he was clearly in remission, anticipating breakthrough advancements with genetically modified "T" cells. This technology is still   developing. Such treatments show new promise almost every week for cures without relapse as teams of scientists collaborate around the world on refining this approach.   If successful, bone marrow transplants may no longer be needed. Had he postponed or avoided bone marrow transplant, would he be alive and with us today?

We will never know! At some future time, at is believed, computers and diagnostic software might well replace some of the "judgment" of doctors, detecting immediately the effects of drugs and their appropriate dosage, sequencing patient genomes and deploying the patients own stem cells to attack and destroy mutant cancer cells. At some future time, the cure for leukemia and other cancers might well be as an outpatient receiving simple injections, much as killer pneumonia, tuberculosis, polio, influenza, all big killers of the past have now been subdued to the point that they are no longer life threatening on a large scale.

The computer might then become the true patient advocate. Until then, except for the mega-wealthy, independent patient advocates will remain out of reach, and the patient will continue to remain "trusting" of the opinions of human medicine men.

38. Honors For Scott's Memory

IN RAPID SEQUENCE, Scott and Terry's friends elected to honor his memory with five special events.

Already noted was the establishment of the SCOTT GARRETT LEUKEMIA RESEARCH FUND in the Froedtert hospital foundation. Friends and foundations from all over the country quickly built the fund to over $60 thousand dollars. It has continued to grow in the months since. It is intended for use in funding at least some part of cutting edge stem or T cell research into cures for leukemia and its complications.

Second, Scott's friends from within the Christ King Church community and the Blue Mound Golf Club, devised an annual 36 hole charity tournament, titled "The Scott Garrett Memorial Cup", to be played each Spring at Blue Mound, with proceeds benefitting Christ King School, in Scott's name. The inaugural tournament and dinner were held in early

June 2012, with great success. At the private dinner that evening, Brian Bessler, Scott's friend and MC for the dinner, presented me with a special golf ball he had found on the course that afternoon. It was imprinted with the words, "Scott Garrett". I will keep it near me forever.

Third, the students and staff of Christ King school initiated the "Pennies for Patients" week, during which students contribute money of their choosing each day for five days, and, at the end of the week, the total funds collected are matched by the parents of students. Students start on Monday of the week with nickels and dimes, on Tuesday with quarters, Wednesday with half dollars, and the last two days with dollars. Significant funds were raised the first year, all donated to the Scott Garrett Leukemia Research Fund.

Fourth, Wisconsin Junior Achievement, where Scott served as a Board Member, held "Scott Garrett BizTown day" on May 21, 2012, and issued a proclamation dedicating the day to Scott. Jack and Audrey and their classmates were present, with Aud playing the role of disc jockey and announcer, and Jack serving as the Biztown policeman. On the one-year anniversary of his death, Jim Stern and his entire legal department volunteered for the day at Junior Achievement, in Scott's honor.

Finally, the annual Christ King "Texas Hold em" poker night at Blue Mound was held December 29, 2011, and dedicated to Scott's memory. I was designated, to my great surprise, as the guest of honor for the night. Some thirty loyal friends honored Scott this way, indicating the wide swath of warm relationships he and Terry had built during less than four years in Milwaukee. Most every man in the room spoke privately to me of their enjoyable friendship with Scott.

Scott would be justly proud of these actions taken on behalf of his memory by his many good friends.

As the months have passed since his death, his family and friends have observed other special days as he might have done, including all family birthdays, his and Terry's wedding anniversary date, and his own 48th birthday on August 30, celebrated with a replica of the cake he ordered for himself on his 47th birthday. The birthday song was sung, and his life was celebrated happily with him forever in our heads and hearts.

Still, his absence from his children's birthdays, their sports competitions, their school plays, from tucking them in with hugs at night, from hugs in the morning as they go off to school, from watching them grow so quickly into fine young people, shades every day with tears just below or on the surface. Jack and Audrey must feel this too, in mostly unspoken ways, but, almost 16 months after his death, he does surface in their memories, in their conversations, in their thoughts of good times with him. They speak freely about him and his humor and the fun things they did with him as a family. He is never far away, always as close as Terry asked him to stay.

As 2011 drew to a close, all are aware that Scott will forever belong in this year, not in 2012 and the years that follow, and that he will always be 47 years of age. He will not leave a footprint in the new year,

Scott's picture displayed at his service.

his voice will not ring out nor his eyes be seen, he will not wrap his wife and children in his arms and tell them he loves them. 2012 will be a demarcation. His years of bringing joy and laughter to so many will now be left behind.

Mourning empties the mind of all normal thoughts, preoccupies and devours normal reactions, normal relationships, causes physical damage through shortened breath and more rapid heartbeat, closes off expected interactions with people and things, tortures the heart. This is our state of mind and heart as we meet at his home on New Year's eve. As he left us, we saw no angels on his shoulders, none of the thousands of prayers being answered, no God saving this kind, decent, upright, responsible Father, husband, and son who had so much remaining to give.

This afternoon, Joan and I delivered the special 10 X 14 inch rectangular box, with Scott's initials gold-leafed on the top, to the funeral director and asked him to place our son's ashes in it. Joan had made a red, soft velvet lining with drawstring. When we see it next, it will contain the remains of our son's body, his essence, his beautiful strong hands. Tomorrow, we will come back with Terry and take this beautiful, sad box to his home. Terry will cradle it lovingly on its way there, saying, "This is what it has come down to."

His genes will be his legacy. He will live on, unknown to his grandchildren as a person. But they will read about him and see his pictures in memory books, know his smile, hear his recorded voice, and recognize him in themselves. They might sculpt, paint, write a poem, compose a symphony, build a Murphy bed, assemble a trampoline, design a room addition, build a patio, or drive a Porsche, become successful attorneys, and realize that these desires and talents came from him, and be proud of their grandfather, Scott Edwin Garrett, and they will have his lovely, strong, perfectly tapered hands.

Tonight, Jack and Audrey are animated and hungry at a restaurant, showing little stress. References are made to him, but not in a sad way. Jack says he misses him, matter-of-factly, as if he were away on a business trip. Jack wears his Dad's gold chain with jade Buddha pendant. Audrey cries some. Their classmates had brought them cards and presents today, sympathizing.

"Give me a year", said Dr. Jeanne Palmer, counseling Scott and Terry on the course of treatment required for achieving remission and recovery from Bone marrow transplant. Very gradually, from home, he would be able to reconnect with his life, his work, albeit with travel restrictions, avoidance of large gatherings, limited hours, and follow up booster medications and monitoring. His legal career would have to be modified, his goal of becoming a General Counsel no longer realistic. He would play more of an advisory role in litigation cases, limited hands-on, remote location participation. International travel would be mostly out. He would always need to be in close proximity to follow up care, needing perhaps more anti-rejection drugs, more antibiotics, the occasional transfusion. He would be lower profile.

He was prepared to accept this plan, with all its trade-off, in exchange for life. For the gift of being with his wife and children, he would live a different routine, form a different philosophy, smell the roses, realize internal peace instead of striving upward. He saw the joy and appreciation he would feel in having another chance.

That was the plan.

The reality was the nightmare we all faced, with his doctors admitting defeat and asking us to do the same. It was not a shortened or altered career...It was the end of life.

Watching Jack's team play basketball tonight, Jack was absent, mourning his Father. But there was Scott, bouncing down the court at that age, long blond hair flying, scoring goals in soccer or hockey, riding his special bike, windsurfing on the Sound, being cradled as an infant. Images of him were everywhere, in every movement of the boys on the court.

39. The Long Trip West

JOAN AND I LEFT MILWAUKEE ON JANUARY 14 with heavy hearts, starting the long trek back to our home in the California desert. The trip was mostly silent, as we reflected on the many dark months in our recent lives, our terrible losses, and our sadness and regret at leaving behind our loves Jack, Audrey, and Terry. Now, they must continue alone in trying to rebuild their day-to-day lives even as their grief persists and invades most of their waking hours. Jon was already in Las Vegas, four hours from California, so we knew we would see him from time to time. But we would not see our Milwaukee family until Spring break, in April, a very long interval under the circumstances.

We felt the greatest need to be near them, to hold them, to cry with them, to help them through this most difficult time in their lives. Yet circumstances of the moment meant that we must tear ourselves away and go back home, and make a start at righting our upside down emotions, at pulling ourselves back together. Alone, in our car for many hours each day, driving greater and greater distances away from them, the closer our psyches clung to them and to the memories of Scott. Our last conversations with him, his golf shoes, his caps, the jackets he gave me, words he spoke, his laughter....all now quiet....made mute by our isolation inside this machine. We had left a part of ourselves behind, permanently, never to be recovered.

Before leaving Milwaukee, we made contact with the owner of a home just two houses away from them which was for sale by owner, but not on the market until April. Joan left him a note inside the front storm door saying we might be interested. Our thinking had been initiated by Scott and Terry, who wanted us to have a summer home near them. In fact, Scott had identified this very house, at 9706 Ridge Boulevard, as one we should own. We had rented apartments in Milwaukee for the past four summers, and Scott felt it was time for us to invest in a place of our own. The house was one level Lannon stone construction, three bedrooms, with two-car garage and good corner property, more than enough space for us and guests. We decided to give serious thought to making a bid for the house, consistent with our needs and Terry's needs to have family nearby for mutual support, at least for the next few years until the kids go to college.

Our travels west took us to Texas and visits with my siblings there, brother Raby, sister Dora, and sister Shirley, and many nieces and nephews and their families, all coming to offer support. We went by Lubbock to see old college roommate Dan Hagood and wife Nancy, he with advanced Parkinson's Disease. Then on to Odessa, Texas and lunch with our oldest dear friends, John and Annette Long, he also with advanced Parkinson's, in very tough shape. From Odessa, the long drive up through El Paso and on to Tucson, where, exhausted, we spent the night. It was here that Joan literally fell apart in grief, repeating over and over the words, "Scott died", bringing disbelief each time she said it. We endured restless sleep.

The next day, we drove on to nearby Phoenix and stopped for a three days rest, much needed. On the fourth day in Phoenix, we visited friends Dick and Joanne West, former neighbors in California, now living in Arizona. Dick and Joanne lost their oldest son Mike to a sudden heart attack early in 2011, and we shared stories of grief and happiness remembered with both our sons. Finally, on January 24, we arrived at our home in La Quinta, California, unpacked, and settled in for our long, forlorn winter, seeing the landscape and our surroundings as we had never seen them before, with perspective formed by all that had happened since we left there last May 9.

Back home, we called friends Mike and Eleanor Miller at their home in Rancho La Quinta, two miles from us, and resumed our weekly dinners together. Gradually, we learned that Eleanor's cancers had worsened, and that doctors were pessimistic that conventional therapies could do more to save her from the ravages of her five-year battle.

Slowly, her condition deteriorated, and, in mid April, Mike chartered a private jet to take them back to St. Louis, where Eleanor was to pass away within about two weeks, on April 27. We had developed a tight bond of friendship with Eleanor and Mike, loving her humor and grace, and losing her after losing Scott was another deep blow.

As the joyless weeks dragged by, we tried to cheer ourselves. Each phone talk or shared email with Terry and the kids was a treasure. We spent time with friends Dennis and Mary Lou Green, who did their best to keep our spirits high. I golfed a little with Paul Chavin, had lunches with Alex Korn and Dennis, but found myself mostly without energy. I forced myself to keep up an exercise routine at the gym, now physically more exhausting, due no doubt to my mental state.

We tried movies and new restaurants, and new books, but spontaneity had gone. We could see little forward purpose, more acutely mindful of our own mortality and the frailty of all humans. As noted by Hitchins, paraphrased here, "We are going in slow motion to the same end as those who die suddenly, out of the natural order."

Terry and the kids came from Milwaukee for Spring break, and we repeated much of the routine we had been following each year during their visit. But this time Scott's absence was the conspicuous void as we went horseback riding, swam, and ate special dinners. Mostly, the week was without heavy tears, including the Easter egg hunt and Easter dinner, but everyone's thoughts were clearly on the past with him present during these activities, the joy of which was never to be taken for granted again.

The owner of the Milwaukee house, Jim Melton, called us and said he was now ready to sell, and since we were the first to inquire, we would have the right of first refusal.   I hired an appraiser and a home inspector before making our bid, and we negotiated very little before agreeing to buy the house, with a closing date of May 11, 2012, just days past the one year anniversary of Scott's leukemia diagnosis. We buttoned up the house in California and left on May 4 for the trip East, this time taking the Northern route through Kingman and Flagstaff, stopping in Kingman for an overnight for a visit with son Jon, who drove down from Las Vegas to meet us. Then on to Texas for two nights visiting relatives, then east to St. Louis, and finally, to Milwaukee on May 9, where we greeted our loved ones we had been missing so much.

Two days later, we closed on the house and moved in, with little more than a bed and a couple of chairs. The floors were refinished and stained before the closing, and the interiors painted to Joan's taste, Furniture had been ordered through our friend Harriet, and would arrive soon. Other furniture was ordered and delivered locally within a couple of weeks, as were rugs, end tables, basic supplies, linens, kitchen utensils, silverware, a kitchen table from Penny's outlet store, odds and ends from neighborhood garage sales, hand me downs from Terry's attic and basement. Joan refinished and antiqued our 47 year-old oak dining table, long in use by Scott and Terry and now stored in their basement.   It became the attractive centerpiece of our new dining room, flanked by six beautiful dining chairs from Restoration Hardware. Lamps and coffee tables from Crate and Barrel filled out the living room.

Old landscaping was torn out and replaced, and a new sprinkler system installed. Exterior painting spruced up the trim, but the Lannon stone was as beautiful as the day the house was built in 1951.

We relish living just two houses away from Jack and Audrey and Terry, and wish son Jon were closer to us. We see our grandchildren almost every day, and hopefully act as stand-ins for their Father at their school sports, plays, concerts. We are thrilled when they have a meal with us or spend the night, or we go to movies together. We want to spoil them in every way possible. I golf some with Jack. Joan takes Audrey to lunch. We honor their special days with dinners or breakfasts out, and make sure they get attention as much as possible from us. Their mother is the best, a smart and effective psychologist to them...their primary counselor. We, the grandparents, also want them to grow up feeling warmth and love and some guidance, never alone with their grief, which surely is just there, beneath the surface.

This is our new mission in life, taking precedence over all other purposes. They need us and we need them equally, seeing them grow in the image of their father, our dear son. Now 77 and 79 years old, Joan and I will hope to see them and wrap them in love at least to their college years and beyond, and become one of their fondest memories when all is done.

40. Up to Now

In the months since his death, our lives and hearts have not mended. We are still disbelieving, stunned, as disabled as we were on December 14 of last year.

We have tried isolating our downcast hours to certain times of day, blocking grief from as much time as we can to allow some normal thinking and functioning, out of sheer need to accomplish the necessary. We have not yet succeeded very well, but must keep trying. Scott remains in our every thought.

Perhaps the most damage is his younger brother, who has not come to terms with Scott's death. His grief is expressed as anger. They were three years apart in age and sometimes at odds, but got back together during his long illness. Jon's outlook and purpose have dimmed, he sees no satisfaction in ordinary work, and resents the hand that fate has dealt. He has given up his job, declaring it demeaning and pointless. He says he wants isolation, freedom from social and employment interaction. Deeply pessimistic, he wants solitude and seclusion. His future is uncertain.

There are moments of clarity when we know to be grateful for the time we had with Scott and the gifts he gave us. We know he would want us to heal and become whole again, with lots of laughter. But crushed spirits revive slowly. Our horizons are limited. We no longer dream grandly or plan for the distant future.

The house in Milwaukee is a challenge and offers a degree of fulfillment. It gives us purpose with our grandchildren. It gives us at least a five-year goal to help them reach the magic plateau when they no longer need us emotionally as much as they do today. Our satisfaction now must be in seeing them grow, assuring ourselves that this is what Scott would have wanted.

We indulge ourselves because we have no choice at this point in time. Later, we will adapt and learn to coexist with our grief, and, in the adage for sailors in a storm, "Press on Regardless."

HIS PHILOSOPHY:

At his service, prayer cards were given to each mourner,
quoting Scott in his own words.
"Don't be a victim...you always have a choice."
"Boredom comes from within"
"Can't never did anything."
"Nothing happens until you go outside." (Put plans into action)

There was also his adopted Optimist's Creed, written over a hundred years ago by Christian D. Larson. It is as relevant today as when it was composed in 1912.

Promise yourself...
To be so strong that nothing can disturb your peace of mind.
To talk health, happiness, and prosperity to every person you meet.
To make all your friends feel there is something in them.
To look at the sunny side of everything and make your optimism come true.
To think only the best, to work only for the best, and to expect only the best.
To be just as enthusiastic about the success of others as you are about your own.
To forget the mistakes of the past and press on to greater achievements in the future.
To wear a cheerful countenance at all times and give every living creature you meet a smile.
To give so much time to the improvement of yourself that you have no time to criticize others.
To be too large for worry, too noble for anger, too strong for fear, and too happy to permit the presence of trouble.

Scott lived by these words, and fervently hoped his family would adopt them as their rules to live by. Accordingly, our greatest challenge is now to lift our heads and seek every shred of happiness we can find. We must force optimism until it becomes habit, searching for the good, viewing and embracing good deeds as gifts from Scott and his memory.

Every shard of light must be sought out, the song of every bird heard, the bloom of every flower caressed with our eyes, as every bad memory slowly fades out, replaced by Scott's view of life. We must strive never to be victims, always keep options open, and take responsibility for straightening our own spines, and standing and walking erect,....seeing through his eyes. We must focus on the joys he was able to realize in his life....a strong marriage, fatherhood, achievement of career goals, respect of his fellow man, his strong friendships, his fulfilled responsibility to his community.

41. Dissecting Grief

We have learned that random tragedy strikes every family sooner or later, and each family thinks of their particular burden as unique. Rationally, in context, it is not. In Wisconsin in December 2011, there were over 4500 "unique" deaths, more than 60000 for the full year. California and Florida each had more than 20000 deaths last December, and New York and Texas were close behind. Obviously, death and suffering are endemic, and, to those not directly involved, a routine or less than routine closing of the life cycle. There are no exemptions, no cheating providence or fate through wishful thinking or the power of prayer.

In line with how we think our lost loved one would want us to live out our own lives, there may be hopeful ways to think about the many ways we have been affected, and about the future. Each family's reactions to crisis and loss will differ, and professional counselors may tailor specific ways to deal with devastating illness and death. But after almost two years of our lives spent dealing with Scott's illness and death, a road map exists which may be helpful to others in going through grief's many phases.

When it happens, shock takes over along with a blanket of gloom, during which every thought is consumed with what has happened. Nothing in life seems worthwhile. A part of life has simply died, and the feeling is so dark that survivors think a full life can never be restored. The gloom stretches across the past, the present, and the future, making all our strivings seem worthless, and our lives of little consequence.

We realize that modern medicine has not eliminated suffering and pain while the patient is still fighting illness. Only in the final hours can this pain be stopped through morphine and other drugs. The anguish and stress of watching this decline can be dangerous to the health of survivors.

There will be guilt and anger. Guilt that we continue living while our dearest loved one cannot. Guilt that we might not have been strong enough advocates , not protective or demanding enough on his behalf. Shift changes, doctor rotations, wrong computer entries, can and do lead to wrong drugs and surgical errors. Suspicion creeps in that any number of mistakes might have contributed to the needless death of the loved one. Anger builds at the randomness of fate allowing many less worthy to continue their lives, with families, careers, and dreams.

Anger that God or a higher power has singled out this good person and allowed this awful thing to happen. Concern and anxiety about his/ her family who survive, and especially the children and their futures. Regret that thoughtless or careless words spoken in the distant past cannot be retracted. Resentment that this death is out of normal sequence…that the parent cannot take the place of the child. There will be resentment that the loved one's life and memory are slowly fading to oblivion, while we live on. We don't want memories to dim.

There will be distress at our own mortality and fragility and vulnerability after watching the decline of the loved one. We will obsess with our own health. There will be blame that we, the survivors, might have been the cause, through faulty genes or perhaps careless lifestyles.

There will be the reality that survivors are not capable of moving on, of righting themselves, while others, less close, have done exactly that. Their lives have resumed with their own set of cares and responsibilities. They no longer want to talk about our trauma, and, in fact, avoid discussing it for fear it will upset and dampen the mood. There will be some references to it, but with the intent and tone of avoiding sadness or tears.

There will be moments of delusion when the mind imagines ways to reverse what has happened….to correct the obvious mistake which has been made. Saving his clothes, his shoes, being unable to sit in his chair or use phrases he commonly used, or drive his car, are emotions which barge in…a sort of unconscious admission that these items must be protected, for what purpose? They are tangible evidence that he existed, and we don't want to violate or damage any thread of the life he had. Are we thinking that he might need them again? The grieving mind invents novel solutions for curing the now incurable, and keeping him close through objects he possessed.

The family may want to talk with a professional, who are really paid listeners when no one else wants to anymore. Continuing to talk about the death with trusted friends or paid advisors, is essential to working through the event, and finding new footing over time. *Trapped grief, we see objectively, is corrosive and damaging.*

Distraction from grief in some activity, project, or trip, can be a temporary escape, bringing the knowledge that outside their family inner circle, life moves on for friends and business associates. They can't share your depth of grief. Forced activity of this kind can bring a new perspective on mourning. New associations, new acquaintances, new hobbies, new work, and volunteering may help in moving beyond narrow daily concerns.

There is great power in a strong support community such as church or club or affinity group, friends of the deceased and his family, who rally round with great kindness during the illness and perform vital support with prepared meals, childcare, household functioning, transportation, and aid in making arrangements. They also provide love. Being willing to accept these gracious acts from friends is very important, recognizing that their closure happens much sooner.

There will be dreams that the loved is still present and recovered from the illness through some miracle. There will be the sudden illusion during wakefulness that the person can still be talked to about something, and the dialogue is vivid, or that a song or event may be shared with them, immediately followed by the reality that, no, this day dream is just a wish.

Archived memories and images will suddenly spring into the conscious mind, triggered by an automatic response to scenes being viewed in real time. Seeing a young family together, a young son holding his father's hand, a young blonde boy walking with his mother, a young father coaching his son's or daughter's sports team, a family together in church, are examples of images which are instantly matched by similar scenes stored in the brain placing the lost loved one in exactly those situations.

Young survivors have a much longer scope of life ahead of them in which to recover and pursue their own dreams of family and career. Older survivors will have much less to look forward to, and will likely be diminished for the remainder of their lives. A vital part of them has been torn away, and there is not enough time to rebuild. In this connection, faith helps many find comfort in thinking of the deceased as being in a more desirable place and state. If faith confers this benefit and sense of comfort to some, so much the better.

Many families will not want conventional funerals or memorials. There are no rules. Most end-of-life services conform to community or religious practice, but in the end are just rituals. Each family should choose its own course.

Writing or blogging about the illness can be therapy. It allows thoughtful exploration of what has happened, how it happened, emotional and physical reactions to each phase of treatment, and an analysis of what might be done differently. It is intellectualizing the event, tearing it apart, as a route to understanding.

Finally, compartmentalize mourning to the degree possible, increasingly so as time goes on. Try to force optimism all the major hours of each day, limiting grief consciously to specific times. We have hope that this may become easier with time, remembering that this is very likely what the loved one would want. They are not forgotten, just focused on at specific times.

We cannot say that these bromides have worked yet to lessen our own grief, but a path has been identified to lead to better, less mournful days.

42. Two Octobers

The leaves of this October 2011 were brilliantly colored.

That was the month when he was flying high, believing, certain that he would be well again. He was home and in remission, with only maintenance appointments at the hospital. He was free of his Picc lines, therefore free to golf, eat out, drive his children to school, visit his office occasionally, and talk details of legal cases with his staff. He and his family were free to drive to St. Louis to see friends and Terry's family there.

He played at least six rounds of golf at Blue Mound club, two with me, and at least one with Jack. His scores, mostly in the 70's, gave no hint that he had been hospitalized all of June and parts of July and August with a life threatening illness.

He drove his Porsche daily, and he and Terry and the kids took a day trip to Lake Waupaca. He relished food, both at his club, and at Eddie

Martini's restaurant, and at the Harbor House on Lake Michigan. He and Terry drove to Madison, Wisconsin for a consultation on the Bone Marrow transplant procedure, and he came back more convinced than ever it was the right thing to do.

October 2011 was a treasured month when everything seemed to be going just right. There were family gatherings, laughter and good humor to share. He and I finished the Murphy bed project and declared it perfect. He talked about the many other home projects he wanted to pursue, and began to make plans to do them. He planned aloud his 50th birthday party at Pebble Beach, and family trips in between, as well as weekend trips he would take with Terry alone. He talked about Jack's and Audrey's futures.

And he began to see a path back to his legal career, perhaps different but still satisfying. His company and his General Counsel, Jim Stern, were solid in their support, assuring him that he would come back stronger than ever. He would make Vice-President after all. He could now see the light at the end of the tunnel. He would see his children graduate college and marry and begin careers and families of their own. He could see a fulfilled life, and see it with new-found perspective.

OCTOBER 2012 saw only dull grey leaves.

There would be no legal career, no competition for the club championship, no parading in his Porsche, no watching his children grow and marry. He would not see his grandchildren, nor complete his many home projects. He would not play Pebble on his 50th. He would not hug his wife or talk to his parents or friends again.

October 2012, ten months after his death, saw no plans made for the future. Optimism faded. Horizons were much shorter, dreams scarce or nightmarish. His children played many of the same games as last October, but they seemed less important now. His son had become a teenager in August and had largely lost interest in golf, partly due to teenage distractions, but his enthusiasm likely damaged by the absence of his Dad and their playing time together. His daughter, 12 years old, continued her acting, singing and dancing, but no doubt missing their traditional Father/Daughter dinner dance. And Terry went back to four days weekly at Junior Achievement of Wisconsin, more of the need for distraction than compensation.

His Porsche sat silently in the garage, started only once each week to keep the battery charged, and a constant reminder to his family of an expression of his personality. October 2012 seemed harsh and biting in its early cold. The leaves fell earlier. Last October's beauty had faded, and would not be back.

On Sunday, October 14, the family walked in a slow drizzle for the cause of ALS disease, which Terry's uncle, Dr. Mark Lochner, suffers. His large family gathered the night before at Scott's and Terry's house to visit and prepare for the Sunday morning walk. There, many of them remembered Scott, spending time with him, golfing with him, and missing him. He had been embraced by the very large Lochner clan, who recalled his energy and his sportsmanship during their gatherings at the family compound on Lake Waupaca, Wisconsin. Their comments were very gratifying to us.

On the 16th Joan and I attended an appreciation dinner at Froedtert hospital, held for those friends and families of Froedtert patients who have established funds or endowments in honor of loved ones who have been treated at Froedtert for cancer and other illnesses. The SCOTT GARRETT LEUKEMIA RESEARCH FUND is one such fund. Arriving at the dinner, Joan and I were surprised to be met by Dr. Jeanne Palmer, Scott's lead doctor in the BMT unit, who came to honor Scott and pay her respects. The sight of Dr. Palmer after 10 months revived all the images of Scott's long hospitalization, and we were overcome.

After the dinner, Joan and I located the bronze engraved plaque "In memory of Scott E. Garrett" posted atop the memoriam wall in the Froedtert hospital main lobby. The plaque was a reminder that this memory is what was left behind of our son… this and his ashes were what his life finally came down to. The moment was emotionally draining.

Simply entering Froedtert again was like visiting the scene of a horrendous crime, the death scene where a loved one had been lost. Thoughts of his months of painful suffering within these walls could not be avoided, and brought renewed sadness. Terry skipped the night. She was not yet ready to set foot in Froedtert, where her most painful memories are housed. Her hurt is still too great. She thinks the coming Christmas season will be even more difficult than last year because last December and for months afterward, she was in shock, moving robot-like through the season.

43. November 2012

November 1 marks the one-year anniversary of the infusion of drugs to "condition" Scott's body to receive new bone marrow. Intensive Busulfan chemo began today and continued for five days, a standard protocol. It was this dosage of toxic chemo that destroyed his liver, and, within 45 days, caused his death. This realization came some three weeks later, two weeks after infusion of his new bone marrow, when his weight suddenly ballooned 30 pounds, a consequence of the liver's inability to process fluids from his body. Looking back, the battle had been lost in the first five days of November, when the fateful drug was administered.

Was this preventable? Perhaps, but we will never know. Could more experience treating VOD liver disease have given doctors the tools to deal with this rare complication successfully? The rarity of VOD liver disease at Froedtert meant that doctors there had very little experience in dealing with it. Would doctors at M.D. Anderson, or Johns Hopkins or

Massachusetts General have taken different, life saving steps. We can never know.

The market for potential drugs targeting VOD is so small that drug makers are unwilling to invest the estimated $ One Billion needed to take experimental drug candidates through the three phases of human clinical trials necessary to get FDA approval. Doctors resort to trying unapproved experimental drugs intended for other diseases, since they have no other options. They simply don't have the tools at hand which might have delivered a different outcome. Defib turned out to be a useless and pointless end game...an impotent weapon against an overwhelming opposing force.

In a real sense, Scott's death was the result of an enigmatic malady, about which little is known. He was the victim of circumstances, with doctors grappling with inadequate tools in a life and death situation. He lost!!

We will forever mourn what happened the first week in November, 2011. And a full sixteen months later, the events are every bit as fresh and surreal and unbelievable as they were then. The stark reality of the ending of these days still cannot be processed. Disbelief still trumps actuality. We hear his voice and impulsively think of calling him to discuss some current event. We dream of talking with him. We see him daily in his children. He is missing in settings where he would normally be present, but we still see his image there. There is no healing yet. We built memories of him over 17,259 days, every day of his life. The 480 days since December 14 of 2011 cannot begin to erode any of those treasured memories.... memories held in the data bank of our minds, instantly producing images of his vital, exciting, energy-filled existence.

44. December 2012
One Year and Counting

Jim Stern wrote me at Thanksgiving to point out that, one year ago on this day, Scott was diagnosed with fatal VOD liver disease. He called again, during the first week of December, just after his legal department's office party observing the holidays. Jim rose to express his thanks to his staff, then began to acknowledge the important contributions Scott had made to the A.O. Smith financials during 2012, the impetus for which began in early 2011.

He choked up unexpectedly, and could not continue, and sat down. Jim and Scott had a "brotherly" relationship of mutual respect and admiration. Jim's older brother, Bill, had died a few years earlier of cancer. Scott became for Jim a sort of stand-in for his lost brother, and now, losing Scott was more than Jim could speak about. We talked for an hour and cried together.

December 13, 2011 was the last full day of Scott's life. On that day, he was in ICU, in a coma, unconscious from morphine and propofol, intubated, helpless, unaware that the next day, his team of doctors would meet with and persuade his family that his case was now hopeless, and that he should be allowed to die.

And he did die, words we still cannot say or process without physical weakness, and deep heartbreak. He did not see 2012.....did not see his son stand in his place and become Godfather to a new cousin. He did not see his son become thirteen and cross over into young manhood. He did not see his daughter, twelve, sing solos in church or perform in THE MUSIC MAN, or dress in her Halloween costume or score at the top of her class in school.

He did not see Terry's loneliness, struggling to find the right path with two children in need of fatherly guidance, or deal through tears with managing the mountains of forms and legal papers, and family financial decisions.

And he did not experience the joy Joan and I felt in buying a house two houses away from his own, to be near and lend support to Terry and Jack and Audrey through their darkest, loneliest, neediest years.

He never knew 2012, and now, 2013, begins his second year in eternity. No footprints, no laughter, no hugs, no fatherly guidance, no companionship.

But our love for him remains as real and as vivid as if he were standing next to us. This will remain, always.

ON DECEMBER 14, we attempted to console each other by telling ourselves that Scott would want us on a more positive path after a full year of terrible grief. His words have meaning, "Don't be a victim, you always have a choice". He believed in looking forward, not back, in seeing the possible in every situation, not the barriers. He would want us to focus on the gifts he gave us, especially his humor and optimism, which could light a brighter outlook and spirit to build on. After a full cycle of living without his life force, he is still with us every day, not in form, but he is surely beside us and within us, our fail safe when we are falling back, our encouragement to keep moving and smiling and doing and achieving. We do not have to wait or guess whether we will see him again. He is with us now, urging us onward, telling us and his children never to give up or give in. He knows of our love.

Jim Stern and his legal team at A.O. Smith, volunteered to work at Junior Achievement this day, dedicating the day to the memory of Scott, who served on the Junior Achievement Board. It was a thoughtful, touching, fitting one-year memorial, the only such ceremony held. His family held memorials in our hearts.

Terry is reclusive on this day and most of this month. She cannot talk with anyone without tears. Joan and I chose to go to a party with friends as a deliberate distraction, but neither of us could complete the day without giving in to our emotions. We did not announce the day to our friends, or the time, which was 3:25 PM Pacific Time, but they somehow knew and tried to cheer us up. I tried briefly to talk to someone about Scott, but could not complete a sentence, and threw up my hands and quit trying.

Friends wrote us emails of condolence, I had lunch with Alex who wondered if my acceptance might have been easier in any way if Scott had died suddenly in an accident, with no prolonged suffering. I could not answer. I had no clue.

My sister Sharon called from Texas, aware of the day, and she was in tears both over Scott and for the young children who had been shot by a mad man at the Newtown, Connecticut, elementary school.

Howard Roughan wrote thoughtfully. He was a true, good friend of Scott's. Joan's friends wrote and called her with similar messages. We will never forget friends like these who record with us our moments of greatest loss.

Verne and lee Westerberg called from Florida for long talks. They comfort us as old friends, aware exactly of what is going on in our heads.

Jack and Audrey carry on with school and their sports and music schedules, aware of the date and its impact on their mother, who they cuddle close to at night and try to make comfortable. They talk openly of DAD, almost in present tense. They are not afraid of eliciting sadness. He was theirs, and he is still theirs.

This same time next year, we will mourn again the same way, reviving all the images we treasure but would like to soften, but never want to forget. What if we had not been there? That would have been a cause for lasting regret.

While we work at building a new, brighter path based on our 47 fortunate years with him, his is staying close to us, just as Terry pleaded over and over for him to be. We feel him everyday, as he talks to us.... strengthens us....encourages us.

45. The Legacy Of Character

In his entire time on earth, Scott was equipped with all the armamentaria to forge a successful life. He possessed a decent mind, well educated. His body was coordinated, strong, and healthy. He had a strong desire to use both to succeed….a willingness to work hard to achieve. His career path and goals were clearly defined, and his path until his illness indicated complete accomplishment.   He had married well to an intelligent, beautiful woman who supported his dreams and was his best helpmate in the broadest, most complimentary sense of the word. He had all the necessary assets.   Their two children, Jack and Audrey, were healthy, smart, energetic, and on a growth trajectory.   Scott and Terry could see them similarly equipped with the tools needed for a good life, of reasonable means.

With it all, he, like every human, was imperfect in some aspects of his complex personality.   He could be impetuous and opinionated, obsessed, convincingly arguing his strongly held views. He was ambitious and strategically and tactically capable in his planning to further his career and his family's financial future. He could be pedantic, verbose, at times distracted by technology, yet taciturn and reflective at other times.

Balancing these traits, he was consistently resolute, loyal, analytical and skillful in strategizing legal cases, sincere, memorable and magnetic in drawing people toward him and into lasting friendships. He was adaptable and driven, rising to challenges, bent on finding solutions. As a father and husband, he was loving, thoughtful, a gentle disciplinarian, a forger ahead, decisive in personal and work matters.

He was a talented athlete, good at tennis and often excellent at golf, his favorite. Many of his friendships were made through tennis and golf. He had natural musical ability and some familiarity with the piano and guitar. He was a determined ethicist, moral in his approach to life and business, fair in his dealings. He was principled and quite outspoken when dealing with what he perceived to be borderline or questionable behavior.

He was given to some excesses, especially in his formative, growing up years, when, like virtually everyone in the midst of physical and emotional growth, he experimented with youthful adventure. He was a product of the massive cultural transition underway as he and his peers cut their teeth on maturity and manhood. He grew up with hard rock and its accoutrements. He swam with the youth of his youth, and carried over some remnants of that culture into his adult life.

He was tenacious above all, never admitting defeat, never giving it never giving up. He tried to teach his children this trait above all others... never be defeated by quitting. Paraphrasing a verse posted in his kitchen:

"It may not be possible to win and be heroic every day. But it is possible to say, I will try again tomorrow".

One of his favorite inspirational passages was an excerpt from a Theodore Roosevelt's speech delivered in Paris in 1910, known as "The Man in the Arena", recited early by his friend and partner Gina Von Oehsen. When he and Gina opened their law office in Stamford, I delivered to him a framed copy, which hung prominently near his desk. The passage mirrored his philosophy of doing. of striving, of being proactive rather than criticizing those who do the heavy lifting in life.

Finally, he had a star quality about him, a Ryan Gosling/Bradley Cooper leading man appeal. People noticed him. He attracted watchers. People engaged him. Friends almost always were seen talking and laughing with him. He found some common thread...some shared experience to bond him with almost anyone. His entourage of friends and admirers was large, as a consequence. Friends listened to him, and shared with him.

These were some of the elements of his character. There were other "toppings" to his character and personality which combined to constitute his legacy. He had a lightness of spirit and heart, an effervescent youthful humor always at the ready. He had a charitable side, excited about pro-bono legal opportunities, while serving on the board of directors of Wisconsin Jr. Achievement. He had willingness, devotion to duty, commitment to youth and community.

He leaned toward doing rather than talking about doing. He had unwavering love for his family, concerned always with their future.

His sartorial tastes were uniquely his, insisting on specific brands of shoes, shirts, and ties. He had the shape of a male model and wore clothes gracefully. He looked good in whatever he chose to put on.

He used his culinary skills almost daily in shopping and preparing foods for his family. He competed in cooking ribs on his smoker. He was a perfectionist in many areas of his life, food and golf among them. His golf swing was almost picture perfect, and his putting stroke a model to emulate. Whether golfing, cooking, building a Murphy bed, planning a home addition or new driveway, or analyzing a legal case, details were never overlooked. Scott was a team player, sharing credit readily.

He had ambition to make his mark, to leave his imprint on whatever he undertook. He was insightful, intuitive, and inventive.

Together, they were sturdy, dependable, reliable, and sought after characteristics. They made his strong personality, his zest for life, his leaning forward day to day, seeking and expecting the best of himself and others. This jumble of great and weak, good and less good, high achievement, sometimes falling short while daring greatly, trying again tomorrow, made up our Scott. We grieve for every aspect of his character and life, taken from us by the most mystical of all human maladies.

46. Christmas Day 2012

Terry and Jack and Audrey made a SKYPE call to us this morning to show us their many presents. The kids paraded their new outfits across our I Pad screen. Madison, their puppy, was also in the picture with her new toys. The mood was happy, as we hoped it would be. Terry talked about their Christmas Eve schedule with friends, getting home at 1 AM, then up at 7AM to see what Santa brought. The kids are long past believing in Santa, but play along for the most part. They were especially pleased that "Santa" had brought them the new mini iPad. The house looked festive, with flowers and decorated trees everywhere.

Unspoken but deeply felt during the call was the missing image who would have made the scene complete. We were keenly aware that DAD, SCOTT, was not part of the happy call. He had missed his second Christmas. His stocking was hung, and no doubt filled, but sadness pervaded that he could not share his children's joy, laugh at their silly toys, watch their parade of new clothes and shoes, share in the fun of a new/old phonograph player of 50's vintage, play their new video games with them, or admire Terry's new pink robe given her by Jack, or her new necklace from Audry. She says her kids are "the best", and it is true.

DAD is never far from their thoughts, or ours, and this particular day, with all its gifts and happiness, cannot mask the terrible loneliness and sadness of events of one year ago. Christmas will forever follow closely the anniversary date of his departure from this earth, and, therefore, Christmas will always have this association. For us, it was always a secular holiday, but now it is a time for remembering and grieving anew.

2011 now seems so far away, so distant.. As the years move on, our thoughts and memories of him will bring him forward with us. He will never be away from our hearts and minds.

NEW YEAR'S EVE: 2012

Thus ends the first full year in which he did not leave his imprint. No voice, no footprint, no smile, no touch. Just an imaginary hologram where he should have been. Terry and Jack and Audrey are at the Stern's lake house tonight, attempting to be cheerful with their family, but not really. There is too much for them to remember and think about.

We are at home in California.. Our son Jon left us today to return to Las Vegas, lost, angry, and depressed by Scott's death which has deeply affected his own life and future.

Auld Lang Syne sung tonight as a song of farewell will never be more forlorn. Its words are in remembrance of those who have departed for other places, and tonight, the words are for Scott and for Jon. The words have meaning deeper than we have ever recognized in singing it a thousand times before.

47. Afterglow

April 14, 2013, and sixteen months have passed. Each day brings an awareness of the same lingering sentiments. Redundant, clearly, but these sentiments will not go away.

I began writing daily notes for this journal on June 7, 2011, the day of his leukemia diagnosis. With contributions from many of his friends, my intent was to leave a record of Scott's life for his children and grandchildren, and their children, and extended family. The actual book began July 1, 2012. Going through it day by day, reliving some horrific moments, I have tried to capture the essence of Scott and what he meant to us. I hope the book does him justice. Writing it was a true revelation for me in at least three important areas.

First, in the course of writing about Scott, I searched my memory for all the interactions with him during his life. Long forgotten, precious images surfaced, which, viewed in context of happenings of the past year, allowed me to see nuanced shadings of his personality and character I had

not fully considered before. I may have been vaguely aware of them, but I
have now come to realize these were traits others felt represented his
greatest strengths. Parents are often least aware of the portrait others paint
of their sons and daughters.

One example: People were drawn to him, seeking his company,
embracing his humor and optimism, much more so than I had realized.
Over and over, his friends and business associates used the same words to
describe his appeal. Loyal, thoughtful, fun to be with, high energy,
adventuresome, aware, fearless, caring, helpful, talented, thorough,
inventive, and great friend, were just some of their superlatives. These
lovely words, of course, would make any parent very proud. There were
many others, all strong and positive, which gave me new insights into
what made Scott tick, and why his friends loved him so. I treasure this
enlarged picture of Scott.

Second, Joan and I came to know grief and mourning in a new
dimension. We had lost parents, siblings, friends and family before,
grieved for them and their survivors, eulogized them, and gradually
recovered our balance and moved forward with our lives. Losing Scott,
we now realize, was a blow which turned the natural sequence of life and
death on its head. Our grieving is the pathological variety, not ordinary, an
illness not diminishing, but with some days of increasing intensity. Scott's
death brought emotional paralysis from which, with time, we had expected
to gain perspective. We anticipated healing to some extent,
compartmentalizing the tears, loneliness, and emptiness. With each
passing month that was hoped to bring improvement, the gloom; the hurt

and imagery of his illness remained fresh, as reality tells us that he has gone and can never come back.

Joan has dreams about Scott. In one, she sits at a lunch counter having food, and suddenly realizes she has no money. She is about to explain her dilemma to the waitress, when Scott suddenly appears at her side and says he has money. He then jokes with her about leaving home with no "mad" money. As suddenly as he appeared, he is gone, and she leaves without paying to look for him. Outside, she sees him in the distance, then she wakes up.

I have "awake" dreams, in which I have an impulse to call Scott to discuss something I have read or heard. At those times, even today, the fact that he actually died is totally incomprehensible to me, as if his death could not possibly have happened to him...to us. It must have happened to someone else, not us.

For parents who have lost a son, for Terry and Jack and Audrey who have lost a needed husband, and father, damage from grief can be life altering, change long held values, twist attitudes. The young will recover and move on with time, but the old have too little time remaining to outlive this darkness. Scott's death was the death of a star, and the black hole it created has sucked us in.

We understand that our darkness is self-indulgent, a form of self- pity. Mourning has its price....deep mourning can be debilitating . A doctor friend describes us as post-traumatic stress disabled. The label fits.

Third and last, when Scott became ill, Joan and I had very limited understanding of leukemia, its many types, and the entire field of cancers and cancer treatments. In the course of living day to day with his illness, we gradually expanded our meager knowledge of cancer, its long history and its treatments over the centuries, advancing in tiny steps with each generation of research and specialists and pharmas, but always falling short of "the cure". The previously referenced book, "The Emperor of all Maladies", by Doctor Siddartha Mukherjee, is a sort of bible on this broad subject. The medical literature available online, and conversations with hospital specialists and nurses, have also been useful.

Cancers, including leukemic cancers, are heterogeneous, extremely diverse in type, with potentially mutant genes in each cell of our bodies. Mutant genes, we learned, can be activated by external carcinogens like cigarette smoke or soot or concentrated benzene, or activated by unknown internal forces such as age, infection, or injury. Once treated with the latest medical tools, including many types of chemo and other drugs and surgery, stronger evolutionary mutant genes escape to other areas of the body and begin dividing out of control once more, requiring entirely new medical paradigms.

Great advances are being made in sequencing individual human genomes to identify mutant genes which may be treated with engineered T-cells, stem cells designed to fight the specific mutancy. The medical profession seems to believe that this is the direction leading to the most likely cures for many cancers, and specifically for cancers of the blood.

Normal blood cells have finite and short lives....they divide for a period of time and then die and are carried out of the body as waste. Mutant cancer genes keep migrating and multiplying and piling up into tumors or altering the necessary mix of white and red cells and platelets in the blood, leading to relapse, and starting the entire treatment sequence over again.

In treating any major illness, it is clear that hospitals are houses of disease, and the staff human. They subscribe to and administer plans of treatment which can differ greatly from those of other equally qualified doctors in other hospitals in other cities. Great areas of medical practice are based on sound science, but scientific facts have short half-lives before being superseded by newer, more advanced science and theories. Medical practice employed in treating cancer combines science with human judgment, and, clearly, doctors in different locations under different tutelage arrive at different conclusions.

To the patient and his family, doctors are the highest authority available. The patient is not usually equipped to know when science ends and judgment takes over. In an ideal world, the best route for the patient is to have his own advocate, his own coach in his own corner, his very own independent medical authority capable of questioning both the science and judgment being dispensed.

The take-away from this primer on cancer is that we are all vulnerable to it at any point in our lives, and while this vulnerability can by reduced by healthy living and exercise, there is no predicting avoidance. Every cancer patient is surprised by his affliction, just as Scott was on June 7, 2011, six months and seven days before cancer caused his death.

48. Tributes From Friends

Scott Edwin Garrett led a restless, impactful, high-energy life filled with achievement, marriage, and a family he loved dearly. His life took a path different from his forebears, away from the soil and into the city bound life of law and rules for society. He made his mark in this arena, while gathering great friends and supporters each step of the way.

"Half-life" is a scientific/mathematical term used metaphorically here as a count of his time on earth. But time is only one small measure of life's value. He filled his shortened years with action and dedication to achieving his goals, ethically and morally. He earned the respect and love of his family, his associates, his neighbors, and his community.

In doing his best as he knew how, he has given his children and his fellow man a template to follow, which is the greatest compliment any man can be awarded.

Eulogies:

Our dear Scott.

We can still hear that voice, can still hear him laugh, can sstill see him lighting up the room with his stories and love of life. We were blessed to have him in our life, if only for a short while.   We believe that we were meant to know him and love him.   He made that easy.   When our little guy, Liam, was first diagnosed with Leukemia, Scott and Terry were so supportive and Scott's words of encouragement for the little guy were direct—telling him that he was strong and tough.   Ironically, these were the same things Liam would come to think of "Mr. Garrett."   He has always so candid and caring and the love he had for his family and friends gave us all something to strive for.   Each day now, we feel like he is watching over our family, ensuring that little Liam stays strong.   While every day we miss him humor, laugh, and sassiness-those are things that can still put a smile on our face when we think of him.   He is our angel and our love for him is eternal.   Our love and support of Terry, Jack, and Audrey is never ending as we will work each day to hold them up and give them love and strength.   Love

*---**The Merz Family***

To Jack and Audrey:

Scott was a wonderful, energetic person! I remember him constantly bringing warmth, happiness, and chili. He brought joy and music. He loved you both very much. We miss him but he is always with us.

--Uncle Jim Bowers

Scott knew no strangers-everyone was a friend to him. He was kind to all people and greeted them as a friend. He embraced all people and enjoyed their presence. May you always feel his spirit with you. He will protect you and lead you through life.

---The Dahm Family

To Jack and Audrey:

Your Dad came into my life when I was only 15 years old. In 31 years of knowing him, I have never met anyone-and don't think I ever will-who made those around him feel so completely special. It was like the world outside of "a Scott Moment" evaporated, and all there was, was you and him, and whatever crazy, hilarious, mischievous undertaking you were engaged in. That's the gift he gave to so many people.

--Love, Ken Hurley

Scott was my cousin. He was quite a few years older than me, but every time I was around him as a child, I was in awe of him. Scott was the "golden boy" and all the cousins looked up to him even though we didn't know why. He always had an aura around him that was tough to explain.. It seemed he had the perfect life, successful career, and wonderful family. He was an inspiration to so many people. There is a favorite picture of Scott and Jon when they were kids on a sail boat, smiling and laughing into the Sun. That is how I will remember him, smiling and laughing, happy and content. I will miss him dearly, but will meet him again some day. Of that—I have no doubt.

--Tami Ayres, cousin

How impossible to sum up who Scott was and always will be to us...How do we put a finger on just how this man touched our lives the most? Scott's effect on us is profound, and yet at the same time, so simple.

Scott exuded joy! He was one of the happiest people I've ever met. I don't have one memory of him without a smile on his face and a gleam in his eye that literally shined with that joy. He loved life, he loved people, he loved to laugh, he loved his work, he loved golf, he loved planning and building and singing. He LOVED Terry and Jack and Audrey. He just loved.

He was a genius at that! An absolute genius. People talk about how to live well, how to see what really matters and embrace it....celebrate it. Scott was one of those rare and truly wise people who really did this. His love of life was contagious. You would leave from having spent any amount of time with him and everything looked different. You'd wonder how you could possibly have missed the fun and goodness that had been there all along. He made you take notice. I will never forget the look on Scott's face when he would enter a room. The beauty of it was that Scott was constantly looking for the good. He would look around with that mischievous little smile on his face, the one that always seemed to hold a secret, and search that room for the good.

And now I know what the secret was. The secret was that he GOT it!. He, way beyond anyone else around him, got it. He got the fact that everything we need to be happy is right here, now, surrounding us. He could see it. Clearly. He was always looking for it. And he always found it.

Anyone who knew Scott knows that one of his favorite statements was. "It's all Good!" We will forever hear him saying that! But what made it even more fun to be around Scott was that if he didn't immediately see the good in a situation, he took such pleasure in creating it. He had a great sense of humor, and an easy way of finding the funny view of everything.

He made our lives great while he was here with us. And, as is true with all great people, his influence on us will continue and evolve and grow forever. We miss Scott deeply and always will. We know how blessed we are to have gotten to have him in our lives, to have loved him. And how blessed we are to have him and his example forever guiding us. We know he lives through you, in perfect combination with you mom, Jack and Audrey. We see that joy and wisdom shine in your eyes, too. It's so obviously there.

Always remember that your wonderful Dad will always live within you. We love you, and always will.

-- Love, The Mosses

*"The greatness of a man can nearly always be measured by his willingness to be kind."---*George W. Young

This was Scott...so kind, so caring, such passion for each day of his life. In the short time we were blessed to have Scott in our lives, he managed to leave an indelible mark in our hearts. He never took one minute of his life for granted. Seizing the moment for a phone call, visits to our house, trips to Glorioso's market for some Italian eats, hosting an impromptu gathering because, he had "fired up the smoker"...he never sat and watched life happen...he jumped in with both feet and made life happen.

His love for the three of you was amazing to watch...he knew how blessed he was to have your love...you could see it. He had such gratitude for the life he had been given.

Scott was also a true friend in every meaning of the word. He was an amazing listener and truly cared about every word we shared with him...as though there was no one else he would rather be talking to. And there was always such beautiful

laughter wherever Scott would be…his smile, his voice, his spirit could light up a room. Scott was contagious in a way. You would want to be a better person after spending time with him. From his seersucker pants (Hamptons), to our favorite leather chair…many great times together…but not nearly enough.

He will forever be loved. Thank you Terry, Jack, and Audrey, for sharing him with us.

*-- **All our love, Karen, Mike, Jake, Mia & Ella***

I love being at Audrey's house because her dad would sing a lot. It always made me laugh. We love you, Audrey.

*--**Tess Phillips***

I was so glad to get to go to St. Louis from Texas for Scott & Terry's wedding, along with my brothers and sisters and two of my daughters, Misti, and Stephanie. We had a wonderful time and Joe, Joan, Scott and Terry and the Bowers family entertained us and made us all feel so welcome. They were all so gracious, and of course, Scott kept us all laughing! Scott grew up to be such a wonderful, funny man, with a wonderful wife and precious children, and we will all miss him so much. He was a special member of our family and we cherish all our times with him, both as he was growing up, and as an adult. Thank you for being such a good friend to Terry.

*--**Love, Dora Garrett McBee & Larry Mcbee (Scott's aunt and uncle)***

To: Terry, Jack, and Audrey:

Since we live in Texas, our face time with Scott was limited, usually with his parents. However, he did have one summer visit alone, at about age 10, to get acquainted with his Texas roots.

As a child, Scott was as he was as an adult, so full of life and the joy of every new adventure. He seemed to see every experience as an adventure. He just loved hanging our with his cousins and going to the convenience store for a treat...and always laughing. I remember one driving trip from Plainview to Lubbock, he any my daughter Susan laughing all the way and singing "Don't go Breaking my Heart."

He loved going to his uncle Raby's farm, spending time with cousins Stan and Brad, and finding out what his country cousins did for fun. Since his visits were so rare, my mom and Dad (his grandparents) pretty much gave him free reign to do as he pleased. When Joe came at the end of summer to take him home, he chafed at the return of parental restrictions, and proclaimed, "I knew it. I knew when you got here, you would take complete control."

We love every one of the minutes we had with Scott and were always thrilled to see him. I am so grateful that he was in our lives for the time we had. He is my model for living life to the fullest.

--Shirley Dean (Scott's aunt on the Garrett side)

Singing in the car on the way to the pool with Audrey and Uncle Scott. And when I was little, he used to sing me a song. And in St. Louis at that hotel, he gave me a one-of-a-kind American water heater hat that I still have.

--Melissa Bowers, Niece

I met Scott in 2009 when he asked me to come to work for him at A.O. Smith. He was so friendly and excited to have me come that it made me feel very valuable and welcome, and he never stopped making me feel that way. Although our lives will go on at work, I will always remember him fondly.

--Jay

Our family lived next door to the Garretts in Riverside, Connecticut, during the five years when Scott was between the ages of three and eight. We were a large family, with three girls who did some baby sitting of Scott and Jon, and my younger twin brothers who were about three years older than Scott. Scott must have enjoyed mayhem to keep coming over to our house. My brothers and their friends must have taught him many things...hopefully some of them beneficial.

He loved my mom and would come right in the kitchen door, climb up on a stool at the counter, and help himself to the cookie "closet". Mom didn't have a cookie jar....she needed a closet to feed our army. My mom just considered him one of her own. My Dad loved to kid around with him, too. He considered him a mini Eddie Haskell. (I do hope some of you are old enough to remember that name)

We had a wonderful time in the best neighborhood in the whole world. Everyone knew everyone...in a good way.

I know that Scott is up in heaven with my folks and is already at home. I bet my mom has already emptied her "closet" and is making cookies from scratch in his honor. Please know that I will keep all of Scott's family in my prayers now and forever. Scott fought a very brave war and is now at peace.

--Bevan Connett Kinney

When we meet people, you may not remember what they did, or what they said, but you will always remember how they made you feel. Scott always made us feel wonderful. We will miss him.

--The Anguils

Mr. Garrett would always drive by our house and honk his horn in his Porsche. It always made my family happy.

--Abby Barczak

Your dad was always the most cheerful guy in the office, and had drawings of you guys all over the walls.

--Charlie Adams, A.O. Smith

I met your dad when he had already been diagnosed with leukemia. However, he was incredibly cheerful, and determined to enjoy life. The first thing he said to me was, "Hi, I'm Jack and Audrey's dad." He was so proud of you. God Bless You.

--Mr. Meuler

One of my favorite memories of Scott were his delicious RIBS! We knew if we were going to the Garrett House and the smoker was out-it was going to be an awesome meal.

--Love, The Harringtons

Dear Scott: You were such a wonderful nephew. I loved you with all my heart. My heart is broken that I will not see you again in this life, but I will see you again some day, I have no doubt. I loved your wonderful smile and your love for all the Garrett family.

The last time we were together, we were at Aunt Dora's house, and we aunts were all standing visiting in the den. You came in and told us all to sit down. Gosh, we were scared you were going to tell us something bad. We said, "What's wrong?" You said, "Nothing, I just want to visit." We were relieved.

You were precious to us. I love your mother and dad and your sweet wife and children with all my heart. Your Aunt Sharon and Uncle Tom will always miss and love you forever.

--Sharon Garrett Prutzman

Scott was a guy that as soon as you met, you felt like you knew him for years. From the day he came to my 39th birthday party not knowing a single person there- but instantly fitting into the last dinner club we had with Scott doing wheelbarrow races with our wives, egg toss and drinking Choco Vino (or, as Scott would say, "shocko Vannnnnnn"....I will always remember his great spirit and his joy for life.

--Bret Barczak

S mart. Scott's wit and intelligence were immediately evident.
C aring. He was kind and generous..always lending a hand.
O ptimistic. He saw the best in people and had a zest for life.
T enacious. He was focused in work, golf, family and using his smoker
T erry. A beautiful couple, inside and out, who created two wonderful legacies, Jack and Audrey.

--With much love and great memories. Sue Doherty

49. Acknowledgements

Ideas included in this Journal for Scottie came from many. Mary Lou and Dennis Green were great friends in publishing the book. Conversations with Jim Stern and Howard Roughan helped me in seeing the scope of the book. Howard, Lance High, Nick Mark, Stan Cribbs, Greg Wesner, Gina Von Oehsen Cleary, and Jim Stern wrote individual and very touching chapters about Scott and their times with him. Maureen Stern supported Terry and Joan in many ways throughout Scott's illness. Their memories were invaluable in forming the larger picture of his life.

His brother Jon told me fun stories of Scott I had not known. Friends Don and Petie McKinley and Barbara English shared memories of our times together in St. Louis, skiing in Colorado, and tubing on the Black River in Peidmont, Mo.. Steve Bethke had played golf with Scott in California, and offered solace, as did Mike and Eleanor Miller, even as dear Eleanor was losing her last long battle with cancer. Paul Chavin talked me through my grief over many cups of tea. Many of our oldest friends from high school and college years have offered prayers and warm thoughts over these many months. Jerry and Billye Jones, Phil and Joyce Thompson, Travis and Millie Goree, Weldon and Helen Hayes, Bobby and Linda Williams, Roy and Kay Poage, Jake and Paula Finny, and especially, John and Annette Long, have stayed in touch, as have Billy Williams, Sarah Mickey Hudson, Yvonne Ragle Sinclair, Wayne and Pat Miller, Dan and Nancy Hagood, and others. I am grateful to them.

Scott and Terry's loving neighbors in Wauwatosa painted joyful stories about Scott's humor and optimism, themes which were found throughout his life in comments from anyone who ever came in contact with him. Kathy Barczak has been particularly helpful in providing pictures, and in preparing a loving picture memory book of Scott, which we treasure. Kathy, Karen Bressanelli, Holly Anguil, Shelly Harrington, Kate Moss and many others provided emotional support to Terry.

The Connett sisters, Stacey, Bevan, and Kate, our next door neighbors in Connecticut, remembered the most loving and fun traits of his childhood nature. John and Harriet Roughan, our friends of more than 50 years, sparked many forgotten memories of Scott's earliest years. Verne and Lee Westerberg gave love and attention as the project progressed. Alex Korn was steadfast in friendship as I stumbled along after Scott's death. My Texas brothers and sisters, Raby and Lanell, Dora and Larry, Shirley, Sharon and Tom, Cal's wife Jan, and Norma's husband Ronald and their families have been caring, concerned, and supportive always.

Betty Lou Snyder, Joan's Pan Am roommate from 50 years ago, and Scott's Godmother, found and provided Scott's original baptism certificate. Milwaukee Gym friends Arnold Sims and Tom Briggs offered prayers and encouragement during Scott's illness.

Very special credit goes to my dear wife Joan, Scott's loving mom, and Terry, Scott's devoted wife and Jack and Audrey's mother. Both have been very patient, and somewhat anxious, I am sure, as I wrote the book without their review over these past nine months. The book will renew their sadness, as it has mine. In a longer time frame, this small monument to his memory will, I hope, help them, and Jack and Audrey, to continue to feel his enduring love and his joyful legacy, as so many others have.

Finally, and most importantly, to the sweet memory of Scott Edwin Garrett, our beloved son, husband, father, brother, and friend, who's life inspired this book. His rich life story could not go untold.

JBG. 4/12/13/13. La Quinta, California...........